Making Music with Java

An introduction to computer music, Java programming, and the jMusic library.

By Andrew R. Brown

© 2005 Andrew R. Brown

All rights reserved.

Version 1.0

Brown, Andrew R.

Making Music with Java: An introduction to computer music, Java programming, and the jMusic library / Andrew R. Brown

cm.

Includes bibliographical references(p.)

ISBN 978-1-4092-8133-7

Composition (music). 2. Java language. 3. Computer programming. 4. Generative art.

786.7/13

http://jmusic.ci.qut.edu.au/

http://explodingart.com/mmwj/

http://explodingart.com/arb/

Java is a trademark or registered trademark of Sun Microsystems, Inc. in the United States and other countries.

Contents

Preface *11*
    Representing Music *12*
    Integrating Java into your Musical Workflow *14*
    The Computer as a Musical Instrument *14*
    Acknowledgements *16*

1: Getting Started *17*
    Installing Java *17*
    Installing jMusic *17*
    Java Basics *18*
    Making it go Bing! *19*
        Compiling *19*
        Running *19*
    Introducing Object-Oriented Programming *20*
    The Anatomy of a Class *22*
        The shell of a class *22*
        Fields *23*
        Methods *23*
        Importing existing classes *24*
        Knowing where to start *25*
        Accessing methods in other objects *25*
    Following the Flow of Control *26*
    Comments *27*
    JavaDoc *27*
    Documenting Java Code *28*

2: Sound as Digital Audio *31*
    Digital Audio *31*
        Java audio *32*

Accessing recorded sound	33
Saving samples as an audio file	34
Digital Audio Details	***35***
Clipping	36
Aliasing	36
Quantization	37
Interpolation	38
Audio File Types	***38***
Audio Dynamics	***39***
Volume	40
Normalize	40
Fading	41
Limiting	42
Compressing	42
Java Details	***43***
Java Data Types	44
Arrays	44
Iteration	45
Casting	46

3: Manipulating Digital Audio 47

Dividing and Combining Audio	***47***
Mixing	47
Dividing audio files	49
Lopping	50
Inserting silence	51
Envelopes	51
Zero crossings	52
Random recombination	53
Audio Data Parameters	***55***
Resolution	55
Changing the bit depth	56
Resampling	***56***
Changing sample rate	56
Changing the number of channels	57
Pitch shifting	58

Interpolation 60
Pitch shift through interpolation 61
Resampling details 62

Java Details 62
The Math class 62
A method's return type 63
And, or, not 64

4: Music as Digital Data 65
Musical Components and Structure 65
The jMusic data structure 66
Notes and rests 66
Phrases 68
Parts 70

The MIDI Standard 71
Playing many parts 73

Building Musical Structure 74
Phrase phasing 74
Scores 75
Repetition 76
Phasing 76
Piano phase 78
Musical data structure 79

Java Structures 82
Import statements 82
Constructors 83
Instance variables 83
Local variables 84
Scope 84

TheGrid: A Rhythmic Phrase generator 86
TheGrid1 86

5: Playing with Polyphony 91
Managing Musical Parts 91
Making a cannon 93

Creating the musical data	*96*
Making duplicate phrases	*96*
Transposing	*97*
Structuring the music data	*97*
Saving and playing the cannon	*99*

The jMusic Mod Class *99*

Arpeggiator	*101*

Java Details *103*

JavaSound playback	*103*
Keywords	*103*
Methods	*104*
Passing arguments	*104*
Access modifiers	*106*
Accessor methods	*107*
Method overloading	*107*

TheGrid: Playing several parts *108*

TheGrid2	*108*

6: Design and Layout 111

Viewing and Arranging Music *111*

HelperGUI	*112*
Random notes	*114*
Start times	*115*
Automatically appending phrases	*117*
Panning	*117*
Dynamics and mixing	*118*
Viewing as a piano roll	*119*
Viewing as printed data	*120*
Viewing as music notation	*121*
Scattered phrases	*122*
Random walk	*122*

Structure *125*

Program Structure – Arranging code into two classes	*126*

Java GUI Classes *131*

Introducing the AWT package	*131*
Listeners	*131*

Introducing the Swing package *132*
Components *133*
Frames *133*
Buttons *133*
CheckBoxes *134*
Sliders *135*

TheGrid: Adding a Visual Appearance *136*
TheGrid3 .... *137*
TheGrid4 .... *138*

7: Building Interfaces **143**

Graphical User Interfaces *143*
Adding GUI details *145*
Adding music *146*
Changing variables via the interface *147*

Reading MIDI Files *150*

Java Details *150*
The 'this' keyword *150*
The 'static' keyword *151*
Static variables *151*
Static methods *151*

TheGrid: Connecting Music and Vision *152*
TheGrid5 .... *152*
TheGrid6 .... *159*

8: Combination and Recombination **165**

Musical Chunks *165*
Chords *165*
CPhrases *165*

Recombination *167*
Assembling rhythms *167*
Phrases and form *168*
Macrostructure & microstructure *171*
Appending sections *171*
Granular organization *172*

TheGrid: Organizing Files and Audio Playback 174
TheGrid7 175
TheGrid with audio 175
TheGrid8 175
TheGrid9 178

9: Following Rules 183
Music From Text 183
Guido 184
Serialism 187
Arvoish 188
Java Details 192
if then else 192
while and do 192
switch statements 193
TheGrid: Controlling Parameters 193
TheGrid10 193

10: Uncertainty 207
Aleatoric and Stochastic Music 207
Music from randomness 208
Probability and music 208
Gaussian distribution 209
Random walk 210
Markov process 211
Viewing histograms 216
Noise 218
Java Randomness and Determinism 220
Math.random() 220
The Random class 220
TheGrid: Random Velocities 221
TheGrid11 221

11: Emergence 223
Inspired by Nature 224

A Life *224*
Evolution *228*

Cellular Automata *231*
CA rhythms (1 dimensional cellular automata) *232*
CA phrases (2D) *236*

12: Making Waves *241*

Describing Musical Gestures as Curves *241*
Sketch *241*

Generative Music *243*
Music from functions *243*
Sine wave melody *244*
Fractal music *245*

Audio Instruments *247*
Audio rendering *249*
Seeing the audio data *250*
Print instrument *250*
SineTest *253*
Rendering with samples *254*
Rendering audio with any file *255*
Audio and the HelperGUI *256*
Adding audio to an arpeggio program *256*

Java Data Structures *258*
Arrays *258*
Vectors *259*
Inheritance *259*

13: Sonic Spectra *261*

Music in the Physical World *261*
Pitch in hertz *261*
Microtonality *262*
Tuning systems *263*

The Harmonic Series *267*
Additive synthesis *267*
Score-based spectrum *268*

More jMusic Instruments *269*
    Instrument-based spectrum *269*
    Timbral morphing *272*

14: Interactivity 275
    Real-time music generation *275*
    Real Time GUI Control *279*
    External Control *286*
    MIDI input and output *287*

Appendix A: Constants in the JMC 289
    RhythmValues *289*
    Pitches *289*
    Dynamics *290*
    Panning *290*
    General MIDI program changes *290*
    General MIDI drum and percussion sounds *290*
    Scales and modes *291*
    Tuning systems *291*
    Audio waveforms *291*
    Audio noise types *291*
    Phrase position alignments *291*

Appendix B: Methods in the Mod class 293

Appendix C: Installing jMusic 299
    Install Java *299*
    Install jMusic on Linux / Unix *299*
    Install jMusic on Mac OS X *299*
    Install jMusic on Microsoft Windows *300*

References 303

Preface

This book introduces you to music making through software development in the Java programming language using the jMusic library. It explains the musical and programming concepts in a co-ordinated way. Programming languages, such as Java, are powerful tools for music making because they allow you describe music structures and sound processing in a precise way, they also enable you to construct software applications that can generate music automatically and/or be played as musical instruments. Therefore, as you make music with Java you can be the composer, sound designer, instrument builder and performer. Making music with Java can be challenging, particularly at first, but it is very empowering, because it allows you to design both your music and the tools which shape your music. This provides a great degree of control, but also responsibility, attributes that are rewarded by persistent study and practice. This book will start you on that path. It will take you on a journey through a variety of music-making activities using Java and the jMusic library. As you work through this book, you will be exposed to a repertoire of well-established compositional and programming patterns and techniques (as well as a few novel ones). You are encouraged to pick and choose from them as contributions to your own music making style and then, hopefully, go on to create new patterns of your own thus continuing the evolution of computer music culture.

This book is for the musician who wishes to learn about Java programming and computer music concepts, and for the programmer who is interested in music and sound design with Java. As such, it assumes little musical or programming experience and introduces topics and issues as they arise. Sections on computer music and programming are interlaced throughout, but kept separate enough so that those with experience in either area can skip ahead as required. You may like to augment this book with specialized books on Java or computer music to follow up topics in more detail than there is space to cover here. For example; *Learning Java* by Patrick Niemeyer & Jonathan Knudsen (2000) or *The Computer Music Tutorial* by Curtis Roads (1996).

The code examples in this book make use of the jMusic library, a music extension to Java co-written by the author. There are instructions for installing jMusic in Appendix C. The jMusic library is a powerful open source toolkit for composing, synthesis, instrument building, analysis, and computer music education. More detailed information about jMusic, including examples and updates, is available from http://jmusic.ci.qut.edu.au and http://sourceforge.net/projects/jmusic/.

The code for examples and their associated files are available for download from http://explodingart.com/mmwj.

Representing Music

Writing music using Java code is simply one way of representing, or encoding, musical information and ideas. Other symbol systems for representing music include common practice notation (CPN), matrix/piano roll displays, guitar tablature and Musical Instrument Digital Interface (MIDI) messages. Each system of representation has strengths and weaknesses, and each enables different methods of music making. Figures i to v show a whole-tone scale represented in different symbols systems.

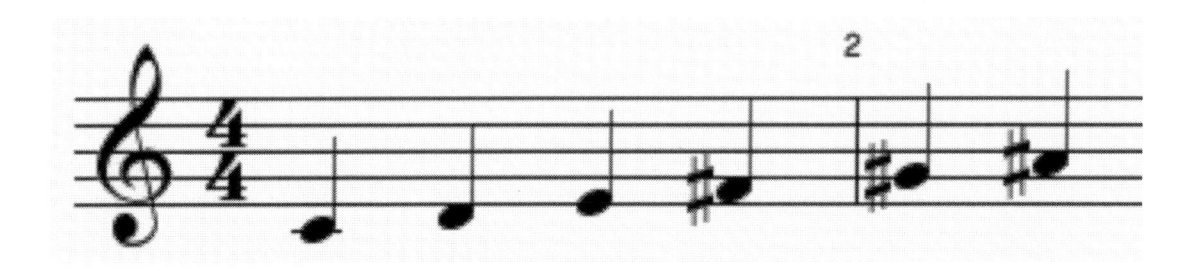

Figure i. A whole-tone scale in CPN.

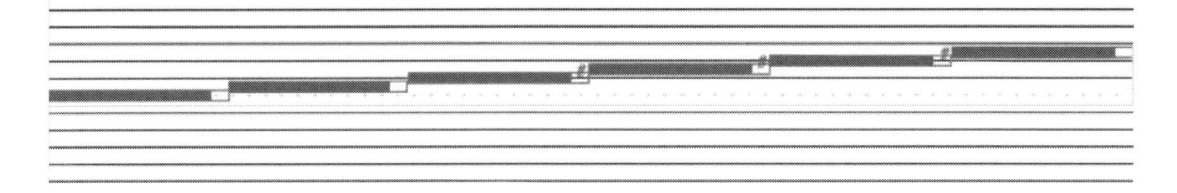

Figure ii. A whole-tone scale in piano-roll view.

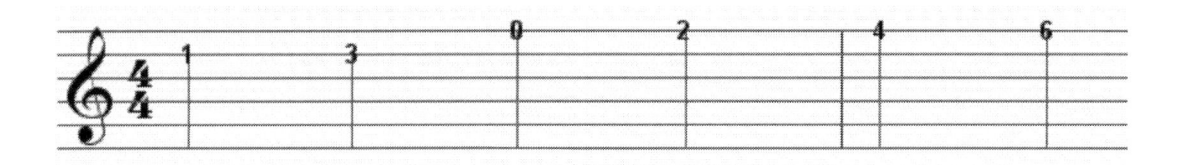

Figure iii. A whole-tone scale in tabalture.

Status	Pitch	Velocity
5	60	100
5	60	0
5	62	100
5	62	0
5	64	100
5	64	0
5	66	100
5	66	0
5	68	100
5	68	0
5	70	100
5	70	0

Figure iv. A whole-tone scale as MIDI data.

```
Phrase phr = new Phrase();
for (int i=0; i<12; i = i+2) {
    phr.addNote(new Note(60 + i, 1.0));
}
```

Figure v. A whole-tone scale as Java code.

Music representations have a number of purposes. They assist musicians by externalizing musical thinking, which allows for further reflection and action. They are a convenient method of storing music, either to assist memory or for archival purposes. And, they enable musical communication in circumstances where sonic communication is not practical or desirable. Normally, musical communication is between humans, and so representation systems such as CPN and guitar tablature are designed to be human readable. When we want to communicate with computers we use systems such as MIDI that are designed to be machine readable, and therefore may look confusing to us. Java, and most computer languages, are designed primarily to be human readable but in many ways reflect the underlying machine structures, thus enabling efficient translation to machine code. Java uses English-like keywords and mathematical symbols that are familiar enough to us, such as `class`, `public`, `void`, `double`, + and /, but relies heavily on logical structures that underpin computer system design, including loops, jumps between sections, and strict syntactic rules. Java keywords have special meanings and are reserved for those purposes and should not be otherwise used. The jMusic libraries, which extend the Java language, provide additional words and structures based on musical practices to aid in the representation of music in Java. Additional keywords in jMusic include data types such as `Note`, `Phrase`, `Part` and `Score`, and constants such as `QUARTER_NOTE`, `FORTE`, `C4`, and `PENTATONIC_SCALE`. Additional musical structures or processes added to Java by jMusic include `repeat`, `elongate`, `transpose`, `invert`, `accent` and `crescendo`. So, representing music in Java combines elements of our linguistic, mathematical, logical and musical histories, even though at times the meaning of terms in Java may differ from your previous understanding of them. The way in which these elements can be combined to make music is vast but also constrained and so, like music representation systems from the past (and those yet to be invented), Java has its syntax and grammar which need to be understood in order to become musically expressive with it.

Integrating Java into your Musical Workflow

To make the most of your Java-based music making skills it is important to think about how they can be integrated into your existing music making practices and tools. Your music making activities probably already include a number of software components, perhaps a MIDI/Audio sequencer, hard disc recording software, and software samplers. The examples in this book include saving the Java-based music as standard MIDI files and audio files. These can be imported into your other software for further elaboration. This means that you don't have to immediately create an entire musical work in Java, but you can create small sections or components that are combined with other elements into a final whole. In this way your music making with Java adds to and leverages your existing musical skills. This interoperability between software works both ways because jMusic and Java include routines to read MIDI and audio files as well. Therefore you might start working in other software, then import your files into your Java applications for manipulation or enhancement, then export them back out to other software environments for arrangement and mastering. As your Java skills increase you can find an optimal balance between making music with Java and other software or hardware devices at your disposal, using each in the way that maximizes its features and potential.

The Computer as a Musical Instrument

When making music with Java it is useful to approach the computer as a musical instrument. As an instrument the computer becomes a vehicle through which you express musical ideas. Like all music technologies, instruments (including the computer) have tendencies, or pathways, for the musician to follow. For example, most acoustic instruments are easier to play in some ranges than others, and many orchestral instruments play only monophonic music. However, these are tendencies rather than limitations, the skilled performer can play notes over a wide pitch range and techniques such as double stopping and multiphonics enable homophonic textures from monophonic instruments. The computer has limitations imposed by the hardware and software but, when viewed as a musical instrument, you can look beyond these limitations or considerations of the computer as simply an efficient tool, to see that the computer is a partner in the music making process. Viewing the computer as an instrument recognizes that music making moves beyond simple human-directed activity to become collaboration with the computer—by assisting, the computer has an influence. However, the more responsibility a computer music system has over the music production, the greater the expectations on the composer using the system. This might seem counter-intuitive but put more simply; a greater emphasis on the unintelligent (even perhaps unskilled) computer requires more of the (presumably) intelligent programmer and composer.

As with traditional musical instruments, such as the guitar, intimate engagement with the computer as an instrument increases with your familiarity with the computing medium - as you increase your programming skills. As with any musical instrument, the greatest satisfaction will result when you learn to *play* the computer well. This involves studying the principals involved, regular practice, and an immersion in the computer music culture through listening, reading and discussion.

Musical instruments are normally associated with their use in real-time performance. The computer can be used in this way, however, you can approach the computer as an instrument in non real-time interactions also; such as the algorithmic computation of musical parts which can take from a few seconds to a few minutes depending upon the amount of data to compute. Engagement is maintained through these drawn out processes when there is sufficient interest in the results of the processes. Another indication of your engagement with the computer as an instrument is the effectiveness with which you can express music with it, which requires a good operational ability and fluency with the music representation system. When these are achieved you can operate directly with the computer to create music without the need for deliberate translation from some other musical language or way of thinking. You just play the computer.

This book focuses more on music composition than performance and it may seem that for composers the computer acts more like a tool or medium, while this is true, the idea of the computer as an instrument is still valid because it denotes a special relationship often witnessed between performer and instrument that can still be found between composer and instrument. In this book you will be introduced to the areas of skill and knowledge necessary for you use the computer as a musical tool, as a medium for musical communication and, as well, you are encouraged to approach the computer as a musical instrument.

Acknowledgements

I would like to thank those in the jMusic community who have contributed to the development and robustness of the library and the tutorials that underpin this book. Worth particular thanks in this regard are the efforts of Andrew Sorensen (co-creator of jMusic), René Wooller (who assisted with proof reading), Andrew Troedson, Adam Kirby, and Tim Opie (who contributed substantially to development of the jMusic library).

Concept Quiz

1. What attributes are suggested as helping gain control over Java as a music making tool?
2. What is the relationship between Java and jMusic?
3. What are the suggested purposes of music representations?
4. What is special about Java keywords?
5. What features does a computer share with other a musical instruments?
6. Improvements in what skill increases your familiarity with the computing medium?
7. What is meant by the term 'engagement' in this chapter?

1: Getting Started

This chapter provides a whistle-stop tour of the Java language, the jMusic library, and installing and running Java programs. If you are already familiar with Java programming feel free to skim this chapter and move directly to chapter 2 where music and audio issues are discussed. If you are new to Java programming then this chapter will provide an overview, but may appear somewhat confusing. Take your time, read carefully, and consult a more detailed Java text when more clarification is required.

Installing Java

Java has two main parts that can be installed (often with the one installation process), the Java Virtual Machine (JVM) which runs Java applications and the Java Development Kit (JDK) which includes the tools required to create java programs. When you do a complete Java install using Sun's installers. Both the JVM and the JDK are installed, and possibly an Integrated Development Environment (IDE) as well, depending upon your choice.

The JVM and JDK are specific to each operating system and you need to install the appropriate version for your computer. Sun Microsystems, the inventors of Java, provide installers for Java on many platforms including Windows and Linux. Apple Computer provide Java tools for Mac OS X and a Apple and number of Linux distributions provide these tools as a standard part of the operating system.

For download and installation instructions visit the relevant link:
- Sun Microsystems: http://java.sun.com
- Apple Computer http://apple.com

Installing jMusic

jMusic is a library that extends Java to provide increased music functionality. The jMusic library must be installed separately from Java, and is usually stored separately from other Java classes. Some set up is required after installation to make Java aware of the jMusic library. This involves setting the classpath; the location(s) on the hard drive where Java should look to find classes and class libraries.

See the details on installing and setting up jMusic in Appendix C and visit the jMusic web site, http://jmusic.ci.qut.edu.au, for further information about installing and using jMusic.

Java Basics

Java is a computer programming language developed and owned by Sun Microsystems. In many respects it is quite similar to other programming languages such as C++, C#, and even Fortran. Java has become quite popular for a variety of good reasons, some of which make it useful for music programming and others which are sometimes a hindrance. In this section I will outline a number of these Java features.

Java programs run on the Java Virtual Machine (JVM), a software layer that sits above the operating system. In this respect it is similar to Lisp and C# but different from C++ and Fortran. JVM's are written for each operating system and, as a result, Java programs only have to be created once and can run on any platform with a JVM. This portability of Java programs is particularly useful to programs distributed over the internet, but is also convenient for people working in computing environments with a mix of platforms. As for example in music communities where it is common to find both Windows and Macintosh users in large numbers, and some musicians running Linux or Unix.

Java is an interpreted language. This means that the Java compiler generates byte code that the JVM can translate into instructions for the local operating system. This interpretive step means that Java programs may be slower to run than those written in C++, for example, but in most cases this presents little practical problem and as computers increase in processing power performance problems due to interpretation requirements decrease.

Java is a modern language that employs many leading architectural features. It is object-oriented, dynamic, robust, secure and multithreaded. While there is not space to explain each of these features in detail, the message is that your Java programs will be quick to write by leveraging other people's efforts (such as using the jMusic library), will take good advantage of your computer's capabilities, will be well behaved internet citizens, and should be relatively robust.

There is a great deal of support for Java as a teaching language. Dozens of "how to program" books have been written for Java and many Universities teach computer programming using Java. You should have no trouble finding help with your Java questions as you work through this book, and I encourage you to have good Java reference by your side (or on your computer) to supplement the explanations in this book. You may also supplement that material in this book with the online Java tutorials at http://java.sun.com.

Making it go Bing!

Let's get straight into it and write our first Java music program with jMusic. Type the code below into a text file and save it as *Bing.java*.

```
import jm.music.data.Note;
import jm.util.Play;

public class Bing {
    public static void main(String[] args) {
        Note n = new Note(60, 1.0);
        Play.midi(n);
    }
}
```

Compiling

To compile the program using a terminal (command line) application use the java compiler, `javac`. Open a new terminal window and navigate (using the cd command in Unix/Linux systems) to the directory that contains your `Bing.java` file. Type `javac Bing.java`, and hit return. This should create a file called `Bing.class` in the same directory. If there are errors, then check for typo's in the file or consult Appendix C to ensure Java and jMusic are installed correctly.

Running

To run the *Bing* program from the terminal, use the *java* application. Type `java Bing`, and hit return. Notice that the `.class` suffix is not required. A single note should sound from your computer's speakers. If you are using an IDE such as *NetBeans* or *jBuilder* for your Java programming, consult the manual about how to compile and run you programs.

This may seem like a lot of trouble to produce just one note. As you work through this book it will become clearer how to leverage algorithmic processes to shift the balance of effort to produce vast quantities of music with modest amounts of code. Here is an example to whet your appetite, that uses the simple algorithmic processes of repetition and randomness and the power of Java's `for` loop to generate hundreds (potentially thousands) of times more music than the *Bing* program with just three more lines of code.

```
import jm.music.data.*;
import jm.util.Play;
```

```
public class BingLoop {
    public static void main(String[] args) {
        Phrase phr = new Phrase();
        for (int i=0; i< 200; i++) {
            Note n = new Note(60+(int)(Math.random()*24), 0.125);
            phr.addNote(n);
        }
        Play.midi(phr);
    }
}
```

Programming Practice

Create `BingLoop.java` file from the above code. Compile the java file with the terminal command `javac BingLoop.java` to create a class file. Run the class file with the terminal command `java BingLoop`.

In the remainder of this chapter the details of how these, and other Java programs, work will be unpacked as the basic concepts of Java programming are introduced.

Concept Quiz

1. What is the difference between the JVM and JDK?
2. What does a *classpath* specify?
3. What does it mean to say that Java is an *interpreted* language?
4. What are the URLs of the Java and jMusic web sites?
5. What is the *javac* program?
6. Does the *java* program execute a .java or .class file?

Introducing Object-Oriented Programming

It was mentioned earlier that Java is an object-oriented language. This design feature involves a particular way of structuring a program and has implications for the way Java programs operate. This section will focus on a few object-oriented concepts that are important to get clear from the start, and others will be discussed in more detail later in the book. Thinking about the world in an object-oriented way is based on the notion that things can be categorized and described, that we objectify things in the world. Categories of objects are often hierarchically arranged. Take, for example, automobiles where there is a category of objects we call cars. All cars are part of the broader category we call vehicles, which can include bikes, trains, and so on. Vehicles are objects that are part of the transportation category, along with airplanes, boats, and the like. This partial object-oriented structure is depicted in figure 1.1.

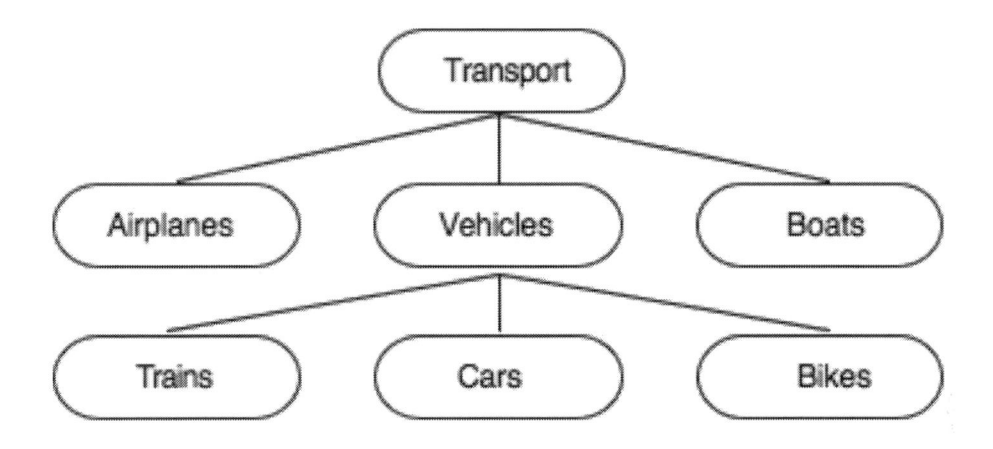

Figure 1.1. An object hierarchy.

At each layer of the hierarchy there are features that describe the objects at that level. For example, all transportation objects share the feature of movement and a mechanism of propulsion; therefore a house does not normally fit in that class of object, whereas a skateboard does. Vehicles, add more precise features, such as the fact that they move on land. The class of cars inherits those transportation and vehicles features and adds more specifics. For example, cars generally have four wheels, are designed for domestic transportation, and so on. Similarly, we can subclass cars into more specific classes of objects, those with four wheel drive, those with six cylinder motors, etc. This object categorization process can be extended as required.

Using object-oriented programming languages a description of the features of an object is called a *class* declaration. A class inherits all the features of the classes that it extends, it describes the types of *data* it will hold, and contains *methods* for manipulating that data. A class description is like a blueprint for objects of a certain type. For example, the four wheel drive car class is a template for producing those vehicles, each of which may have a distinctive set of data values, such as a different brand, model, color, and motor size. These individual objects (four wheel drives) are said to be *instances* of the four wheel drive class, they are specific exemplars or versions of the class.

In Java, we write classes that describe objects. These classes define what the objects will do. The *new* keyword is used to create an instance of a class. A class includes a *constructor* that is run when the object is created, and includes *fields* (variables or constants) that hold data about the object, and includes *methods* which are descriptions of what the class can do to data.

The creation of instances of a class is called *instantiation*. As a musical example, let's look at the `Note` class from jMusic. There is only one `Note` class, and it describes the category of objects we call musical notes. `Notes` have variables including pitch, rhythmValue, and dynamic, and each variable has a data value. `Notes` have methods to act on those data, like `setPitch()`, and methods that act on the entire object, like `copy()`. A piece of music can have hundreds of notes, but these are all instances of the one `Note` class. Each note object (instance) is unique but they all share the same features and behavior. The single `Note` class can be used to create any number of note objects. Now, it's time to see how a Java class is organized.

The Anatomy of a Class

Java programs are made up of one or more classes. As mentioned above, a class is a template or blueprint for creating objects. When programs are run objects are created from these blueprints, these objects are called *instances* of the class and are created using the *new* keyword.

The Java code files are text files designed to be human readable and writable. Each Java file you write is compiled into a class file of the same name. Class files are only machine readable. By convention class names, and their files, start with uppercase letters, use uppercase letters at the start of each new word in multi-word names and do not have any spaces. The source file *MakeMusic.java* produces a *MakeMusic.class* file when compiled. The class files are binary files, designed to be executed by the JVM. You use the source files to write your program and the class files to run your program.

The shell of a class

```
public class MakeMusic {

}
```

Java classes are declared with the `class` keyword, followed by the class name, in this case `MakeMusic`. When the file is saved it must have the same name of the class with a .java suffix, in this case *MakeMusic.java*. The *public* keyword indicates that this class is available for use by any other classes. There are other keywords that can be used instead of public to limit the availability of this class, these include *protected* and *private*. The code within the class is delimited by the opening and closing curly brackets {}. Other sub-sections of the program can also be bounded by these brackets.

Fields

Classes can contain data. Data is stored in fields, usually these are *variables* whose values can change, but they may be *constants* whose values cannot change. The *MakeMusic* class has one variable, a Note named n. Additionally, the variables within the object n can be assigned values when it is created by passing arguments. In the example below, the arguments are a pitch of middle C (C4) and a rhythm value of one beat (QUARTER_NOTE). In summary, n is a variable of type Note belonging to the *MakeMusic* class, and the note n contains variables including a pitch of C4 and a rhythm value equal to a quarter note.

```java
public class MakeMusic {
    Note n = new Note(C4, QUARTER_NOTE);
}
```

Methods

A class can also have methods, which are sections of code that describe a process or algorithm. Methods usually act on the data within the class. By convention method names start with lower case letters – this makes them easy to distinguish from class names. In this example a method called playMusic() has been added to the class.

```java
public class MakeMusic {
    Note n = new Note(C4, QUARTER_NOTE);

    public void playMusic() {
        Play.midi(n);
    }
}
```

Method names are followed by brackets "( )" which may contain indications that data (arguments) are required by the method. Methods must also indicate the type of value they will return (*int, double, String, Note*, etc.), or *void* if they return no result, as in this example. (Types will be discussed in more detail later in the book.) This method does not accept or return any values, it is self-contained; it simply plays the note object n.

Importing existing classes

One of the advantages of modern computer languages is that rather than having to write all the required code there are many libraries of existing classes and methods you can draw upon. jMusic is one such library, and there are many that are part of the Java language as well.

To access existing classes, or groups of classes called *packages*, you *import* them at the beginning of your program.

```
import jm.util.Play;
import jm.music.data.*;
import jm.JMC;

public class MakeMusic implements JMC{
    Note n = new Note(C4, QUARTER_NOTE);

    public void playMusic() {
        Play.midi(n);
    }
}
```

There are three `import` statements in this example, they point to particular sections of the jMusic libraries that are used by this class. The first imports the `Play` class. It is in the *util* package, inside the *jm* directory. Next, the `jm.music.data` package is imported. The asterix (*) indicates that all classes in the `data` package should be available for use, these include the `Note` class. Lastly, the `JMC` (jMusic Constants) class is imported. This class has many fields that are abbreviations and synonyms that map standard musical terms to numbers required by jMusic. Being Java constants, the values of these fields cannot be changed. For example, C4 is a JMC constant equaling the value 60, and `QUARTER_NOTE` is a JMC constant with a value of 1.0. The use of constants makes the code more human readable, and save you having to remember arcane numbers when you would rather think in musical terms.

Additionally, the class declaration *implements* the JMC class. This is required because the JMC is actually an *interface* rather than a normal class. In Java an interface is a kind of abstract class that declares variables and methods but does not implement the methods. When implementing an interface, a class inherits all its fields and should override any abstract methods. In this case we use the JMC interface to inherit many fields with English-like names that can be used in the code to make it more musically meaningful when read, and the JMC interface does not have any method definitions to override. The important thing to understand for now, is that implementing the JMC allows you to use musical terms throughout your code making it much easier for musicians to understand.

Knowing where to start

Every Java program must have one `main()` method. The method can be contained in any one of the program's files. The main method is where the program begins execution and everything follows from that point. In a simple program like the *Bing* example the `main()` method can be the one and only method. In this example we'll see how the `main()` method can be in a different file.

```java
public class MyProgram {
    public static void main(String[] args) {
        MakeMusic musicObject = new MakeMusic();
        musicObject.playMusic();
    }
}
```

The `main()` method has an additional keyword, *static*. This indicates that there can only be one copy of this method and when instances of this class are created this method is not duplicated. This is the formal way of ensuring that there is only one `main()` method and that a program is not confused about where it will begin.

The `main()` method always accepts one *argument*, a list of words, a string array `String[]`, that can hold a list of alphanumeric characters, called `args` (short for arguments). This allows words to be passed to the program when it beings. These words may be used to provide data for the program to work on or parameter settings that can be specified each time the program runs. We do not use this feature of the main method in our program, but Java requires that the `main()` method accepts this argument. The main method in this example creates a new *MakeMusic* instance then calls it's `playMusic()` method.

The *MyProgram* class creates an instance of the *MakeMusic* class named `musicObject`. It then calls (runs) the `playMusic()` method of that object. How is this 'remote' control of another class achieved?

Accessing methods in other objects

Notice that the syntax for calling the `playMusic()` method uses a 'dot' between the instance name and the method, `musicObject.playMusic();`. This can be read as, call the `playMusic()` method from the `musicObject` instance of the *MakeMusic* class. Or, more simply, call `musicObject's playMusic()` method.

Programming Practice

To run this example program, create two new files. Into the first type the final version of the *MakeMusic* code and save it as `MakeMusic.java`. In the second text file type the *MyProgram* code above and save it as `MyProgram.java`. Compile both Java files and run the *MyProgram* class. You will get the same result as the *Bing* program earlier, but it has been achieved in an object-oriented way. This, somewhat convoluted object oriented program structure will pay dividends as the programs become more sophisticated.

Following the Flow of Control

The way the running of the program unfolds is depicted in figure 1.2. When the *MyProgram* class is run the *main* method is executed first. It creates a new instance of the *MakeMusic* class which automatically results in the creation of a new `Note` object called n. The main method then calls the *playMusic* method which creates a single note and plays it using Java's software synthesizer (more on these musical details later).

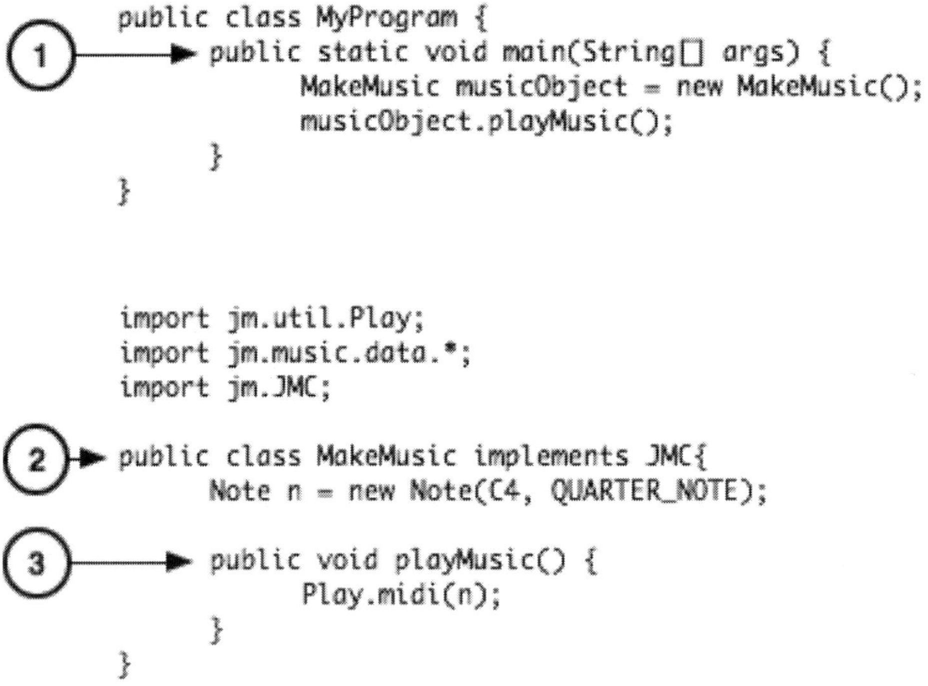

```
public class MyProgram {
    public static void main(String[] args) {
        MakeMusic musicObject = new MakeMusic();
        musicObject.playMusic();
    }
}


import jm.util.Play;
import jm.music.data.*;
import jm.JMC;

public class MakeMusic implements JMC{
    Note n = new Note(C4, QUARTER_NOTE);

    public void playMusic() {
        Play.midi(n);
    }
}
```

Figure 1.2. Flow of control between the program's two classes.

Comments

Like most other programming languages Java lets the programmer write remarks into the source code. These sections are called comments, and are ignored by the compiler. There are a couple of ways that comments are indicated.

```
// Single line comments start with two back slashes.
/*
        Multiple line comments start with an astrix and star and
        end with the opposite, an astrix and a slash.
*/
```

JavaDoc

One of the most helpful sources of information about Java is the documentation. Learning to use Java easily relies upon becoming familiar with accessing information from the java documentation. There are too many classes and methods in the Java libraries, let alone adding jMusic libraries, for most people to ever remember, and so a successful strategy is being aware of the general capabilities of the language then looking up the fine details in the documentation as required.

Fortunately, there is a standard format for Java documentation, therefore once this is understood finding information about new libraries and packages will not be difficult. The Java documentation is in html format and should be installed alongside Java, but can also be accessed online or downloaded from http://java.sun.com. Below, in figure 1.3, is an example of the Javadoc index page for Java 2 SE.

On the left are index panels, the top one selects a particular package and the lower one displays all the classes in the selected package. By default 'All Packages' is selected and so all the Java classes are shown in the index in alphabetical order. Selecting a class in the index panel displays it in the larger right panel. There are a large, and increasing, number of classes in Java and, as a result, the documentation can appear overwhelming at first. The trick is to understand the simple organization of the documentation and for the time being ignore the classes you have not yet encountered.

The organization of the class documentation that displays in the right panel is always similar. First is the class name and its package location in the library, after this is a short description of the class and how it can be used. Following the description is a summary of the fields (variables and constants), constructors, and methods. These summaries are one-sentence descriptions with a column to the left that indicates the type of data involved (the type of the field or the return type of a method). The summary may also indicate fields and methods that have been inherited by the class from any super (parent) classes. Finally in the documentation page are detailed descriptions of the fields, constructors and methods.

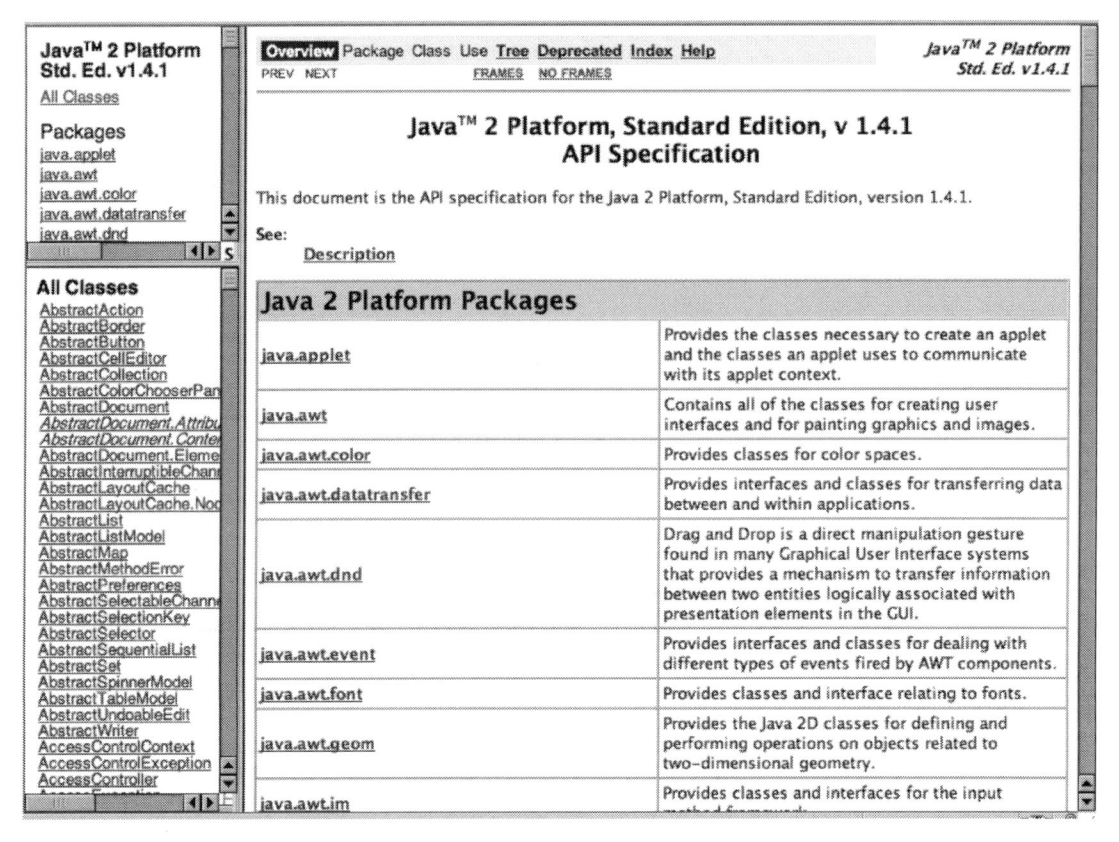

Figure 1.3. The java documentation index page.

It is good programming practice to have a browser with the documentation open at all times while you are working and to access it regularly when you need reminding of the details of a class or method. There is similar documentation for jMusic. It can be downloaded from `http://sourceforge.net/projects/jmusic/` or viewed online from the jMusic web site, `http://jmusic.ci.qut.edu.au/jmDocumentation/index.html`.

Documenting Java Code

A neat feature of the Java documentation is that it is semi-automatically created from comments in the source code. While this is not the place for a detailed discussion of Java documentation procedures, the simple story is that all documentation comments that start with `/**` (rather than the normal `/*` or `//`) and ends with a `*/` are included in the Java documentation. A program called `javadoc` searches through source files and builds the HTML pages. Further details on Java documentation procedures can be found at http://java.sun.com/.

Concept Quiz

1. What is an object oriented approach?
2. Objects derived from the definition are called an _____ of it.
3. There are two types of fields that hold data within objects, what are they?
4. What are sections of code that act on data called?
5. What does the public keyword indicate?
6. What does the import keyword indicate?
7. When we implement the JMC what does that add to the program?
8. Which method is always the first to be run?
9. What will the file name be for a program that starts, public class Test implements JMC ?
10. Where does all the text for the Java documentation come from?

2: Sound as Digital Audio

While symbolic representations of music, including notes and phrase, assist in compositional tasks and in thinking about large musical structures. In the end the computer produces a sonic outcome from a digital audio stream based on these structures. In this chapter we will examine how sound is represented as digital data and how that data can be directly manipulated to vary the sound. Along the way we will learn about important Java language features and how they can be utilized for digital signal processing. In this and other early chapters of this book the symbolic and sample-based representations of music are being discussed separately, but in later chapters they will be interconnected into a complete computer music system with even more potential for music making than either of the constituent parts.

There are two main sources of digital sounds, recordings and synthesis. Recorded sounds are captured from the acoustic world with microphones and we tend to treat them at a macro level, as entire files or wavetables. Synthesized sounds are generated by an algorithmic process and can be produced (computed) as required. In this book, we will look at how to deal with recorded sound material and how to generate sounds via synthesis. But, whichever way a digital sound is created, at a fundamental level they are all the same kind of data, and so it is useful to briefly describe the basics of digital audio.

Digital Audio

Computers are digital devices, meaning that they deal with number or digits. The reason they work this way is because fundamentally they are built with switching devices, called gates. These gates have one of two states, on or off. As a result, all numbers in the computer have discrete values rather than continuously varying (analogue) values like other media; such as water volume, electrical current or a magnetic field. Digital audio data, like all other computer data, is simply a stream of numbers. When recording a sound, an analogue-to-digital converter (ADC) measures the amplitude (loudness) of the sound input thousands of times every second in a process called sampling, and the list of sample values is the digital audio data. When synthesizing digital sound the sample values are computed rather than measured. In the digital domain there are two considerations with respect to audio quality, sample rate and resolution.

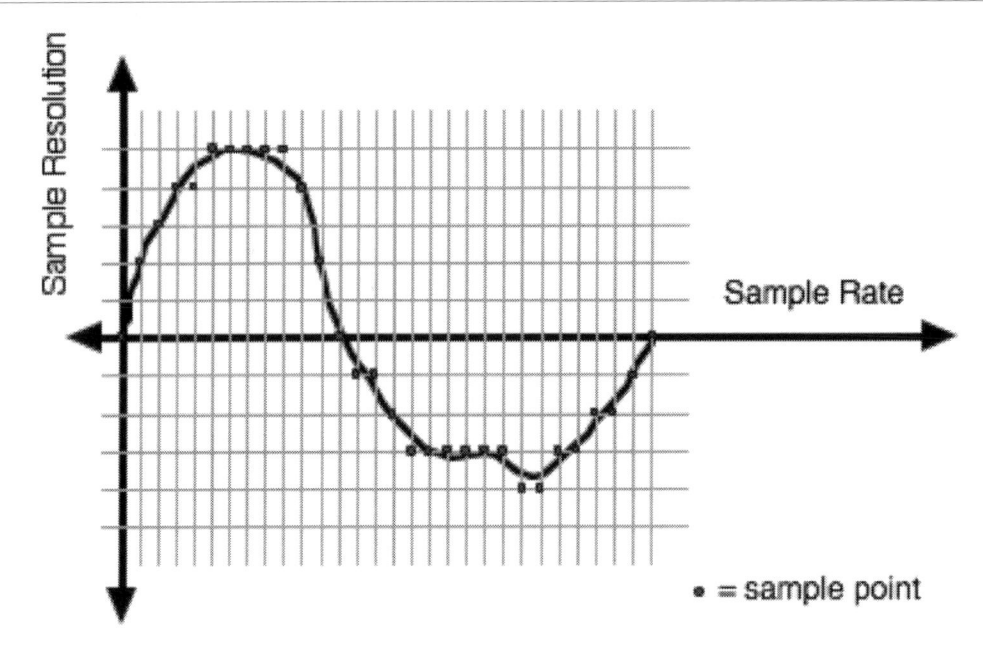

Figure 2.1. Converting an analogue signal to digital values.

The more frequently samples are taken the more accurately the sound is represented, remembering that an analogue/acoustic sound is infinitely variable, and this measurement regularity is called the sample rate. Typical sample rates vary from 11 to 96 thousand samples per second, but the most common sample rate is 44100 samples per channel per second; as used for CDs.

The resolution of a sample refers to the accuracy of measuring its amplitude. The finer the resolution the higher the audio quality and the greater the dynamic range. In computer sound the resolution is generally related the number of bits used to store the sample. For example, in a sound with 8 bit resolution the amplitude scale has 256 steps, in a 16 bit sound this increases to 65,536, and for a 24 bit sound 16,777,216 steps. When the sample rate and resolution are increased the sound quality improves, but the memory required to store the sound data and the time taken to process them also increase. A trade-off between quality and file size is always in play, and the best choice depends upon the importance of the features in each circumstance. For example, voice over IP applications trade quality for low bandwidth data transmissions, while professional music studios trade hard disk storage costs for undistorted audio clarity.

Java audio

Java provides classes for reading and writing from audio files in the AU, WAVE and AIFF formats. jMusic provides some simple read and write utilities that deliver and accept audio data as an array of floating point numbers. Specifically, the Read.audio() and Write.audio() methods, in the jm.util package. The reading method operates in two ways, one returns an array of floats, the other accepts an existing array and fills that array. Both methods require the name of the file to be read.

Note that in programming terminology, a 'float' means a floating point number; that is a number with decimal places such as 12.345.

```
float[] data = new float[1];
Read.audio(data, "Welcome.au");
```

or

```
float[] data = Read.audio("Welcome.au");
```

The writing method has only one argument format, it requires an array with the audio data in it and the name for the saved file.

```
Write.audio(data, "SavedAudio.aif");
```

Accessing recorded sound

A program to access an audio file simply needs to wrap the Read.audio() method with a class structure. Here is one of the simplest jMusic classes that imports and uses the Read.audio() method.

```
import jm.util.*;

public final class ReadAudio {
    public static void main(String[] args){
        float[] data = Read.audio("Welcome.au");
    }
}
```

During the reading of the audio file, the **Read** class prints some feedback out to the terminal window. This includes information about the file.

```
-------------------- Reading Audio File --------------------
File 'Welcome.au' read in. Details:
Channels = 1 Samples per channel = 47492 Sample rate = 44100 Bit depth = 16
------------------------------------------------------------
```

It should be noted that these methods are designed to enable stand-alone manipulation of audio data and that many additional audio features in Java and jMusic allow for integration of event-based and audio-based music making processes.

To access the audio samples, simply read from the float array `data`. For example, adding a for-loop after the `Read.audio()` line can print out all the sample values to the terminal window.

```
for (int i=0; i< data.length; i++) {
    System.out.print(data[i] + " ");
}
```

In order to see a more visual (but still textual) display of the sample data, replace the previous for-loop with this one, recompile and run.

```
for (int i=0; i< data.length; i+= 10) {
    for (int j=0; j-40<data[i] * 40; j++) {
        System.out.print(" ");
    }
    System.out.println("o");
}
```

Saving samples as an audio file

The compliment to the `Read` class is the `Write` class, whose `audio()` method will create an audio file from an array of floats. In the class below, samples are read from one file and immediately written out to another. Notice that the written file is of a different type to the input file. So this program performs a simple file type conversion from an AU to AIFF file.

```
import jm.util.*;
/*
* Read an audio file into an array and write out
* an audio file from the array.
*/
public final class WriteAudio {
    public static void main(String[] args){
        float[] data = Read.audio("Welcome.au");
        Write.audio(data, "SavedAudio.aif");
    }
}
```

As a final code example in this section, we'll manipulate the samples before they are written. A simple change is to reverse the order of the samples, thus playing the sound backwards.

```java
import jm.util.*;
/*
 * Read an audio file into an array and write out
 * a reversed version of the array.
 */
public final class WriteReverseAudio {
    public static void main(String[] args){
        float[] data = Read.audio("Welcome.au");
        // reverse the order of samples
        float[] reversed = new float[data.length];
        for (int i=0; i< data.length; i++) {
            reversed[data.length - i - 1] = data[i];
        }
        // write
        Write.audio(reversed, "ReversedAudio.wav");
    }
}
```

Programming practice

Type up each of these short classes in a text editor, save, compile and run them to hear the results. You may also like to experiment with some different processing of the audio data after reading and before writing it. There is no end to the types of signal processing functions you can apply.

Note that the JavaSound library in Java also has classes for reading and writing files, but these are not interoperable with jMusic. The jMusic library was developed before JavaSound existed (in the days of Java 1.0 in the late 1990s) and while it has integrated many of JavaSound's MIDI features jMusic audio processing remains somewhat parallel to JavaSound audio until the final input-output stage.

Digital Audio Details

When audio data comes from recordings, the process of digital recording involves an change from continuous analog signal to a quantized digital one; a process called sampling. The device that does this is called a analogue to digital converter (ADC). Representing waveforms as digital samples is often referred to as pulse code modulation (PCM) data. The sample data stored in this way is often called PCM audio. This process of sampling provides audio data in an easily manipulated form as a simple list of amplitude values, but may be prone to properties that may corrupt the signal including clipping, aliasing, quantization and interpolation.

Clipping

The range of audio data needs to be kept within specific limits to accommodate the limits of the data types or the specification of the D/A conversion. In a 16 bit audio file the data is stored as signed integer values, with a range from −32,767 to +32,767. If the values are larger or smaller than the allowed range they will usually be truncated to the values at the out limits of the range. This is known as *clipping*.

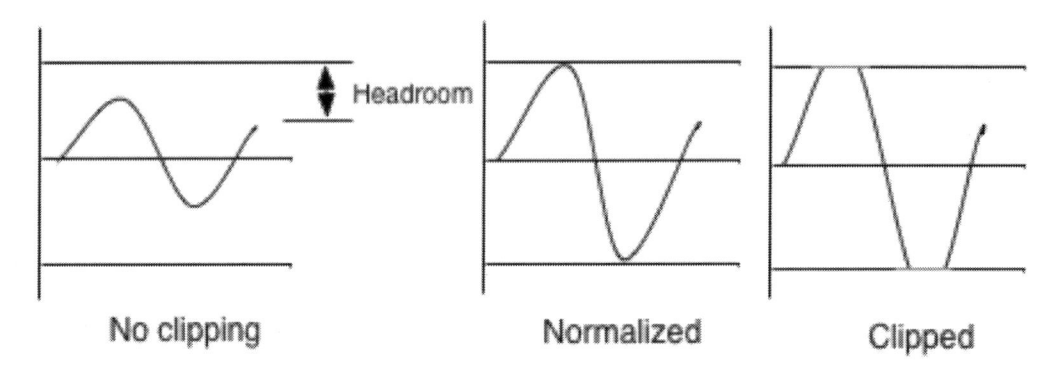

Figure 2.2 Audio file amplitude examples.

The degree to which the maximum sample values are within the audible range is referred to as the *headroom*. If the maximum data values are close to the maximum range then it is said there is little headroom, if the data is well within the possible range there is said to be a lot of headroom in the signal. It is good practice to have only a small amount of headroom in the data because that maximizes the dynamic range of the audio. The process of amplifying the data so that it occupies the full range, so that the loudest sample is equal to the maximum value, is called *normalizing* the file.

Aliasing

Acoustic audio signals contain a spectrum of frequencies, the particular characteristics of which determine the timbre, or color, of the sound. When recording a sound it is important, for sound quality considerations, to capture the entire spectrum and it is the higher frequencies that are the more difficult to accurately capture. The sampling rate determines the highest frequency that can be captured. The physicist Henry Nyquist (1889-1976) showed that in order to capture a frequency of x hertz and sample rate of 2x samples per second was the minimum required (and even this was not high quality). Hence the highest frequency capable of being sampled by a particular sampling rate is half the rate, and is called the *Nyquist* frequency. Given that human hearing ranges up near 20,000 hertz a sampling rate of more than 40,000sps is required. This consideration played a large part in determining the 44,100sps sampling rate used on CDs. The effect of using a sample rate lower than twice the highest frequency in the signal spectrum is *aliasing*. In effect, the frequencies above the Nyquist 'fold over' and re-emerge as low frequency components that are usually non-harmonic. The result is an undesirable change in timbre. Aliasing is usually prevented by the use of low-pass filters in the sampling process to prevent frequencies that are too high from entering the process.

Quantization

When measuring a sample, a fixed number of bits (binary digits) are used to store the value. In an 8 bit sample, for example, 256 values are available to represent the dynamic range. An analogue recording source will have an infinite number of values which are rounded or truncated to the closest available digit. This rounding is *quantization* which introduces some inherent inaccuracy, referred to as quantization error.

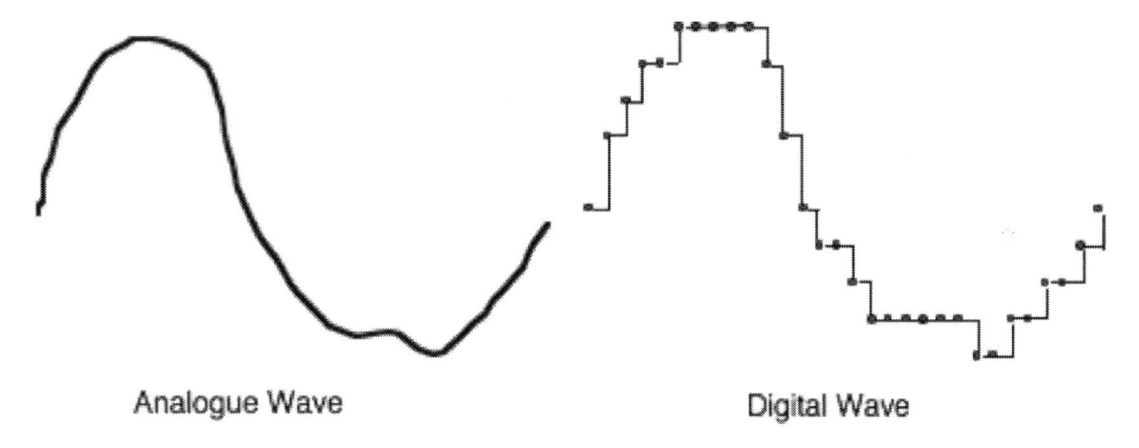

Figure 2.3. Severe quantization of a recorded waveform.

As shown in figure 2.3, the digital representation of the wave is less smooth than the original signal. Just as a square wave has a richer harmonic spectrum than a sine wave, so the more jagged digital signal will introduce some higher harmonics that were not in the original. This quantization noise is usually heard as additional high frequency hiss. The main solution to minimizing quantization is the use of higher bit rates, 16 and above, so that the number of steps in the digital values are so numerous that the rounding is insignificant.

Interpolation

Sampled audio comprises a series of discrete values. At times when replaying or manipulating the sample data it is necessary to work out what values between the samples might be. This process is called *interpolation*. The simplest form of interpolating is to calculate a sample value by looking at both its neighboring samples and imagining a straight line between them and finding the value of the appropriate position along that line. This is called linear interpolation. However, because waveforms are usually curved rather than straight, whenever greater accuracy is required a number of more sophisticated interpolation methods can be used.

Audio File Types

While the details of the audio data remain the same, different types of audio files are often incompatible as a result of the way in which the data is stored in the file. Just as text can be saved differently from each word processing application, so audio data files vary from format to format. In general the differences are in three areas. First, the file has a header that contains details about the data, and different file types have different headers of different sizes and with information stored in different orders. Secondly, the data itself can be arranged in a number of ways. A multi track audio file may store all the data for one track, followed by the data for the next, and so on. Or, it can store the first sample of each track, then the second of each and so on – these types of files are said to be *interleaved*. Interleaved files are very common, CD audio is in this format, but there are some notable exceptions where split channel files are used.

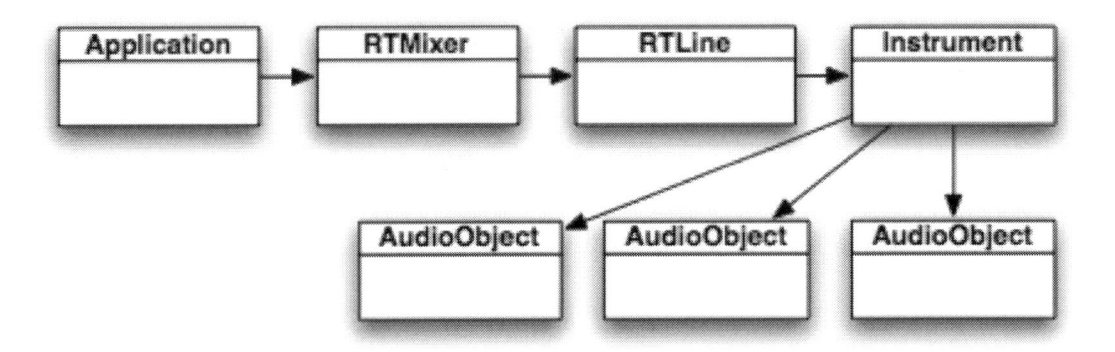

Figure 2.4. Stereo audio data file format examples.

Thirdly, the data can be stored as raw numbers just as they were captured or created, or it can be stored in a varied form usually designed to assist in compressing the data size. It is normal for audio files to store values as signed integers, however, it is more convenient to process audio as floating point numbers because the precision is very high and the risk of clipping audio is almost negligible. The JavaSound libraries leave the decision about the audio processing data type to the programmer, while the jMusic audio routines always work with audio data as floating point values. The floating point values are assumed to be normalized between –1.0 and 1.0 and so data read from files will be scaled within that range and, to avoid clipping when saving, all data should be normalized (see below) prior to saving.

Understanding the details of digital audio is important because even though the JavaSound and jMusic packages contains classes for reading and writing the audio file headers, when we create audio streams in Java we must be aware of the rate, resolution and formats supported by the language, the computer hardware and the file formats we are using. To a large extent, both Java and the jMusic libraries take care of many of these digital audio details, but once we move beyond the simplest programs, an understanding of these details will become essential.

Concept Quiz

1. What is the difference between sample rate and resolution?
2. What is the sample rate used by CD audio?
3. Is the bit depth of the file related to sample rate or resolution?
4. Do the jMusic `Read.audio()` and `Write.audio()` methods deal with samples as integers, bytes or floats?
5. What is the audible result of clipping?
6. Would normalizing floating point audio data prevent clipping in the saved audio file?
7. What is the audible result of aliasing in an audio file?
8. Does the sample rate or sample bit depth influence the possibility of quantization noise?
9. How many samples are required to calculate a linear interpolation?
10. 1n an interleaved stereo audio file how many samples are between the 1st and 3rd sample of the first channel?

Audio Dynamics

At their essence audio samples have only one parameter, loudness. Other musical attributes, such as a pitch and timbre, are a result of combinations of samples over time. Given, that loudness is the basic attribute of samples this section will focus on the way's in which this can be usefully manipulated.

Volume

Changing the volume of a wave is simply a matter of multiplying each sample by the same value. If this value is greater than 1.0 then the volume will increase and if it is less that 1.0 the volume will decrease. As you play with this, remember that data with values larger than 1.0 or less than −1.0 will be clipped when written to an audio file.

```java
import jm.util.*;

public final class VolumeChange {
    public static void main(String[] args){
        float[] data = Read.audio("Welcome.au");
        float gain = 0.5f;
        for (int i=0; i< data.length; i++) {
            data[i] *= gain;
        }
        Write.audio(data, "VolumeChange.aif");
    }
}
```

The f after the number 0.5f indicates that this should be a floating-point value. Without the f a decimal number would default to being a double. Try some extreme gain values to see what effect they have. What effect will a negative gain value have?

Normalize

To normalize a file is to change its volume such that it is as loud as it can be without clipping. The process takes two steps. First, find the maximum value and determine the difference between it and the 1.0 maximum. Secondly, amplify the data by that amount.

```java
import jm.util.*;

public final class Normalize {
    public static void main(String[] args){
        float[] data = Read.audio("Welcome.au");
        float maxGain = 0.0f;
        float gain;
        // find max
        for (int i=0; i< data.length; i++) {
            if (Math.abs(data[i]) >maxGain)
                maxGain = Math.abs(data[i]);
```

```
            }
            // calulate the change in gain required
            gain = 1.0f / maxGain;
            System.out.println("MaxGain = " + maxGain + " gain = " + gain);
            // change the volume of all samples
            for (int i=0; i< data.length; i++) {
                data[i] *= gain;
            }
            Write.audio(data, "Normalized.aif");
        }
    }
```

Remember, that there are negative values in the data and the loudest sample may be a negative one. This is why the `Math.abs()` method is used to find the absolute (positive equivalent) value of each sample.

Fading

In this program each sample is changed by a different value in order to achieve a fade out effect. The first sample is at full volume, then each subsequent one is at an ever decreasing level. The ramping effect is linear, and would look like a straight line if plotted on a graph.

```
    import jm.util.*;

    public final class Fading {
            public static void main(String[] args){
            float[] data = Read.audio("Welcome.au");
            float fadeIncrement = 1.0f / data.length;
            for (int i=0; i< data.length; i++) {
                data[i] *= (data.length - i) * fadeIncrement;
            }
            Write.audio(data, "Fading.aif");
        }
    }
```

Only small changes are required to make the audio fade in rather than fade out, or to fade over a shorter period than the whole file. Try making those adjustments.

Limiting

A simple limiter will put a ceiling on the maximum (positive or negative) value for any sample. The code example below does this. In practice such 'brick wall' limiting is not very musical and simply results in clipping. The resulting data is also reduced in volume.

```java
import jm.util.*;

public final class Limiter {
    public static void main(String[] args){
        float[] data = Read.audio("Welcome.au");
        float maxValue = 0.3f;
        for (int i=0; i< data.length; i++) {
            if (data[i] > maxValue) data[i] = maxValue;
            if (data[i] < -maxValue) data[i] = -maxValue;
        }
        Write.audio(data, "Limited.aif");
    }
}
```

Notice that two if-statements are used, one for positive and one for negative values. A more musical result is achieved by limiting through extreme compression of the dynamic range.

Compressing

A compressor reduces the volume of samples above a specified threshold. It reduces the dynamic range overall and the difference between soft and loud parts of the file. The reduction is specified as a percentage of the value above the threshold. For example, a compression ratio of 4:1 is a reduction of the sample value by one-quarter of the amount above the threshold. If the sample value was 0.6 and the threshold was 0.2 then the compression reduction would be applied to the 0.4 above the threshold which, give a 4:1 ratio would result in a final value of 0.3 (0.2 + 0.1). Because there is always a volume reduction with a compressor it is normal to include a compensating volume gain on all samples.

```java
import jm.util.*;

public final class Compress {
    public static void main(String[] args){
        float[] data = Read.audio("Welcome.au");
```

```java
            float threshold = 0.2f;
            float ratio = 2.0f;
            float gain = 2.0f;
            for (int i=0; i< data.length; i++) {
                // positive values
                if (data[i] > threshold) {
                    data[i] = threshold +(data[i]-threshold) *
                        (1.0f/ratio);
                }
                // negative values
                if (data[i] < -threshold) {
                    data[i] = -threshold + (data[i]+threshold) *
                        (1.0f/ratio);
                }
                // apply the gain to all samples
                data[i] *= gain;
                if (Math.abs(data[i]) > max)
                max = Math.abs(data[i]);
            }
            Write.audio(data, "Compressed.aif");
        }
    }
```

Experiment with the ratio, threshold and gain variables to achieve different compression effects. Using a ratio of less than 1:1 will turn the compressor into an expander.

Math Moment

The human ear does not respond to loudness in a linear way. This means that a gain reduction of 0.5 in the `VolumeChange` class will not result in a perceptual halving on the loudness, in fact a much larger change is necessary to produce that. Perceived loudness is measured on the logarithmic decibel scale. All the variations in dynamics would need to substitute different formulae to achieve the appropriate psychoacoustic effect. For example in the compressor, rather than the simple (1.0f/ratio) ratio calculation the math should be `(float)Math.min(1.0, (Math.abs(Math.log(1.0 - 1.0/ratio) * 0.2 )));`.

Java Details

There have been a few new Java concepts introduced in this chapter. In this section we'll examine them in more detail.

Java Data Types

Data types are the basic elements that a computer language can use for expressing numbers and letters. Therefore they are critical to the computer's operation. In this chapter we have looked at some of the musical data types in jMusic and in this section we will examine some of the data types native to the language Java. These Java data types are sometimes closely matched to the basic operations of the computer's CPU itself, although the JVM does shield Java programmers from many of the CPU issues that earlier languages needed to navigate. Java data types include the following:

Type	Meaning	Size	Range (approx)
boolean	Two state value	1 bit	True or False
byte	An 8 bit number	8 bit	-128 to 127
short	Small integer number	16 bit	-32,768 to 32,767
int	Integer number	32 bit	-2^{31} to $2^{31} - 1$
long	Large integer number	64 bit	-2^{63} to $2^{63} - 1$
float	Floating point (fractional) number	32 bit	10 decimal places precision
double	Large floating point number	64 bit	Massive precision!
char	Alphanumeric character	16 bit	a-z & A-Z and many more
String	An array of characters	N/A	variable
Array	A list of a fixed size	N/A	variable

In Java some of these data types are primitive and some are objects. The difference is subtle but important, and will be covered in more detail later in the book. Numbers characters and boolean types are primitive in Java. In the type list above, the ones starting with lower-case letters are primitive, the others are classes and their name, following the Java class naming convention, start with an upper case letter. There are object versions of each of these primitive types provided in Java when that is required. For example, the `int` primitive type has a related `Integer` class and the `float` type has a related `Float` class.

Arrays

An array is a list of a fixed length. There can be arrays of any type in Java. For example an array of `ints`, an array of floats or an array of Strings.

Arrays are indicated with square brackets [ ]. An array of `ints` is declared in this way:

```
int[] myIntArray;
```

An array with a particular size is declared as:

```
int[] myIntArray = new Array[23];
```

An array can also be declared and filled in the one operation, in this way:

```
int[] myIntArray = {2, 45, 6, 78, 32, 11};
```

We have seen an array of Strings as an argument to the main() method in all our examples so far. This enables the program to accept and list of words and/or numbers as data when the program runs.

Data is accessed in an array by specifying the index in the list you wish to set or retrieve inside the square brackets. Remember that the index starts at zero. For example, retrieving the fourth element from the array:

```
int age = myIntArray[3];
```

Setting the first element of the array;

```
myIntArray[0] = 44;
```

Iteration

Repeating processes is called iteration and is a common and powerful feature of programming languages, including Java. The workhorse iteration operation in Java is the for-loop. Which has the form:

```
for (initial condition; boolean result; iterative update) {
    //code to execute if boolean result is true;
}
```

An example is :

```
for (int i=0; i < data.length; i++) {
    data[i] *= (data.length - i) * fadeIncrement;
}
```

This example starts by setting an integer variable i to a value of zero. Each time around the loop i is compared to see if it is less than the length of the array named data. If so, then the value of i is incremented by one and the block of code is executed once. The Boolean (true or false) test is checked and the loop continues until the result is false, at which time the program moves on to the code after the for-loop.

Casting

Casting is way of changing one Java type into another. This is only legal in sensible cases, such an casting one number type to another. The compiler won't allow a cast from a Note to a Boolean for example. Casting is indicated by a bracketed type name prior to an instance of another type. For example, changing a double to a float `(float)0.5;` or changing an integer to a double `(double)7;`.

Concept Quiz

1. Which math operator is used for amplification of audio data, +, -, / or *?
2. What number results from this code fragment? `Math.abs(-0.2451)`?
3. Is each sample in an audio fade reduced by the same amount?
4. Is aliasing or clipping a potential risk with applying a limiter to digital audio data?
5. What are the stages in a normalizing algorithm?
6. Why is an overall gain change often required at the end of in a compression algorithm?
7. What code will access the 5th element of an array named `myData`?

3: Manipulating Digital Audio

The concept of digital audio was introduced in chapter 2, so now we will turn our attention to processes and techniques for working with digital audio. Because the digital representation of sound is a simple list of numerical sample values, all manipulations will be mathematical functions of various types on those numbers. While some of the manipulations, such as reversing a sound, require straight forward manipulations others are more complex or less obvious. We will look at a number of these processes without attempting to teach digital signal processing techniques in detail, which is the topic of other (many other) engineering texts.

Music Moment

The use of audio recordings as a compositional tool was extensively developed in the middle of the 20th century by Pierre Schaeffer and his colleagues at the GRM studios in Paris through a process they called *musique concrète*. The name was given to reflect the fact that they were making music from static recorded sounds assembled into sound constructions. At the time, recordings were made onto analogue tape and these recordings were 'processed' by cutting and splicing tape segments together into sound collages. This practice was revolutionary at the time, but today we take the capture and manipulation of recorded sound for granted, and it has become widely accepted that such manipulation can be considered an artistic practice.

Dividing and Combining Audio

The methods used in creating pieces of musique concrète by cutting and splicing magnetic tape are now much easier with digital audio technologies. In this chapter we will explore some of these techniques and see how they can be used creatively to make new music.

Mixing

Combining two audio files to hear both sounds together—mixing the files—is simply a matter of adding the sample values one by one. `CombinedSample = file1Sample + file2Sample`. In order to prevent clipping if the combine samples values are above the maximum threshold, a volume change multiplier can be used. So the final formula is; `CombinedSample = (file1Sample + file2Sample) * gainReductionAmount`.

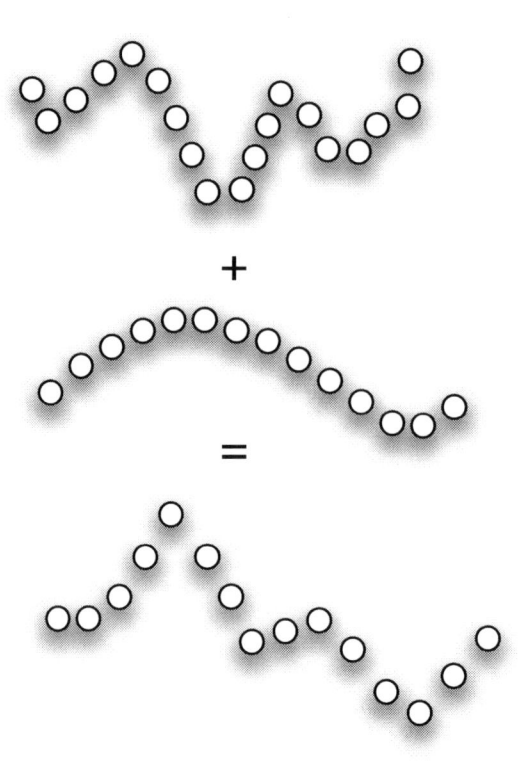

Figure 3.1. Mixing two waveforms by adding samples one by one.

Here is the code for the *Mixer* class that reads two files and adds them together. It looks slightly longer than you might expect because it has to make allowances for files of different lengths.

```java
import jm.util.*;

public class Mixer {
    float[] data1, data2;

    public static void main(String[] args) {
       Mixer m =  new Mixer();
         m.process();
    }

    private void process() {
        // get the data to be mixed
        data1 = Read.audio("Welcome.au");
        data2 = Read.audio("RainStick.wav");
```

```java
        // prepare for calling mix method
        float[] mixedData;
        if (data1.length > data2.length) {
            mixedData = mix(data1, data2);
        } else {
            mixedData = mix(data2, data1);
        }

        // output the resulting file
        Write.audio(mixedData, "MixedAudio.aif");
    }

    private  float[] mix(float[] longest, float[] shortest) {
        float[] tempData = new float[longest.length];
        // combine where file length overlaps
        for (int i=0; i<shortest.length; i++) {
            tempData[i] = (longest[i] + shortest[i])  * 0.5f;
        }
        // pad out with remainder of longer file
        for (int i=shortest.length; i<longest.length; i++) {
            tempData[i] = longest[i]  * 0.5f;
        }
        return tempData;
    }
}
```

Dividing audio files

A common requirement when working with audio files is to isolate particular sections of the file. The *Chop* program creates a new file from a specified segment off the original file. The start and end points of the segment are specified in samples. It is possible to modify the program so the start and end locations are specified as time (in seconds) or beats (taking into account a tempo) locations and then performing the appropriate mathematical conversion to samples.

```java
import jm.util.*;

public class Chop {
    float[] data = Read.audio("Welcome.au");

    public static void main(String[] args) {
        Chop chop =  new Chop();
```

```
            Write.audio(chop.process(1000, 4000),
    "ChoppedAudio.aif");
        }

        private float[] process(int startLocation, int endLocation) {
            int length = endLocation - startLocation;
            float[] tempData = new float[length];
            for (int i=0; i<length; i++) {
                tempData[i] = data[startLocation + i];
            }
            return tempData;
        }
    }
```

Lopping

Repeating segments of audio files can be used at a small scale to help sustain the sound, and at larger scales to create rhythmic effects. The *Loop* program is an extension of the *Chop* program that makes multiple copies of a segment.

```
    import jm.util.*;

    public class Loop {
        float[] data = Read.audio("Welcome.au");

        public static void main(String[] args) {
            Loop lp =  new Loop();
            Write.audio(lp.process(1000, 4000, 5), "LoopedAudio.aif");
        }

        private float[] process(int startLocation, int endLocation,
                    int repeats) {
            int length = endLocation - startLocation;
            float[] tempData = new float[length * repeats];
            for (int i=0; i<length; i++) {
                tempData[i] = data[startLocation + i];
            }
            for (int i=1; i<repeats; i++) {
                for (int j=0; j<length; j++) {
                    tempData[j + i * length] = tempData[j];
                }
```

```
        }
        return tempData;
    }
}
```

Inserting silence

Silence is very quiet audio. To make a section of an audio file contain silence the sample values simply need to be set to zero. It is important to remember that even though it cannot be heard, silent audio sections continue to occupy the same amount of memory and file space as audio we can hear. The number of samples in the file do not change, only their values. The silence program changes the samples values within a specified region of the audio file.

```
import jm.util.*;

public class Silence {
    float[] data = Read.audio("Welcome.au");

    public static void main(String[] args) {
        Silence sil = new Silence();
        Write.audio(sil.process(5000, 20000),"SilenceAdded.aif");
    }

    private float[] process(int startLocation, int endLocation){
        int length = endLocation - startLocation;
        for (int i=0; i<length; i++) {
            data[startLocation + i] = 0.0f;
        }
        return data;
    }
}
```

Envelopes

At the borders between sounding and silent areas of a wave file (including at the beginning and end of the file) a sudden change of sample value can cause an audible click. To reduce this unwanted artifact a short fade in or out can be applied to the sounding section. The curve which outlines the overall loudness of the wave file is called the amplitude envelope of the sound. By changing the volume at the ends of the sounding segments to minimize 'clicks' we are altering the envelope of the wave. Envelope changes can also be used for cross fading segments, or changing the expressive and, sometimes, timbral character of the sound.

```java
import jm.util.*;

public class Envelope {
    float[] data = Read.audio("Welcome.au");

    public static void main(String[] args) {
        Envelope env =  new Envelope();
        Write.audio(env.process(5000, 25000, 1000),"EnvelopedSegment.aif");
        View.au("EnvelopedSegment.aif");
    }

    private float[] process(int startLocation, int endLocation, int fadeSize){
        int length = endLocation - startLocation;
        float[] tempData = new float[length];
        for (int i=0; i<length; i++) {
            tempData[i] = data[startLocation + i];
        }
        // fade in
        for (int i=0; i<fadeSize; i++) {
            tempData[i] *=  (float)i/ (float)fadeSize;
        }
        //fade out
        for (int i=0; i<fadeSize; i++) {
            tempData[tempData.length - i - 1] *=  (float)i/ (float)fadeSize;
        }

        return tempData;
    }
}
```

Zero crossings

Another method for minimizing clicks in cut-up audio segments is to ensure that the cut points occur at samples whose value is zero. Zero crossings are locations in the wave data when the waveform passes through the half-way, zero, value. Using zero crossings for cut locations avoids large leaps from segment to segment or between silence and segments ends.

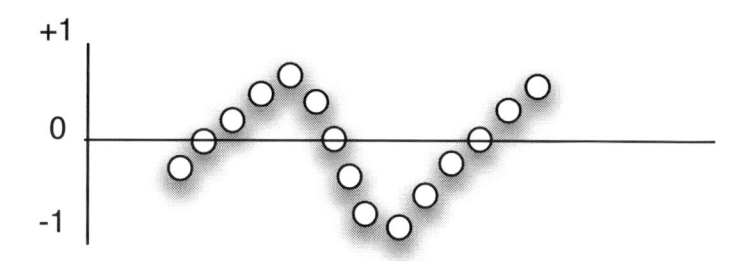

Figure 3.2. A wave section with three zero crossing points.

To search for zero crossing points in your code, simply check the value of each sample until you find one that equals (or is very close too) zero. This code fragment is an elaboration on a section of the *Loop* program that adjusts the loop end point to ensure that it falls on the first zero crossing after the specified loop end location. In practice this difference in loop end time will be so short that it will not effect the tempo of the loop to a noticeable degree. The additional code required is shown in bold in below. It creates an additional condition that keeps the for-loop processing until both the segment length is exceeded and the sample value equals zero.

```
for (int i=0; i<length && data[startLocation + i] != 0.0f; i++) {
    tempData[i] = data[startLocation + i];
}
```

Random recombination

The *Recombine* program chops several segments from a wave file and creates a new file from them. The segments are randomly selected from the wave data, then toped and tailed by changing the segment envelope with a short fade in and out. Because several segments are extracted and processed, the code that does this can be put into a `newSegment()` method which is called three times. Checks are made to the random values to make sure that the ranges for segment size and position are valid.

```
import jm.util.*;

public class Recombine {
    float[] data = Read.audio("Welcome.au");

    public static void main(String[] args) {
        Recombine recomb = new Recombine();
        Write.audio(recomb.process(), "Recombined.aif");
        View.au("Recombined.aif");
```

```java
    }

    private float[] process() {
        float[] seg1 = newSegment();
        float[] seg2 = newSegment();
        float[] seg3 = newSegment();

        float[] newData = new float[seg1.length + seg2.length +
                seg3.length];
        int newDataCounter = 0;
        for (int i=0; i<seg1.length; i++) {
            newData[newDataCounter++] = seg1[i];
        }
        for (int i=0; i<seg2.length; i++) {
            newData[newDataCounter++] = seg2[i];
        }
        for (int i=0; i<seg3.length; i++) {
            newData[newDataCounter++] = seg3[i];
        }

        return newData;
    }

    private float[] newSegment() {
        float fadeSize = 500f;
        int length = (int)(Math.random() * data.length / 2) +
                (int)(fadeSize * 2);
        int startLocation = (int)(Math.random() *
                (data.length - fadeSize * 2 - length));

        float[] tempData = new float[length];
        for (int i=0; i<length; i++) {
            tempData[i] = data[startLocation + i];
        }
        for (int i=0; i<fadeSize; i++) {
            tempData[i] *=  i/ fadeSize;
        }
        for (int i=0; i<fadeSize; i++) {
            tempData[tempData.length - i - 1] *=  i/ fadeSize;
        }
```

```
            return tempData;
        }
    }
```

Programming Practice

After typing in and running the Recombine program try changing the `process()` method and adding a for-loop within in to allow any number of very short segments to be recombined. Whenever you see the sort of repetition of code that appears in the `process()` method there is usually an opportunity to consolidate by reducing the repetitive code and adding a for-loop around the single remaining code block.

Audio Data Parameters

The two key attributes of an audio file are its sample rate and bit depth. In this section we will explore how the sound changes as these attributes vary.

Resolution

The resolution of the audio file depends upon the size, or bit depth, of the 'words' used to represent each sample. Data words are made up of a number of bytes, and each byte is made up of 8 bits – binary digits. Data words are, therefore, multiples of a byte such that a sample value can be represented by an 8 bit, 16 bit, 24 bit or 32 bit word, and so on.

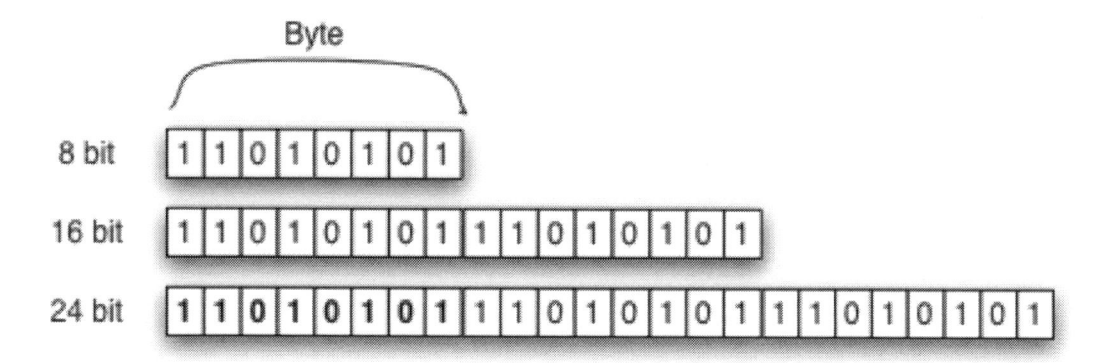

Figure 3.3. Various sample word sizes.

A 16 bit sample has greater resolution and than 8 bit sample but less than a 24 or 32 bit sample.

Changing the bit depth

An audio file can be saved as an 8, 16, 24 or other bit format. The lower bit depths will result in smaller files but the dynamic range will be reduced and the amount of quantization noise may increase. Higher bit depths are desirable to improve audio quality but the additional bytes will increase file size and audio processing overhead. The *SampleBitDepthChange* program reads in a file, assumed to be 16 bit mono, and writes out an 8 bit and 24 bit version of the file.

```java
import jm.util.*;

public final class SampleBitDepthChange {
    public static void main(String[] args){
        float[] data = Read.audio("Welcome.au");
        Write.audio(data, "Welcome44_8.aif",1, 44100, 8);
        Write.audio(data, "Welcome44_32.aif",1, 44100, 24);
    }
}
```

When comparing the audio files, you will notice that the quantization noise in the 8 bit file is quite audible and that the 24 bit file sounds identical to the original - the increase in bit depth from the 16 bit original does not improve the quality of existing data. The `Write.audio()` method can save the data in a variety of formats.

```
Write.audio(data, "Welcome44_8.aif", 1, 44100, 8);
```

The third, forth and fifth arguments to the `Write.audio()` method indicate the number of channels (1 in this case – mono), the sample rate for the new file (44100 sps) and the bit depth of the file (8 bit).

Resampling

The sample rate determines the number of samples per second used to describe the waveform, it also relates to the speed of sample data playback. You may have experienced a tape recording device which lowered the pitch of the recording when playback was slowed down. The same connection between sample rate and pitch exists for digital signals.

Changing sample rate

A clear example of how the sample rate effects the pitch is demonstrated in the *SampleRateChange* program. Here an audio file, assumed to have a sample rate of 44100 samples per second, is read in then new files are saved each with a different sample rate. The lower sample rate results in a lowering of pitch, and the higher sample rate results in an increase in pitch. Here is the important line of code in this program.

```
Write.audio(data, "Welcome22.aif", 1, 22050, 16);
```

The arguments to the `Write.audio()` method indicate that the number of channels will be 1 (mono), the sample rate for the new file is 22050 sps and the bit depth of the file is 16 bit. Here is the complete code listing.

```
import jm.util.*;
public final class SampleRateChange {
    public static void main(String[] args) {
        float[] data = Read.audio("Welcome.au");
        Write.audio(data, "Welcome22.aif", 1, 22050, 16);
        Write.audio(data, "Welcome48.aif", 1, 48000, 16);
    }
}
```

This resampling process changes the duration of the sound as well, lower sounds are longer, while higher sounds are faster. This is quite understandable when you consider that the same number of samples are in each file, but they are being played back more or less frequently, depending on the sample rate.

Changing the number of channels

Another way of changing the pitch and duration of the waveform is to alter the number of samples. In this example we will divide the samples into two channels, thus making it a stereo file. This process will put every second sample in the first channel and the others into the second. Picking alternate channels for each sample halves the playback time, because both channels play back simultaneously. Because the sound file is being stepped through twice as fast the pitch will also increase, even though the sample rate of the file is the same. Figure 3.4 shows how the sample data is organized in mono and stereo files.

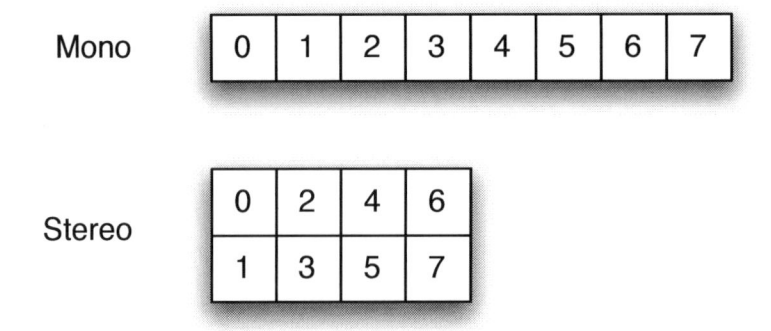

Figure 3.4. Arranging samples in mono and stereo formats.

The *ChannelChange* program reads in a mono file and writes out a stereo file.

```
import jm.util.*;

public final class ChannelChange {
    public static void main(String[] args){
        float[] data = Read.audio("Welcome.au");
        Write.audio(data, "WelcomeStereo.aif", 2, 44100, 16);
    }
}
```

The third argument to the `Write.audio()` method indicates the number of channels, a value of 2 indicates a stereo file.

Pitch shifting

A technique of sample skipping can be used to increase the pitch of a sound. By varying the number of samples skipped the pitch increase can be controlled. Similarly, the pitch of a digital audio stream can be lowered by adding extra samples to the data at regular intervals. By varying the regularity of adding samples the amount of pitch lowering can be controlled. In the *SimplePitchShift* program the pitch of the sound is altered by either removing or duplicating samples at regular intervals throughout the data array. Here is the complete code.

```
import jm.util.*;

public final class SimplePitchShift {
    public static void main(String[] args){
        float[] data = Read.audio("Welcome.au");
        double originalPitch = 440.0;
```

```
            double newPitch = 261.0;
            double resamplingRatio = newPitch/originalPitch;
            float[] newData = new float[(int)(data.length/resamplingRatio)+1];

            int counter = 0;
            for (double i=0.0; i<data.length; i += resamplingRatio) {
                newData[counter++] = data[(int)i];
            }
            Write.audio(newData, "ShiftedPitch.aif");
    }
}
```

Let's examine the code step by step.

First, we make an assumption about the original pitch, or fundamental frequency, of the sound as a reference point. In this case we arbitrarily define the original pitch as 440.0 cps, A4. The target frequency is specified, `newPitch = 261.0`, which is approximately C4. The resampling ratio is the difference between these two frequencies. It will be used to determine how regularly to interrogate the original data and calculate a new sample value. If this ratio is 1.0 each new sample will correspond with an existing one and the result will be identical to the original. If the resampling ratio is less than 1.0, then the new data will have more sample than the original data, and the resulting pitch will be lower. If the resampling ratio is above 1.0 then the pitch shift is upward, and the new data will skip over some of the samples in the original data.

As shown in figure 3.5. The sample ratio increments are `double` values because `int` values would not provide enough granularity to produce all the pitch values we might want. As a result, the new sample positions will not fall evenly on the existing values, so in-between values will need to be created. In the *SimplePitchShift* program new in-between samples are created by duplicating a nearby value.

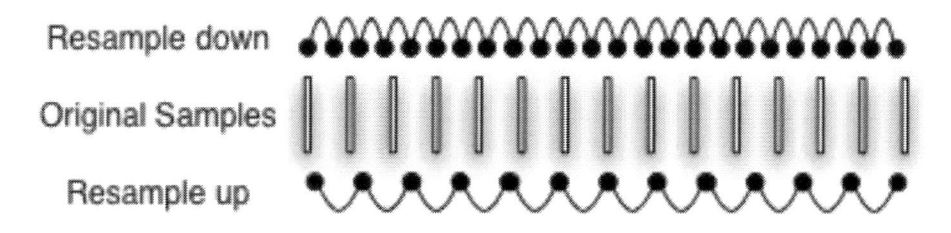

Figure 3.5. Sample data points during interpolation.

Next in the program an array to hold the adjusted data is created, called newData. The array length is a multiple of the resample ratio, if the ratio is less than 1.0 a larger array will be required because extra samples will be generated, otherwise a smaller one is all that is needed. The for-loop iterates through the original sample data. It steps through one resample ratio increment at a time, as shown by the top row of dots in figure 3.5. Any new sample value is determined as being equal to the preceding sample in the original data.

```
newData[counter++] = data[(int)i];
```

The casting of i, a double, to an int will truncate the value. That is, it will remove its fractional component. For example, 243.789 will become 243. Notice that truncating is different to rounding to the closest whole number. Finally, the Write.audio() method is used to save the new data as an audio file. This file should have the same number of channels, sample rate and bit depth as the original file – mono, 44100, 16. Keeping these file attributes fixed ensures that any change in the sound is attributable to the signal processing in our program.

Math Moment

Interestingly, many signal processing and music composition tasks use similar mathematical processes relating to dividing. Division and its related functions are useful for segmenting and structuring tasks from the micro to the macro level of music making. Here are brief descriptions of some of the most often used:

- division - split up into a number of equally sized segments (e.g., 1024 / 8 = 128)
- truncate - remove any fractional amount from a number (e.g., Math.floor(123.654) => 123)
- round - resolve a number to the closest whole number value (e.g., Math.round(123.654) => 124)
- modulus - returns the factional remainder of a division (e.g., 1001 % 10 => 1)

Interpolation

When pitch shifting by amounts that are not simple ratios of the original pitch, the new sample values will fall between the existing samples. When increasing the number of samples in a sound, the amplitude of the new samples should ideally be calculated to fit with the implied curve of the waveform. Calculating the new sample value based on the surrounding sample values is called *interpolating* the value. In the *SimplePitchShift* example the additional samples were only duplicates of a neighboring sample. While this worked after a fashion, it increases quantization noise in the signal because the data curve becomes more jagged as the duplicate samples are added.

Pitch shift through interpolation

The use of interpolation results in a smoother amplitude curve and, therefore, less quantization noise than in the previous simple pitch shifting algorithm. Weather or not this is a desirable result is a musical decision. The most common form of interpolation is linear interpolation, where the value is calculated as a point along the straight line drawn between those existing sample values.

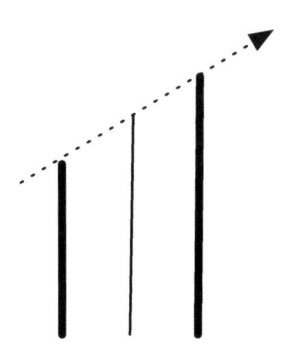

Figure 3.6. Linear interpolation used to calculate the centre sample value.

The bold lines of code in the *Interpolation* program below perform the linear interpolation between the two samples closest to the new sample location. In other respects this example is the same as the *SimplePitchShift* program.

```
import jm.util.*;

public final class Interpolation {
    public static void main(String[] args){
        float[] data = Read.audio("Welcome.au");
        double originalPitch = 440.0;
        double newPitch = 261.0;
        double resamplingRatio = newPitch/originalPitch;
        float[] newData = new float[(int)(data.length/resamplingRatio+1)];

        int counter = 0;
        for (double i=0.0; i<data.length - 1; i += resamplingRatio) {

            float lowerSample = data[(int)i];
            float upperSample = data[(int)i + 1];
            float difference = upperSample - lowerSample;
            float newSampleValue = lowerSample + difference *
                (float)(i%1.0);
            newData[counter++] = newSampleValue;
```

```
        }
            Write.audio(newData, "LinearInterpolated.aif");
    }
}
```

Even though interpolation improves the pitch-shifted audio, it may not eliminate timbral artifacts such as the 'chipmonk' effect when pitch shifting up, especially when the pitch shift distance is large, and it does nothing to prevent alteration of the sound's duration.

Resampling details

When increasing the pitch of a sound, the range of it's frequency spectrum is shifted up. It is possible that the higher frequencies in the 'upsampled' spectrum may be greater than half the sample rate, and so above the Nyquist frequency, which will result in aliasing. To prevent this, it is good practice to low pass filter the sound prior to resampling to remove frequencies greater than half the new sample rate. Resampling can involve even more complex interpolation algorithms that generate a smoother waveform. In his book *Real Sound Synthesis*, Perry Cook (2002) recommends using the `sinc` function as for ideal interpolation.

More sophisticated pitch shifting algorithms often allow the pitch to be shifted without effecting the duration of the sound. These processes require a combination of resampling and delaying, where the sample data is divided into small sections and each part is resampled individually then remixed. For more information on pitch shifting algorithms in Java see Craig Lindley's book *Digital Audio with Java* (2000).

Java Details

The processing of audio data relies heavily on many of the mathematical functions available in Java. While the standard functions—add, subtract, divide and multiply—are often enough for simple changes, more involved math functions are occasionally required. Like other modern programming languages, Java has extensive mathematical capabilities and the `Math` class provides many of them.

The Math class

We have used `Math.random()` quite a bit so far in this book, but it is only one of the methods in Java's `java.lang.Math` class. The class includes methods for rounding numbers, generating sine and cosine values, doing square roots and logarithmic functions, and many more. The methods in the `Math` class are static, which means that we don't need to make an instance of them when they are used. Some of the jMusic classes work this way too, including the `Read`, `Write`, `Play`, `View` and `Mod` classes. This use of static methods is not considered a very elegant design from the perspective of object-oriented programming, but it is a convenient way to access these functionalities. This table summarizes a number of the most commonly used methods in the math class. Consult the Java documentation for a complete list.

- `Math.abs(x)` Int, long, float, double Absolute (positive) value
- `Math.cos(x)` Double Cosine value
- `Math.sin(x)` Double Sine value
- `Math.log(x)` Double Natural logarithm of x
- `Math.max(x, y)` Int, long, float, double Maximum of the two
- `Math.min(x, y)` Int, long, float, double Minimum of the two
- `Math.pow(x, y)` Double X to the power y
- `Math.random()` None Random value, 0.0 to 1.0
- `Math.round(x)` Float, double Closest whole number to x
- `Math.sqrt(x)` Double Square root of x

A method's return type

Method declarations must always specify a return type. Return types can be any data type. When the method does not return (produce) any value the type `void` is specified. The return type is positioned just prior to the method name in the declaration as in this example where the `getCounter()` method returns an `int`.

```
int getCounter() {}
private int getCounter() {}
```

Here are some more examples;

```
float getAmplitude() {
    ...
}
private boolean makeDecision() {
    ...
}
```

Methods that specify a return type are required to pass back (return) a value of that type when they finish executing. This is usually achieved using the return keyword, as in this example;

```
public int getFileType(String fileName) {
    int fileType;
    ...
    return fileType;
}
```

If a method does not need to return a value it uses the void keyword in place of a return type.

```
private void setFilterCutoff(int cutoffValue) {
    ...
}
```

The only important exception to this pattern of return types is a constructor method, which does not include a return type (a type of the current class is both assumed and automatically returned).

And, or, not

When writing software algorithms decisions are often required in the code; most often using if-then or while statements. To support more complex decisions involving several conditions a number of operators are provided for; and, or and not. They have the corresponding symbols &&, || and !. Here are some examples;

"if x is greater than five and y is less than ten"
if (x > 5 && y < 10)

"if vol is less than zero or mute is true"
if (vol < 0 || mute == true)

"while i is not equal to zero"
while (i != 0)

Concept Quiz

1. How much larger would 24 bit file be than the same data saved as an 8 bit file?
2. What might be the audible artifacts that result from lowering the bit depth of a file?
3. Does interpolation effect the timbre or the pitch of the resample waveform?
4. What would be the result of this code? Math.abs(-34);

4: Music as Digital Data

Musical ideas are abstract, and therefore in order to communicate them to another person or to a computer we need to represent these ideas in some way. Languages are formal systems for representing our ideas and Java is a language designed to help us communicate with the computer. Music notation systems are languages (more correctly symbol systems) for representing music. The most well established Western music representation system is Common Practice Notation (CPN), the system of dots and squiggles on five-line staves. Computer music systems usually require a much more accurate and flexible system than CPN because the computer cannot be relied upon to interpret the notation with very much cultural understanding. jMusic's music representation scheme is based on CPN to make it easy to learn, but can be much more elaborate and detailed than CPN when this is required. In this chapter, we introduce Java objects and the way in which they are structured for music making. In particular we look at some of the jMusic music data objects and how they represent musical information.

Musical Components and Structure

Music is made up of structured sounds and silence. But music, as sound or ideas, is not a concrete thing that we can see, grasp or capture. In order to do so we create musical representations. Typically these representations stand for particular musical events and describe the characteristics of these events. But what are music representations for? They serve a number of functions. First, they make music concrete and stable so that it can be stored and manipulated. We can capture music as scores, data structures and files and we can process and modify the representation. Secondly, it allows music to be communicated in ways other than aurally. We can transfer files to other software packages, send the musical representations over the internet, and print them out using music publishing software. Thirdly, a representation is a conception of music, a way of understanding it, a way to think about it. The way we represent music says a lot about what we conceive music to be, and it influences the types of musical transformations that will be evident and available to us. Importantly, the music representation is *not* the music, and so the way a representation is interpreted by software, hardware or humans can vary the outcome significantly by amplifying any distortion present in the representation system.

Over time there have been many schemes for representing music, and in Western cultures the most prevalent has been the use of the notated score. The data structure in jMusic takes this tradition as a starting point and builds upon it. A computer representation of music, or anything else, needs to be quite detailed because the computer's interpretation is very literal, even moronic. As we proceed through this book the level of detail in the music representations will become more fine-grained, but for now many assumptions are made to keep the task manageable.

The jMusic data structure

The musical information in jMusic is stored in a hierarchical fashion based upon a conventional score on paper.

```
Score (Contains any number of Parts)
   |
   +---- Part (Contains any number of Phrases)
            |
            +---- Phrase (Contains any number of Notes.)
                     |
                     +---- Note (A single musical event.)
```

This is a highly orthodox structure where a piece of music is represented as a score, that score has several parts (e.g., a flute part and a percussion part), each part contains phrases (e.g., melodies, riffs, grooves, sequences, patterns) and each phrase is made up of one or more notes (individual sound events). The structure and naming conventions are designed to be familiar to those with some musical knowledge, however, this hierarchy is only a starting point and, as will become clear later, you can represent any style of music within this structure. We will now examine the details of this data structure, starting with the most important and most basic music event, the Note.

Notes and rests

Notes are musical events. These events can have many properties, which typically include pitch, duration and loudness. The `jm.music.data.Note` class is the most basic musical structure used by jMusic. `Note` objects contain lots of useful information including:

- `Pitch` - the frequency of note.

- `RhythmValue` - the length of the note

- `Dynamic` - the loudness of the note.

Each attribute is of a particular Java *type* which has a very wide range of potential values, only a part of that range is used by jMusic. Here are the types and valid ranges for these `Note` fields.

- `Pitch` - integer (0 – 127, lowest to highest frequency of the note in chromatic steps)
- `RhythmValue` - double (>=0.0, shortest to longest length of the note in beats)
- `Dynamic` - integer (0 – 127, softest to loudest intensity of the note)

Creating a note is done using the `new` keyword, and passing the desired attribute values. The most common `Note` constructor takes arguments for pitch, rhythm, and dynamic. This line of code creates a loud, middle C, quarter note that is assigned to the variable **n**.

```
Note n = new Note(60, 1.0. 85);
```

There are helpful constant values for these attributes to make the code easier to read and write. The line above can be rewritten using constants inherited from the JMC interface. A full list of JMC constants can be found in Appendix A.

```
Note n = new Note(C4, QUARTER_NOTE, FORTE);
```

or with constants that are abbreviations,

```
Note n = new Note(C4, QN, F);
```

A special type of `Note` object is a `Rest`. A rest is a silent note, used to create space in a phrase. A `Rest` has a `rhythmValue`, but no `pitch` or `dynamic` (of course).

```
Rest r = new Rest(QN);
```

There is another way to create a rest, as a special type of `Note`. This is useful in algorithms where notes and rests are being created together.

```
Note r = new Note(REST, QN);
```

This code example creates a phrase from a few notes and rests and plays it back.

```
import jm.JMC;
import jm.music.data.*;
import jm.util.*;

public class Beet implements JMC {
    public static void main(String[] args) {
        Phrase phr = new Phrase(0.0);
        for (int i=0; i<3; i++) {
            Note e = new Note(E4, EIGHTH_NOTE_TRIPLET);
            phr.addNote(e);
        }
```

```
            Note c = new Note(C4, HALF_NOTE);
            phr.addNote(c);
            Rest r = new Rest(QUARTER_NOTE);
            phr.addRest(r);
            for (int i=0; i<3; i++) {
                Note d = new Note(D4, EIGHTH_NOTE_TRIPLET);
                phr.addNote(d);
            }
            Note b = new Note(B3, HALF_NOTE);
            phr.addNote(b);

            Play.midi(phr);
        }
    }
```

Programming Practice

Type up this program in a text editor. Save it as Beet.java. Compile the program using javac Beet.java and execute it using java Beet. Notice that the phrase is created first, then after each note or rest is created it is added to the phrase. The order in which notes are added is critical to their playback order. Because this phrase has repeated notes a for-loop is used to more easily add multiple notes of the same value. The phrase is in two parts and the rest is added to separate them.

Phrases

While notes are the building blocks of music, they are often arranged in a series called a phrase. A jMusic Phrase can contain many Notes. Every Phrase object contains a list of Notes that can be added to, subtracted from or moved as a group to a new start location. The Java container class that enables this expanding and contracting list-like behavior is called a Vector and is found in Java's util package, java.util.Vector. Don't worry if you don't completely understand Vectors for the moment, it is enough that you are simply aware that a Phrase class uses one to hold a list of Note objects.

A Phrase has other attributes as well as the list of Notes, in particular it has a start time attribute. StartTime is of type double and is measured in beats. For example, a phrase with a start time of 4.0 would begin four beats after the start of the piece. The length of a beat varies with the tempo, or speed, of the music. The default tempo is 60 beats per minute (bpm) such that one beat equals one second. At 120 bpm each beat lasts half a second. A Note's rhythm value is also in beats, so that note lengths are relative to each other, and so that timing and playback length change as the tempo of the score is altered. We will discuss setting and changing tempi later, when describing `Score` objects.

Creating a new phrase is usually done using just one argument, the start time. In this case the phrase is set to start at beat 0.0, the beginning of the music. This code creates a new `Phrase` object assigned to the variable `phr`.

```
Phrase phr = new Phrase(0.0);
```

Once a phrase has been created, notes can be added to it using the `addNote()` method.

```
phr.addNote(n);
```

Importantly, the list of notes in a phrase is monophonic, that is, notes are stored one after another in the order that they are added to the phrase. This seems obvious for melodies and riffs, but it means that several phrases are required to represent a chord or a drum kit rhythm where more than one note may sound together. Monophonic phrases are not a limitation, but a design choice of jMusic, which aims to keep simple things easy to do while ensuring that complex things are possible. Chords and polyphonic textures are adequately catered for in other ways using multiple phrases or the `CPhrase` class, as we will see later.

Here is an extension of the *Bing* program that creates a phrase, adds three notes to it, then saves the phrase as a MIDI file and plays it back.

```
import jm.JMC;
import jm.music.data.*;
import jm.util.Play;
import jm.util.Write;

public final class BingPhrase implements JMC {
    public static void main(String[] args) {
        Phrase phr = new Phrase(0.0);
        Note n = new Note(G4, EIGHTH_NOTE);
        phr.addNote(n);
        Note n2 = new Note(D4, QUARTER_NOTE);
        phr.addNote(n2);
        Note n3 = new Note(E4, HALF_NOTE);
        phr.addNote(n3);
        Write.midi(phr, "BingPhrase.mid");
        Play.midi(phr);
    }
```

}

Programming Practice

To compile the program using a terminal (command line) application use the java compiler, `javac`. Open a new terminal window and navigate (using the `cd` command in Unix/Linux systems) to the directory that contains your `BingPhrase.java` file. Type `javac BingPhrase.java`, and hit return. This should create a file called `BingPhrase.class` in the same directory. To run the program type `java BingPhrase` and press return.

Parts

In musical arrangements it is common to refer to a musical *part*, for example, the trumpet part, or the guitar part. A jMusic `part` is similar. The `Part` class holds the phrases to be played by a particular instrument, as depicted in figure 4.1. A `part` contains a list of phrases stored in a Vector. A `part` has attributes including a title ("Violin 1" for example), and an instrument (which is >=0), a channel (also >=0). If you are familiar with MIDI systems, then it may help to think of the instrument and channel attributes as corresponding to MIDI program changes and channels respectively. So, if you wish to save the score as a MIDI file the number of channels is limited to 16 but the number of parts is unlimited. When working with jMusic audio instruments the instrument number is used in a similar way but the channel is ignored and, unlike MIDI, the number of instruments and channels is almost unlimited. A visual depiction of how this nested hierarchy of notes, phrases and parts may appear is shown in figure 4.1.

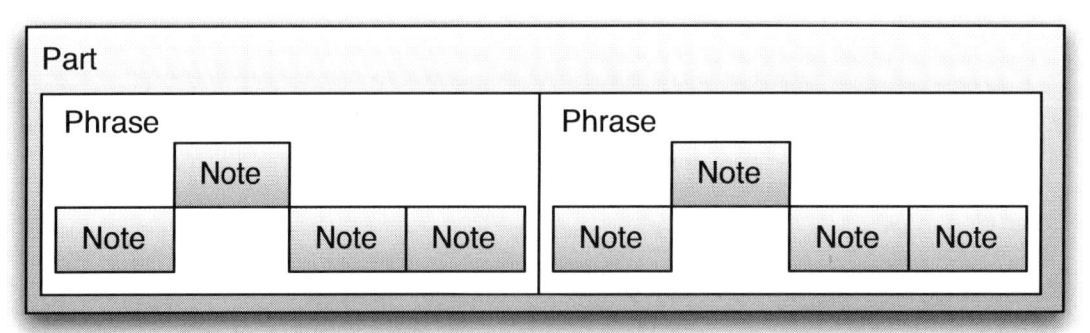

Figure 4.1. An example of how the jMusic data structure can be arrnaged.

When creating a `part` it is usually constructed with three arguments, corresponding to a title, instrument and channel. The title is a `String` (a list of alphanumeric characters), followed by an instrument number or constant, and lastly a channel number.

```
Part part1 = new Part("Flute", 73, 0);
```

There are constants in the JMC for the General MIDI set of instruments. A list of the General MIDI instrument numbers and constants can be found in Appendix A. Notice that by convention in Java, constants are written using upper case letters.

```
Part part1 = new Part("Flute", FLUTE, 0);
```

Adding a phrase to a part is done using the part's `addPhrase()` method.

```
part1.addPhrase(phr);
```

To recap about the music data structure so far; we have `Notes` that are the elemental music objects, many notes can be stored in series within a `Phrase` which has a start location in the music. A `Phrase` can be added to a `Part` which can have an instrument (sound) associated with it. Each layer of this structure adds additional features to the musical whole.

The MIDI Standard

It is likely that you will want to save your music as a file for storage, playback, or use in another application. The most common file format for symbolic digital music is the standard Musical Instrument Digital Interface (MIDI) file. Files saved in this format have, by convention, a *.mid* suffix appended to their name. Some attributes of the `Note` class follow the conventions of the MIDI specification. These include the pitch values which are consecutively number semitones from 0 to 127, with middle C being 60, the C sharp above it is 61, then D is 62 and so on. The jMusic dynamic values that range from 0 to 127, softest to loudest, also mirror the MIDI specification. There has been much debate about the limitations imposed by MIDI (Moore 1991) however the jMusic specification goes beyond the MIDI specification in may areas, as will become clear later in this book. The following of these MIDI conventions assists in the translation between jMusic and MIDI data for playback, makes note values easy to specify for those familiar with MIDI, and enables fluent translation to and from MIDI files.

Here is the *Bing* program, from chapter 1, modified to save its output as a MIDI file. This file can be read by other music software. Compare the *Bing* and *BingFile* programs and notice that two lines are different.

```
import jm.JMC;
import jm.music.data.*;
import jm.util.Write;
```

```
public final class BingFile implements JMC{
    public static void main(String[] args) {
        Note n = new Note(C4, HALF_NOTE);
        Write.midi(n, "Bing.mid");
    }
}
```

The first addition in this code is an `import` statement that notifies the compiler of the existence of the `Write` class. The second bold line saves the note n as a MIDI file called *Bing.mid*.

Math Moment

Bits and binary number systems: Value ranges in MIDI are often between 0 and 127 because this is the range of values that can be specified in 7 bits of digital data. Although 32 or even 64 bit systems are common today, 8 bit systems were common in the 1980s when MIDI was invented. Of the 8 bits, 1 bit acts as a flag indicating a data byte, the remaining 7 are used for the data value. What exactly is a byte of computer information? Well, its eight bits. What's a bit? It's the smallest element of a digital system, that has two states 1 or 0, on or off, positive or negative. A binary number system is one with two values, unlike our decimal system with has 10 values (0 – 9). Given that a bit has only two states how do we represent larger numbers? The same way we do with a decimal system, by using several of them. For example, the decimal number 34 consists of 3 in the ten's column and 4 in the one's column, so the 3 ten's and 4 one's equals 34.

Binary numbers are similar. The binary number `10` (one, zero) consists of a 1 in the 2's column and a 0 in the 1's column, so 1 two's and 0 one's equals 2. In the binary system each column increases by a factor of 2 (unlike the decimal system where each column increases by a factor of 10). So the decimal number `1101` equals, $1 \times 8 + 1 \times 4 + 0 \times 2 + 1 \times 1$, a sum of 13. This is a 4 bit number, the largest value it can represent is 16; written in binary arithmetic as `1111`. An eight bit numbers has twice as many bits. Each extra bit increases the range by double, so a 5 bit number can hold values twice the size of an 4 bit number. An 8 bit number, a byte, holds values up to 255.

Binary numbers made up of multiple bytes are called words. For example, there can be 16, 24 or 32 bit words. Because every additional bit doubles the range of values that can be represented we can see how this will compound such that a 16, 32 or 64 bit word will hold progressively much larger numbers and therefore allow for a very high resolution music or audio values.

Concept Quiz

1. What are the three functions that music representations serve?
2. What does it mean than the music representation is not the music?
3. Name the four levels of the jMusic's data structure.
4. Why do many of the code examples implement the JMC?
5. What is MIDI an acronym for?
6. jMusic `Phrases` have a `startTime` field, what does its value indicate?
7. Is a jMusic `Phrase` monophonic or polyphonic?
8. What is the method used to add a `Phrase` to a `Part`?

Playing many parts

Below is an example program that elaborates on the *Bing* class to play several notes in two different parts.

```java
import jm.JMC;
import jm.music.data.*;
import jm.util.*;

public final class BingPart implements JMC{
    public static void main(String[] args){
        Part myPart = new Part(TRUMPET, 0);
        Phrase topPhrase = new Phrase(2.0);
        Note n = new Note(G4, HALF_NOTE);
        topPhrase.addNote(n);
        myPart.addPhrase(topPhrase);
        Phrase midPhrase = new Phrase(1.0);
        Note n2 = new Note(E4, DOTTED_HALF_NOTE);
        midPhrase.addNote(n2);
        myPart.addPhrase(midPhrase);
        Phrase bottomPhrase = new Phrase(0.0);
        Note n3 = new Note(C4, WHOLE_NOTE);
        bottomPhrase.addNote(n3);
        myPart.addPhrase(bottomPhrase);

        Write.midi(myPart, "BingPart.mid");
        Play.midi(myPart);
    }
}
```

Programming Practice

To compile the program using a terminal (command line) application type `javac BingPart.java`, and press return. This should create a file called `BingPart.class` in the same directory. Run the program by typing `java BingPart` and press return.

Building Musical Structure

As we have seen, musical lines can be stored in phrases. So, it makes sense that polyphonic music requires multiple phrases playing at once. A `Part` class is used in jMusic to group phrases together. Phrases with the same start times will begin playing together, and phrases with widely spaced start times can be used when the parts play sporadically throughout the music. Phrases are the primary grouping structure for notes in music, and they will be the basis for most of the manipulations, modifications processes that will be undertaken allowing a processes to be applied to all notes in the phrase.

Multiple phrases can be put into one part. Because a `part` has a specified instrument associated with it all the phrases in that part are played (rendered) with that instrument. So, for a trumpet trio, only one part would be required and all the phrases could be put into it because they will all play on the same instrument. To represent a jazz trio, three parts would be required, one for the piano, one for the double bass and one for the drum kit. The trumpet trio could be organized into three parts, each set to the same instrument, and while this arrangement would sound the same there may be good reasons to separate the trumpets into different parts set to different channels. For example, when saving the score as a MIDI file, the individual parts would remain separate when imported into music publishing software.

Phrase phasing

A powerful example of how small variations in a phrases can effect the music can be heard in the following example, where a repeated whole tone scale is added to two phrases but one is played slightly faster than the other. This causes a phasing effect.

```java
import jm.JMC;
import jm.music.data.*;
import jm.util.Play;

public final class PhrasePhasing implements JMC {
    public static void main(String[] args) {
```

```java
            Phrase phrase1 = new Phrase(0.0);
            for (int i=0; i<16; i++) {
                for (int j=0; j<12; j++) {
                    Note n = new Note(C4+j*2, SIXTEENTH_NOTE);
                    phrase1.addNote(n);
                }
            }
            Phrase phrase2 = phrase1.copy();
            phrase1.setTempo(130.0);
            phrase2.setTempo(131.0);

            Part guitarPart = new Part(GUITAR, 0);
            guitarPart.addPhrase(phrase1);
            guitarPart.addPhrase(phrase2);

            Play.midi(guitarPart);
        }
    }
```

Scores

If we consider music of the complexity of a jazz trio, with its multiple parts, these parts need to be collected together into a score. The Score class represents the top level of the jMusic data structure and contains (you guessed it) a vector of parts. A score object also has other attributes including a title and a tempo.

The tempo, or speed, is described in beats per minute (BPM) and is set to 60bpm by default, which is quite a slow tempo but has the advantage that each beat equals one second of time, which is useful for music that is time-based rather than beat-based.

A common way to create a new score is with the constructor that takes a title and tempo as the arguments.

```java
Score myMusic = new Score("Opus 1", 135.0);
```

Insert parts into a score with the addPart() method.

```java
MyMusic.addPart(part1);
```

Music Moment

> Minimalism is a genre of music composition where pieces are made from limited material. It usually refers to composers of the mid twentieth century who located themselves in Western Art music culture. Sometimes this can result in sparse works like those of La Monte Young and Phillip Glass. Their minimalist works feature drones and slowly overlapping phrases. Minimalist pieces can result in very repetitive works, such as *Lovely Thing* by Harold Budd which consists of one chord played softly over and over for about fifteen minutes, or Erik Sartie's *Vexations* where a short section in repeated hundreds of times. Another famous minimalist piece is Terry Riley's *In C*, which features repeated C octaves with very limited harmonic changes over about a an hour of performance. Music from non-western cultures also rely heavily on repetition and have had a influence on Western composers. Steve Reich, for example, is a famous American minimalist composer, who was inspired by the repetition of simple phrases and rhythms in the music of Bali and Ghana.

Repetition

Repetition is a common musical technique that can be used to extend music or to create slowly evolving changes like those used by minimalist composers. Computers excel at mundane repetitive tasks and so this section will explore how repetition can be put to effective musical use. Computers have already found a significant role in popular music styles, particularly electronic dance music, where the use of repetition is pervasive. While some exact repetition provides music with coherence and structure, too much repetition can often be dull or boring. Music that relies on repetition often introduces variety in one parameter to provide sufficient interest that we continue to pay attention to the evolving change. Electronic dance music uses small timbral changes to maintain interest - usually, achieved by sweeping a highly resonant low-pass filter over the sound source. A technique of minimalists that adds interest to repetition is *phasing*. Phasing occurs when repeated phrases are of different length such that during playback they progressively change alignment over time.

Phasing

Here is a brief jMusic example where two phrases of different length are repeated enough times so that they realign at the end of the example. In the process, all possible offsets are passed through and the varying interaction between the phrases is the point of interest, both harmonically and rhythmically. The program generates a seven beat long melody and a six beat long chord progression, then repeats then several times. Because of the unequal lengths they go out of phase.

```
import jm.JMC;
import jm.music.data.*;
```

```java
import jm.music.tools.*;
import jm.util.*;

public final class Phasing implements JMC{
    public static void main(String[] args){
        Phrase melody = new Phrase(0.0);
        CPhrase chords = new CPhrase(0.0);
        int[] melPitches = {C5,D5,E5,A5,G5,D6,C6};
        double[] melRhythm = {DQN,EN,QN,QN,QN,EN,DQN};
        melody.addNoteList(melPitches, melRhythm);

        int[] notePitches1 = {C3, E3, G3};
        int[] notePitches2 = {D3, F3, A2};
        int[] notePitches3 = {B2, D3, G3};

        chords.addChord(notePitches1, HALF_NOTE);
        chords.addChord(notePitches2, HALF_NOTE);
        chords.addChord(notePitches3, HALF_NOTE);

        Part kalimba = new Part("Thumb Piano", KALIMBA, 0);
        kalimba.addPhrase(melody);
        Part rhodes = new Part("Electric Piano", EPIANO,1);
        rhodes.addCPhrase(chords);

        Mod.repeat(kalimba, 6);
        Mod.repeat(rhodes, 7);

        Score comp = new Score("Phasing Example", 90);
        comp.addPart(kalimba);
        comp.addPart(rhodes);

        Play.midi(comp);
    }
}
```

Another way of achieving phasing is to independently vary the playback speed of two identical looped phrases. This is a subtle effect and, if the speed variation is only minor, adds timbral variety through phase cancellation to the more obvious rhythmic evolution. This technique, used by Steve Reich in many of his earlier works, is the basis for the next example program.

Piano phase

Reich's first experiments with tempo phasing used two tape recorders. Each with the same loop of pre-recorded material, but one set to a slightly faster playback speed than the other. He then transferred this technique to compositions for acoustic instruments, which included a piece for two pianos, simple titled *Piano Phase*.

In *Piano Phase* two pianists have the same short phrase to play on separate pianos. They begin together, then after a time one pianist speeds up slightly causing the phase effect. When the faster part is one beat ahead the faster pianist reverts to playing at the original tempo. This process is repeated several times and the phase distance increases each time. This provides a staircase effect of stable and phasing sections.

In this example, we isolate a section of the Piano Phase score where the two parts play at different speeds. The speed difference is quite small, 1 bpm, so the phase shift is quite gradual, but nevertheless the result is dramatic.

In order to get the second part to play faster we set its tempo attribute. Normally a part takes on the tempo of the score, but it can also have a different tempo. This is one of the first deviations we have seen from the strict orchestral score metaphor that jMusic is based upon where all parts line up and are under the tempo control of a single conductor.

```
import jm.JMC;
import jm.music.data.*;
import jm.music.tools.*;
import jm.util.*;

public final class PianoPhase implements JMC{
    public static void main(String[] args){
        Score score = new Score("Piano Phase");
        score.setTimeSignature(12,16);
        Part part1 = new Part("Piano1", PIANO, 0);
        Part part2 = new Part("Piano2", PIANO, 1);
        Phrase phrase1 = new Phrase(0.0);
        Phrase phrase2 = new Phrase(0.0);

        int[] pitchArray = {E4,FS4,B4,CS5,D5,FS4,E4,CS5,B4,FS4,D5,CS5};
        phrase1.addNoteList(pitchArray, SIXTEENTH_NOTE);
        phrase2.addNoteList(pitchArray, SIXTEENTH_NOTE);
        Mod.repeat(phras41);
        part1.addPhrase(phrase1);
```

```
            score.addPart(part1);
            Mod.repeat(phras41);
            part2.addPhrase(phrase2);
            score.addPart(part2);
            part1.setTempo(120.0);
            part2.setTempo(120.5);

            Play.midi(score);
        }
    }
```

Musical data structure

You should have a good overview of the jMusic data structure at this stage. Notes describe musical events, notes are arranged in as a list in phrases. Phrases have a start time which positions them within a part. Parts can contain many phrases and also have an instrument assigned to them. All notes within a part are played by that instrument. The parts are added to a score which also sets the tempo of music within it.

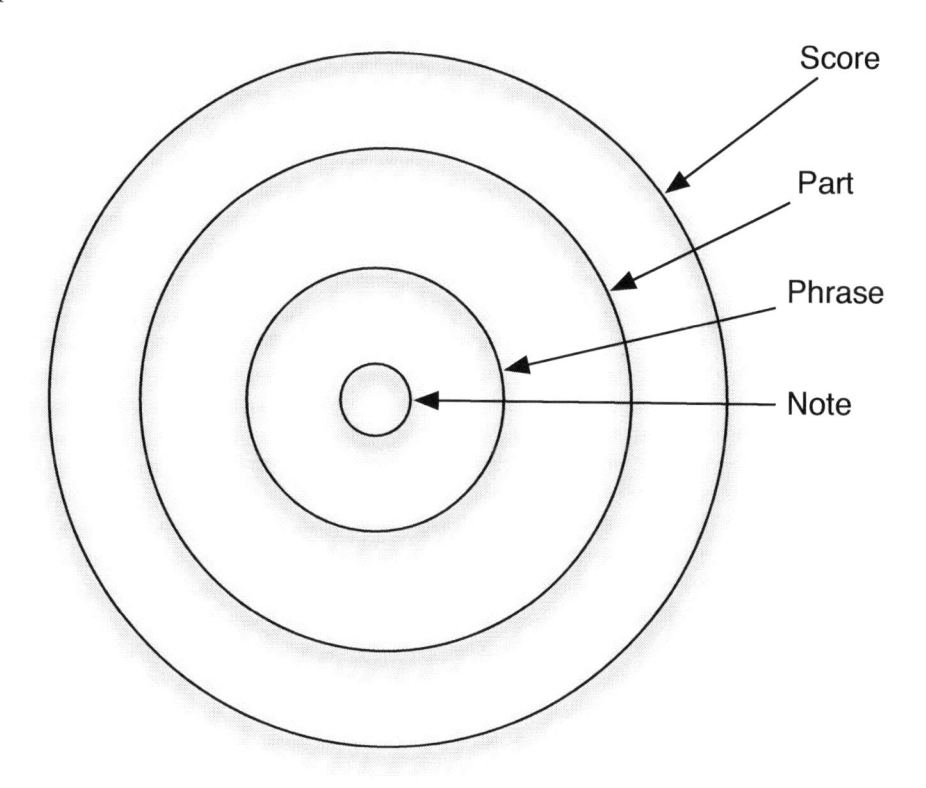

Figure 4.2. The jMusic Data Structure.

The jMusic data structure can be thought of as a set of concentric rings, one within another as shown in figure 4.2. This code fragment is a concise way to generate a score that is equivalent to figure 4.2.

```
Score s = new Score(new Part(new Phrase(new Note())));
```

The 'target' view of the score is a simplification, because in reality a score can contain many parts, a part many phrases and a phrase many notes. More realistically the jMusic data structure can also be represented visually as in figure 4.3.

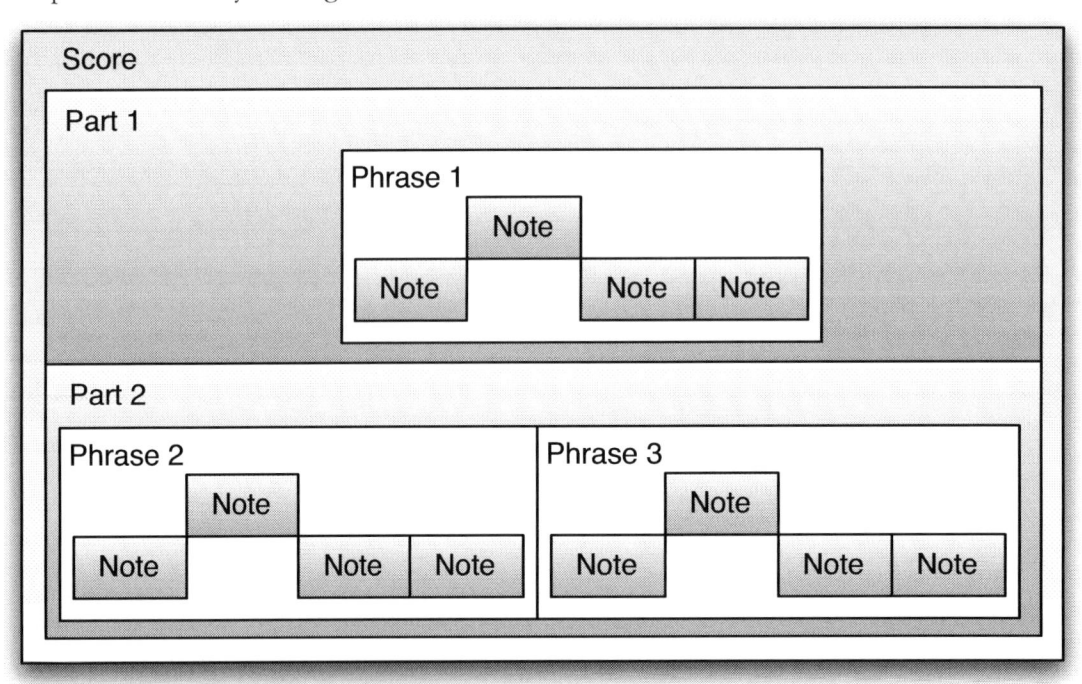

Figure 4.3 Another view of the jMusic data structure.

Below is a program that puts all this jMusic structure into practice. It is program that creates a drum pattern consisting of kick, snare and hi hats. It uses many notes, three phrases, a part and a score, with each layer adding additional functionality. The class consists of five methods and each is called in turn from the `main()` method. To ensure that the music data objects are visible to all the methods, they are declared at the class level as instance variables.

```
import jm.JMC;
import jm.music.data.*;
import jm.util.*;
import jm.music.tools.*;
```

```java
public class MultiPhraseDrums implements JMC {
    // declare instance variables
    Score music = new Score(125.0);
    Part drums = new Part(25, 9);
    Phrase kickPhrase = new Phrase(1.0);
    Phrase snarePhrase = new Phrase(1.0);
    Phrase hatsPhrase = new Phrase(1.0);

    public static void main(String[] args) {
        MultiPhraseDrums kit = new MultiPhraseDrums();
        kit.createKickPhrase();
        kit.createSnarePhrase();
        kit.createHatsPhrase();
        kit.output();
    }

    // the constructor
    public MultiPhraseDrums() {
        drums.addPhrase(kickPhrase);
        drums.addPhrase(snarePhrase);
        drums.addPhrase(hatsPhrase);
        music.addPart(drums);
    }

    private void createKickPhrase() {
        for (int i=0; i<8; i++) {
            kickPhrase.addNote(new Note(C2, QUARTER_NOTE));
            kickPhrase.addRest(new Rest(QUARTER_NOTE));
        }
    }

    private void createSnarePhrase() {
        for (int i=0; i<8; i++) {
            snarePhrase.addRest(new Rest(QUARTER_NOTE));
            snarePhrase.addNote(new Note(D2, QUARTER_NOTE));
        }
    }

    private void createHatsPhrase() {
        for (int i=0; i<16; i++) {
```

```
            hatsPhrase.addNote(new Note(FS2, SIXTEENTH_NOTE));
            hatsPhrase.addNote(new Note(FS2, SIXTEENTH_NOTE));
            hatsPhrase.addNote(new Note(AS2, EIGHTH_NOTE));
        }
    }

    private void output() {
        Write.midi(music, "Kit.mid");
        Play.midi(music);
    }
}
```

Programming Practice

Notice that the `MultiPhraseDrums` class, which is one of the longer program examples used so far in this book, has been divided into separate methods to make it easier to read and understand. This is good programming style because it makes the logic of your code clear, assists in the easy identification of bugs, and makes the code easier to understand for someone else or even for yourself when you revisit it some time later.

- Type up this program, save, compile and run it.
- Experiment with changing the rhythm patterns to get new beats.

Java Structures

Computer programming and musical composition both share a heavy emphasis on structure. In this section we'll examine some of the elements that make up the structure of a typical Java program.

Import statements

The import statements appear at the top of the java file and indicate particular classes that are to be used by the file. A core set of the Java libraries are always available, but others need to be imported. For example, when writing an application with a graphical user interface it is common to import the advanced windowing toolkit (AWT) package.

```
import java.awt.*;
```

The import statement tells the Java compiler where to find the classes required. In this case it instructs the compiler to import all files (*) inside the `awt` directory, which is inside the `java` directory. The JMC class that is imported in all the examples in this book is located within the jm directory - the top level directory of the jMusic library. External libraries, such as jMusic, always need to be imported. In this example the jMusic constants (JMC) interface is imported.

```
import jm.JMC;
```

Constructors

A constructor is a special method that is run when a new instance of a class is created. Up to this point only one example program required the writing of a constructor. Whenever the new keyword is invoked to create an object, that class's constructor is run as the object is instantiated. A constructor is a method with a couple of distinctive syntactic features. Constructors must have the *same name* as the class they are in and, when declared, they *don't* require a return type. Here is an empty constructor added to the *MakeMusic* class.

```
// class declaration
public class MakeMusic {
    // constructor
    public MakeMusic() {
        ...
    }
}
```

The constructor is run only once in the life of the object, when it is created. The brackets "( )" following the constructor name can, as with methods, contain information about data that may be passed to the constructor when it is called. Such data are called *arguments*. In the example above, the constructor does not take any arguments. Even if no arguments are required (there is no data to be passed), the empty brackets are still required.

Instance variables

Variables, as we've seen, can be used to hold objects or primitive data types. For example the variable n may stand for a Note object, and the variable myHeight may contain the number 170. The variable n in the code below is an instance variable standing for a Note.

```
public class MakeMusic implements JMC{
    Note n = new Note(C4, QUARTER_NOTE);

    public void playMusic() {
        Play.midi(n);
    }
```

}

Instance variables 'belong' to the whole object, and can be used or 'seen' by any method within the class. Instance variables are declared within the braces of the class definition but outside of the methods. Each time a new instance of the class is created, a new instance variable is created within it. Therefore, the same variable name in one instance might have a different value than in a different instance of the same class. Pitch is an instance variable in the `Note` class, and each instance can have a different value for the pitch variable. This feature allows one `Note` object to have a pitch of C4 and another to have a pitch of D5, for example.

Local variables

If a variable is declared within the braces of a method, it is called a local variable and can only be 'seen' or used by code within that method. Local variables only have a short life, they exist while the method is being executed, and are recreated each time the method is called. Whereas, instance variables exist for the life of the object within which they reside.

To recap about variables: the difference between instance and local variables is their scope and persistence. An instance variable's scope is the entire class, while the local variables scope is just within the method in which it is declared. An instance variable's life is tied to the object's life, while the local variable lasts only while its method is being executed.

Scope

The scope is a region of code within which a variable is said to exist, or to be visible to other code. As we have said, instance variables have scope across the entire class, while the scope of local variables is within the method or code block within which they are declared. Another way to understand the scope of a variable is to consider that it exists with the code block in which it is declared; that is, between the curly brackets {} within which it is created. It is important to understand the scope of a variable so that you avoid errors by trying to access that variable outside it's scope or try to use the same variable name more than once within the same code block. In the simplified code fragment below, the variable A has scope across the entire class, the variable B has scope within the method `compose()` and the variables C and D have scope just within the for-loop.

```
public class ScopeExample {
    int A; // instance variable  accessible within whole class
    ... you can do something here with A

    public void compose() {
        int B; // local variable accessible within the compose() method
```

```
            ... you can do something here with A or B

            for (int C; ; ) {// local variables within the for-loop
                int D;
                ... you can do something here with A or B or C or D
            }
            ... you can do something here with A or B
        }
        ... you can do something here with A
    }
}
```

IT is important to remember that if a variable is declared within a sub block of code, such as an if statement, it is only visible within that block of code. Remember, that a block of code is often bounded by open { and close } curly brackets but that in the case of the for-loop the `for` statement and conditions are visible within the code bounded by curly brackets that follows, because they are part of the same expression. In this incomplete class below the variable `scaleLength` and `i` are local, however, because of where they are declared, `scaleLength` is visible anywhere within the method but i is only visible within the for-loop block. The phrase `myPhrase` is an instance variable and is visible anywhere in the class.

```
    public class BeatMover {
        Phrase myPhrase =  new Phrase();

        private int chromaticScale () {
            int scaleLength = (int)(Math.random() * 24);
            for (int i=0; i < scaleLength ; i++) {
                myPhrase.addNote(new Note(60 + i, 1.0));
            }
            return scaleLength;
        }
        more code...
    }
```

Concept Quiz

1. How many jMusic Notes can be in a Phrase?
2. Which jMusic class specifies the instrument for playback of the notes?
3. What do we mean by the term musical phasing?
4. Why are `import` statements required?
5. What is the connection between the new keyword and a constructor method?
6. What is a variable?

> 7. How do we know is a variable is an instance variable or a local variable?
> 8. What is the scope of a local variable?
> 9. What does a constructor method construct?

TheGrid: A Rhythmic Phrase generator

It's now time to begin work on an example application called *TheGrid* that we'll build stage by stage as the book proceeds. *TheGrid* is a drum and bass step sequencer application that can even generate it's own rhythms and bass lines! Figure 4.4 shows what the application will look like down the track.

```
Figure 4.4. TheGrid application
```

But first things first, in this chapter we'll create the basic data structure for a drum part and get it to play back.

In chapter 1 it was demonstrated how a Java program can be made up of more than one class file, and that the file with the `main()` method is the one to be executed. In the simple examples in this chapter all of the code was in the one file. Similarly, the code for *TheGrid* classes in this and the following chapters will be in one file for convenience.

TheGrid1

This program creates a rhythmic phrase that contains a series of notes, the phrase is added to a part that is assigned a drum kit instrument, then the part is played back. The source code for *TheGrid* can be downloaded from from the accompanying web site for this book. When you locate and open the file *TheGrid1.java*, it should look similar to the code below, or you can type the code from the book into a new file.

```
import jm.JMC;
import jm.music.data.*;
import jm.util.*;

public class TheGrid1 implements JMC {
    private Phrase hats;
    private Part drums;

    public static void main(String[] args) {
        TheGrid1 grid = new TheGrid1();
      grid.compose();
    }

    public TheGrid1() {
        hats = new Phrase(0.0);
        drums = new Part("Drums", 25, 9);
        drums.addPhrase(hats);
    }

    public void compose() {
        int[] hatsHits = {FS2, REST, FS2, REST, FS2, FS2, FS2,
              REST, FS2, REST, FS2, REST, FS2, FS2, FS2, FS2};
        hats.addNoteList(hatsHits, SIXTEENTH_NOTE);
      Write.midi(drums, "TheGrid1.mid");
        Play.midi(drums);
    }
}
```

Programming Practice

The classes start execution at the main() method, which calls the constructor to create a new instance of the class which, in turn, calls other methods as necessary. Try compiling, running then editing this code. You can change the rhythm by changing the order of notes and rests in the hatsHits array. Run the program by typing java TheGrid1 and press return.

There are three methods in this class, main(), TheGrid1() (the constructor), and compose(). In addition there are two instance variables, hats and drums that are used by several of the methods. The main method creates a new instance of the class which calls the constructor. The constructor instantiates (creates and sets up) an empty phrase named hats and an empty part named drums, then adds the phrase to the part. The arguments passed to the phrase and part set particular parameters.

> `hats = new Phrase(0.0);`

The (0.0) argument indicates that this phrase should start at the beginning of the part – at beat 0.0.

> `drums = new Part("Drums", 25, 9);`

The "Drums" argument is the title of the part. The second argument, 25, is the instrument number. Notice that in the General MIDI specification drum kit 25 is the electronic kit, but unfortunatley JavaSound only has the one 'rock' drum kit so this argument is ignored by the JavaSound synthesizer. When playing back the MIDI file with another General MIDI synthesizer, such as QuickTime, the 'electronic' drum kit sounds will be heard. The third argument, 9, is the channel. Note that in the General MIDI specification, channel 10 is the drum channel – and that equates to 9 in Java because counting starts from zero, rather than one.

Next, from the `main()` method the `compose()` method is called. There is one local variable `hatsHits`, used in the compose method. In the `compose` method notes are added to the phrase and the part is played back. Note pitches are stored in an array called `hatsHits`. There are sixteen notes. The pitch FS2 (F sharp in the octave 2) is the General MIDI position for hi hats. The other pitch used is a jMusic REST constant, indicating silence.

> `hats.addNoteList(hatsHits, SIXTEENTH_NOTE);`

Notes are added to the phrase using the `addNoteList` method. This method can take an array of pitches and a rhythm value as arguments. This will create one bar of music, assuming the music is in common time (4/4).

> `Write.midi(drums, "TheGrid1.mid");`
> `Play.midi(drums);`

A MIDI file of the music is written to disk and, finally, the part is played back using JavaSound's General MIDI sound bank.

Music Moment

A number of ways of generating notes have been used in the examples so far in this book. They include adding notes individually, at random, selecting from an array of note attribute values, and using the `addNotelist()` method. Here is an example of each technique.

Individual Notes

```
Note n = new Note(A4, QUARTER_NOTE);
phrase.addNote(n);
```

Random Notes

```
for (int i=0; i< 8 ; i++) {
    Note n = new Note((int)(Math.random() * 12 +60), QUARTER_NOTE);
    phrase.addNote(n);
}
```

Selecting from a pitch set

```
int[] pitches = {C4, E4, G4, D4, A3, B3, C4};
for (int i=0; i< 8 ; i++) {
    Note n = new Note(pitches[(int)(Math.random() *pitches.length)],
        QUARTER_NOTE);
    Phrase.addNote(n);
}
```

Adding notes using an attribute list

```
int[] pitches = {C4, E4, G4, D4, A3, B3, C4};
phrase.addNotelist(pitches, QUARTER_NOTE);
```

5: Playing with Polyphony

Creating music of significant complexity involves coordinating several musical lines at one time. For example, coordinating a melody, a bass part, and a percussive accompaniment. Music that includes several independent strands at one time is said to be polyphonic. Typical examples include multi-part vocal chorales or string quartets. However, such multi-part coordination is required by music of almost any style. The jMusic part and score classes are provided to assist with this structuring.

Managing Musical Parts

Many experiments have been done by psychologists to determine how we hear musical lines. It should be noted that the tendencies in our imaginative perception are not simply choices about how things appear to us, but are the result of how our brain attempts to group events and always seeks to find patterns in what we hear. In musical terms the patterns that appear in musical lines are the basis for the texture and the form of music. These structural elements are designed by the composer and then described in a medium, for example in Java code. This compositional process requires an imagining of the musical structures and then the describing of them. Interestingly this is the reverse of the listeners experience, where they hear the music unfold over time, then retrospectively construct the form from their memory of the passing events, or more particularly from the lines, shapes and textures they perceived as the events unfolded.

There is a connection between music's structure and its meaning and enjoyment. Understanding some of the psychology of perception that underpins these sound gesture metaphors assists the composer to better create a desired musical experience. The roots of psychological concerns with how people perceived patterns in a holistic way can be traced back to the Gestalt movement that originated in Europe in the early decades of the 20th century. Their experiments were particularly focused on the visual perception of movement, but regular correspondence to audible perception of music were made. The Gestalt psychologies examined a range of phenomenal qualities and derived a series of rules, or laws about bout ways in which humans organize their experiences. These included the law of proximity, where objects that are closer (in space, time, pitch, and so on) are grouped together; the law of symmetry, where things that create a trend or pattern are perceived as a closed region, and; the law of good continuation, where foreground and background are differentiated by degrees of interruption, change or inconsistency. The Gestalt psychologists also tended to associate the recognition of complex patterns with intelligence or creativity, seeing the best thinking as being novel rather than reproductive.

A holistic and schema-based view of pattern recognition was not limited to the Gestalt movement, who tended to believe that the mind operated to impose logical organization upon the world as it was perceived. A more constructivist approach to understanding perception was presented by psychologists such as Jean Piaget and James J. Gibson, one in which mental representations were responses to experiences of the external world rather than the imposition of schema in the mind of the individual. Piaget's work was famously in the area of child development where he conducted experiments and observations to see how the young mind understood the physical world differently as it developed. J. J. Gibson's work focused on understanding as the interpretation of cue's in the environment, what he called environmental affordances. Gibson suggested that these responses were based on instinctive or automatic responses which did not require mental processing at all, but could be refined and elaborated on through learning and experience. More recent work in cognitive science has elaborated on and refined these views (Gardner 1985). However, the fundamental notion that our atomic-level musical structures of notes and phrases will be perceived as having higher-order organization and thus meaning needs to be kept in mind by the composer, particularly one operating at the potentially more abstract level of algorithmic composition.

Music Moment

The contrast between the composer's and audience's experience of music was discussed by Arnold Schoenberg, a 20th century composer who developed a system of serial (algorithmic) music making which broke down tonality by requiring an even distribution of all the 12 chromatic scale tones. On the issue of musical structure existing as space and time he commented that, "Music is an art which takes place in time. But the way in which a work presents itself to a composer … is independent of this; time is regarded as space. In writing the work down, space is transformed into time. For the hearer this takes place the other way round; it is only after the work has run its course in time that it can be seen as a whole—its idea, its form and its content" (Quoted inCook 1990:40). There have been a number of ideas relating to the representation of music, and in the next section a few of these will be presented.

A common conception of music is as a gesture or a sequence of sound events which appear as movement in pitch and time space. Like animation, a series of notes can provide the illusion of movement even though it is only a series of stationary events. For example, a scale of ascending tones may appear as a rising gesture. These musical impressions emerge from the overall effect of individual scale notes, and even when the pattern is interrupted with a brief descending tone, the overall shape the line is maintained. This tendency of musical sequences to be perceived as gestural curves was observed by Roger Scruton, who wrote that, "It

> seems then that in our most basic apprehension of music there lies a complex system of metaphor, which is a true description of no material fact" (Scruton 1983:106).
>
> This metaphorical aspect of musical structures goes beyond the gestural nature of musical shapes in time and space to include the ways in which these combine to indicate musical styles and to trigger emotional states. Particular musical gestures can be characteristic of particular musical styles, or even of individual composers. David Cope called such frequently found gestures stylistic signatures (Cope 2001). Musical metaphors are even more direct when depicting emotional states, for example the slow tempo and wide vibrato that imitate the despondent movement and quivering lip of a very sad person, or the violent staccato bowing of Bernard Herman's score for the stabbing featured in the 'shower' scene from Alfred Hitchcock's film *Psycho*.

There are many types of musical form and structure that are commonly used and the jMusic data structure has been designed to allow for them. In this chapter we will examine one of the oldest musical forms, the cannon.

Making a cannon

A musical cannon, also called a round, is a musical structure where one melody is played against a delayed version of itself. The same phrase is played by several parts whose entries and exits are staggered. We will use as an example the well known round *Row, Row, Row Your Boat*. For a more elaborate example of a cannon you can listen to the first movement of Béla Bartók's *Sonata for Two Pianos and Percussion*.

There are two ways in which to write polyphonic music in the jMusic data structure, and these reflect compositional practices in acoustic music. The first is to allocate multiple voices (phrases) to a single part. This is analogous to a harpsichord fugue where a composer may write two or more simultaneous parts for each hand to play. The second is to allocate a single phrase to each of two or more parts, as you might for a woodwind quintet where each voice is played by a different instrument. Obviously, a combination of both techniques can be used.

For now, we will write our cannon for multiple parts each containing a single phrase. The *RowYourBoat* program is a somewhat longer program so we will deal with it one section at a time. Here is the complete code.

```
import jm.JMC;
import jm.music.data.*;
import jm.util.*;
import jm.music.tools.*;
```

```java
public class RowYourBoat implements JMC {
    Part flute, trumpet, clarinet;
    Phrase phrase1, phrase2, phrase3;
    Score score;
    int[] pitchArray, rhythmArray;

    public static void main(String[] args){
        RowYourBoat row = new RowYourBoat();
        row.makeMusicData();
        row.structureData();
        row.playAndSave();
    }

    public RowYourBoat() {
        score = new Score("Row Your Boat", 120.0);
        flute = new Part(FLUTE, 0);
        trumpet = new Part(TRUMPET, 1);
        clarinet = new Part(CLARINET, 2);
        phrase1 = new Phrase(0.0);
        phrase2 = new Phrase(0.0);
        phrase3 = new Phrase(0.0);
        pitchArray = {C4,C4,C4,D4,E4,E4,D4,E4,F4,G4,C5,C5,
            C5,G4,G4,G4,E4,E4,E4,C4,C4,C4,G4,F4,E4,D4,C4);
        rhythmArray = {QN,QN,QNT,ENT,QN,QNT,ENT,QNT,QT,HN,
            ENT,ENT,ENT,ENT,ENT,ENT,ENT,ENT,ENT,ENT,
            ENT,QNT, ENT,QNT,ENT,HN};
    }

    public void structureData() {
        flute.addPhrase(phrase1);
        trumpet.addPhrase(phrase2);
        clarinet.addPhrase(phrase3);
        score.addPart(flute);
        score.addPart(trumpet);
        score.addPart(clarinet);
    }

    public void makeMusicData() {
        phrase1.addNoteList(pitchArray, rhythmArray);
        phrase2 = phrase1.copy();
```

```
            phrase2.setStartTime(4.0);
            phrase3 = phrase1.copy();
            phrase3.setStartTime(8.0);

            Mod.transpose(phrase1, 12);
            Mod.transpose(phrase3, -12);
        }

        private void playAndSave() {
            Write.midi(score, "Rowboat.mid");
            Play.midi(score);
        }
    }
```

In essence, the steps for creating the cannon are; 1) create a melodic phrase, 2) make copies of that phrase, 3) change the start times so each phrase is offset in time, and 4) add each phrase to parts with different instruments.

Java Moment

When typing up a program you will inevitably make some mistakes, that produce errors when compiled. Interpreting Java compiler error messages is an important skill in working productively in the language. The error messages are the way that the compiler communicates with you about things it does not expect in the code. The errors are not always easy to interpret and, occasionally, they are misleading, but they are the key to assist you to debug your code. Here's an example:

```
AudioPlayer.java:220: cannot resolve symbol
symbol   : class Getopt
location: class AudioPlayer
Getopt  g = new Getopt("AudioPlayer", args, "hlufM:e:i:E:S:D");
        ^
```

The error messages, like the one above, start by indicating the class and line in which the error occurs. Then the error message, in this case 'cannot resolve symbol.' This message indicates that the class Getopt is not known to the compiler. Possibly it needs to be imported at the start of the code. Lastly, the offending line is displayed and a caret (^) points to the section in the line where the error was detected. All in all, this is pretty helpful, especially when compared to error messages in other languages.

Creating the musical data

Now let's examine the interesting sections of *RowYourBoat* code in detail. In the code fragment below from the constructor method all the necessary musical data objects are instantiated.

```
score = new Score("Row Your Boat", 120.0);
flute = new Part(FLUTE, 0);
trumpet = new Part(TRUMPET, 1);
clarinet = new Part(CLARINET, 2);
phrase1 = new Phrase(0.0);
phrase2 = new Phrase(0.0);
phrase3 = new Phrase(0.0);
```

First, a score object is created with a title and tempo, then three part objects are created and set to different instruments and channels. This will enable three instruments to play the round. Finally, three phrases are declared with a start time of 0.0.

The next step is to create the notes. It would be very painful if for a long melody like this one every time we wanted to make a Note object we had to type `Note note = new Note(C4, QUARTER_NOTE);` then add it to the phrase with `phrase1.addPhrase(note);`. Fortunately, jMusic has several nice ways of helping us with this. A convenient way to enter musical information is by using arrays. The pitch and rhythm values for each note can be stored in arrays. The first note we create has a pitch of a C4 (the first element of the pitch array) and a rhythm value of QN (the first element of the rhythm array), the second a C4 and QN, and so on. The number of elements in each array must be the same in order to avoid an error. The pitch array contains `int` values, and the rhythm array contains doubles these arrays are declared at the class level, making them instance variable that are accessible to all methods within the class.

```
pitchArray = {C4,C4,C4,D4,E4,E4,D4,E4,F4,G4,C5,C5,C5,G4,G4,G4,E4,
              E4,E4,C4,C4,C4,G4,F4,E4,D4,C4};
rhythmArray = {QN,QN,QNT,ENT,QN,QNT,ENT,QNT,QT,HN,ENT,ENT,ENT,ENT,
               ENT,ENT,ENT,ENT,ENT,ENT,ENT,ENT,QNT,ENT,QNT,ENT,HN};
```

Once we have specified the arrays we can include them in a phrase using the `addNoteList()` method of the `Phrase` class.

```
phrase1.addNoteList(pitchArray, rhythmArray);
```

Making duplicate phrases

To create a cannon we need to start the melody again and again with a delay between each entry. In this example we want a three part round so use three phrases, each starting on a different beat.

Copies of the first phrase and made using the `Phrase.copy()` method and assigned to `phrase2` and `phrase3`.

```
phrase2 = phrase1.copy();
phrase3 = phrase1.copy();
```

The `copy()` method returns a duplicate of the Phrase object which we assign to the new phrase named `phrase2`. At this stage phrase 2 and 3 are identical to phrase 1, which includes that they have the same start time. However, a cannon needs each phrase to have a different start time. This can be achieved with the `Phrase.setStartTime(double newStartTime)` method which accepts an argument indicating the new start time. The start time is in beats (and fractions of a beat) and remember that the first beat of the music is zero (0.0) not one. This follows the general computer programming convention where counting begins at zero, so if you are not used to it you soon will be.

```
phrase2.setStartTime(4.0);
phrase3.setStartTime(8.0);
```

This code sets `phrase2` to start at the second measure (bar) and `phrase3` to start at the third measure (bar).

Transposing

In order that we can hear the parts a little more clearly we are going to set them to different octave ranges by transposing them. Transposition is a pitch shift up or down. A call to the `Mod.transpose(Phrase phrase, int pitchShift)` method will do this.

```
Mod.transpose(phrase1, 12);
Mod.transpose(phrase3, -12);
```

`Phrase1` is transposed up one octave (twelve semitones) and `phrase3` transposed down one octave

Structuring the music data

At this stage the score, parts and phrases exist independently and are not related to each other. This disconnected state is shown in figure 5.1.

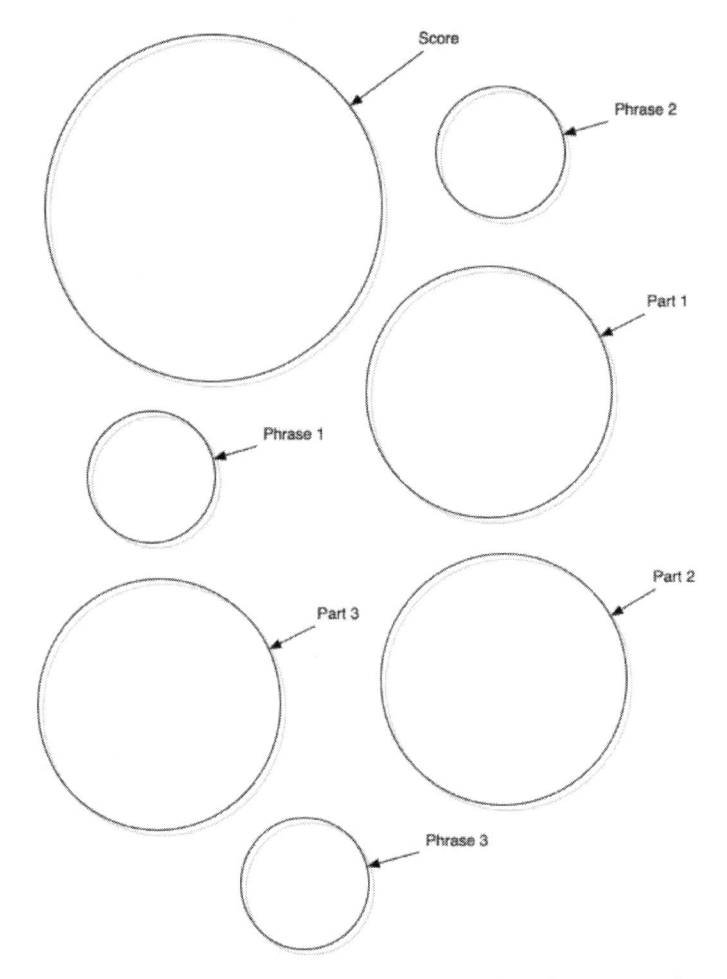

Figure 5.1 An unorganized collection of jMusic data objects.

We now need to add objects to others to create an appropriate hierarchical (target) structure like that shown in figure 4.2.

The part called flute uses its `addPhrase()` method to put `phrase1` into it's phrase list vector. So the flute part then contains one phrase, `phrase1`. To the trumpet and clarinet parts are added `phrase2` and `phrase3` respectively.

```
flute.addPhrase(phrase1);
trumpet.addPhrase(phrase2);
clarinet.addPhrase(phrase3);
```

Parts are added to the `score` to complete the data packing operations. We add parts to a score using the `addPart()` method.

```
score.addPart(flute);
score.addPart(trumpet);
score.addPart(clarinet);
```

Saving and playing the cannon

Finally, the score is written to a MIDI file and played back using static methods in the `Write` and `Play` classes.

```
Write.midi(score, "Rowboat.mid");
Play.midi(score);
```

Programming Practice

Type up the *RowYourBoat* program, compile and run. To make sure you understand the flow of control between methods, print out the source code and draw arrows on the page where one method calls another. Extend the program by adding a fourth part that starts one bar after the third.

The jMusic Mod Class

The `Mod` class contains many methods for modifying, or varying, phrases, parts and scores. The `Mod` class is in the `jm.music.tools` package, and you need to import this package in order to access these methods.

```
import jm.music.tools.*;
```

The `Mod` class uses static methods, so you can call the methods directly from the class and don't need to instantiate a new `Mod` object. It is used in a similar way to the `Math` class, such as `x = Math.random();`. However, somewhat unusually for Java the `Mod` methods are declared as void and do not return any value but modify the data passed to them. As an example the `Mod` class palindrome method is called with the line, `Mod.palindrome(phrase);`. While the arguments for each method vary slightly, the general structure of calls to `Mod` methods are:

```
Mod.methodName(data, [argument1], [argument2], ...);
```

Phrase manipulations are widely used in western composition, and this is reflected in the jMusic `Mod` class having more methods than other data classes. In most cases the method names are self explanatory, but that will not always be the case. Here are some of the `Mod` methods that apply to a `Phrase`:

`repeat();` - play the phrase a number of times through

`transpose();` - shift the pitch of the phrase by a certain number of semitones

`palindrome();` - extend the phrase to add all the notes in reverse order

`retrograde();` - reverse the order of the notes

`inversion();` - flip the pitch of notes in relation to the first note's pitch

`shuffle();` - randomly reorganize the order of the notes in a phrase

`elongate();` - change the rhythm values of the notes in the phrase by a scaling factor

`accents();` - add a sense of meter by emphasizing the dynamic of regular beats

`fadeIn();` - starting at zero volume, add a crescendo to the current loudness over a certain number of beats

`fadeOut();` - starting at the current loudness, add a decrescendo down to zero volume over a certain number of beats

`getEndTime();` - report the beat number following this phrase (where a subsequent phrase might start)

`append();` - extend a phrase by adding another phrase to the end of it

`empty();` - remove all notes from this phrase

These methods are located in the `Mod` class. Here are some examples of this class in action.

```
Mod.quantise(phrase1, QUATER_NOTE);
Mod.repeat(phrase1, 4);
Mod.append(phrase1, phrase2);
```

The first example quantizes `phrase1` to multiples of quarter notes, the second repeats `phrase1` so that it plays four times, and the third appends `phrase2` to the end of `phrase1`. This begins to show some of the power of the jMusic libraries. All the hard work is done behind the scenes, and all you need to access this power are method calls like these.

All the methods in the `Mod` class follow the same syntactic pattern. The first argument is always the musical data that gets modified. Subsequent arguments describe in what way the first parameter should be modified, but then subsequent parameters are never altered themselves. For example in this code, `Mod.append(phrase1, phrase2);` the second parameter, `phrase2`, remains the same. It is `phrase1` that gets updated to include the melody stored in `phrase2`.

Most of the method names in the `Mod` class are *overloaded*. This is programming term meaning that several methods have the same name but different arguments. For example the `Mod` class contains several append methods.

```
Mod.append(note1, note2);
Mod.append(part1, part2);
Mod.append(score1, score2);
```

This framework can be used with all the methods of the `Mod` class. The full list of `Mod` methods, including comments about their use and specifics about their parameters, are listed in appendix B.

Modifications effect existing jMusic objects. So remember to create a `Phrase`, `CPhrase`, `Part`, `Score` before modifying it.

```
Phrase phr = new Phrase();
        . . . add notes . . .
Mod.retrograde(phr); // play backwards

Phrase phr = new Phrase();
        . . . add notes . . .
Mod.repeat(phr, 3); // repeat three times
```

Concept Quiz

1. What do we call music that includes several concurrent lines?
2. What does our brain attempt to find in music we hear?
3. What does the `copy()` method do to a phrase?
4. What effect does changing a phrases start time have?
5. Name three of the methods in the jMusic Mod class.
6. What does the void return type indicate about a method?

Arpeggiator

Arpeggiators have been used in electronic music for many decades. An arpeggiator creates a phrase from a set of notes (a chord) by playing them in a series one after another. In essence they generate a musical order from a group of pitches; providing note-level structure. An arpeggiation is often associated with note sets that are chords, for example C, E, G, and B flat (a C7 chord). Traditionally the arpeggiated phrase is repeated many times to provide both a rhythmic and harmonic layer in the music. A variety of arpeggiation patterns are common; these patterns include playing them in ascending pitch order, in descending order, up then down, or in a random order. Here is a simple Java arpeggiator program called *Arp1*.

```java
import jm.JMC;
import jm.music.data.*;
import jm.util.*;
import jm.music.tools.Mod;

public class Arp1 implements JMC {
    int rootNote = C2;
    int[] pattern = {0,4,7,4};
    Phrase phr;

    public static void main(String[] args) {
        Arp1 myArp = new Arp1();
        myArp.arpeggiator();
        myArp.saveAs();
    }

    public void arpeggiator() {
        phr = new Phrase(0.0);
        for (int i=0; i<pattern.length; i++ ) {
            phr.addNote(new Note(rootNote+pattern[i], SN));
        }
        Mod.repeat(phr, 8);
    }

    public void saveAs() {
        Write.midi(phr, "Arp1.mid");
        Play.misi(phr);
    }
}
```

Programming Practice

You should be able to apply the copy and transfer techniques from the *RowYourBoat* class to the *Arp1* program so that it plays the arpeggio motif in different keys, following a chord progression. For example, try to make it repeat the motif 8 times in C then 4 times in F, four time in G, and another 8 in C. To do this you will need to make copies of `phr`, transpose them as required, set their start times to the right locations, and add all `Phrases` to a `Part` for writing and playing.

Java Details

In this chapter, and previously, a number of Java features have been introduced, and some have been used without much explanation. This section elaborates on a number of these Java features.

JavaSound playback

The playback of jMusic data types with the `Play.midi()` method, uses the JavaSound libraries that have been a part of the standard libraries in Java since version 1.3. When Java is installed on your computer a library of instrument sounds (a soundbank) conforming to the General MIDI instrument standard is included. It is this sample soundbank that is being used for playback. Importantly this soundbank is independent of any computer sound card or external synthesizer that you may have. This provides convenient playback, but with little control over the quality of sound. There is an option to download and install alternate soundbanks from Sun, at http://java.sun.com. Later in this book we will see how you can use your own samples and synthesized instruments to play, and render, music. This will provide much greater control over how the music sounds.

When the `Play.midi()` method is called the jMusic data is converted into a MIDI format behind the scenes before playback. This explains why, after running the program, there may be a short wait before playback begins.

Keywords

Identifying which words in the code are Java keywords, which are jMusic keywords, and which are variable names is important to understanding the code. If you use a text editor with syntax highlighting, then many of the Java keywords will be in a different color to other text. Java keywords include `public`, `class`, `int`, `double`, `static` and so on.

Keywords in java have special meaning and are reserved so you are not allowed to use them for other purposes. This means you can't create your own variable called 'class', for example. The jMusic libraries define various another words to have special meaning, including `Note`, `Phrase`, `Mod`, and `Play` which are class names, and `C4`, `FORTE`, `QUARTER_NOTE`, and `PIANO` which are constants. These words are not reserved, you can redefine their meaning, but when working with jMusic we suggest you don't. Some text editors allow you to add your own words for syntax highlighting, and it is useful with these to make a list of the common jMusic class names, method names, and constants so they are easily identified in the code.

Methods

Methods are blocks of code inside a class that perform some function. Object-oriented programming languages use the name 'method' because they usually define a method of operating on data. Other programming languages have similar structures they call procedures or functions. Methods are defined with a return type, name and required arguments and the contents of a method are bounded by curly brackets { and }. Here is a simple method with three lines in its body. Methods are usually written to manipulate the data with their class, sometimes data passed to the method from outside the class.

```
private void emptyEverything() {
    score.empty();
    part2.empty();
    bassPhrase.empty();
}
```

This method can be called from elsewhere in your class with the line;

```
emptyEverything();
```

or from another class with,

```
className.emptyEverything();
```

One significant advantage of methods is to assist in reuse of code. In this example, the one line method call executes three lines of code, so each time this method is used we are being more efficient about how much code we must write. Methods should be kept small to increase code readability and help localize error detection. Once common way to achieve this is to break large methods into multiple smaller methods.

Passing arguments

When a method is declared the types of data it can receive are specified. These are called method arguments. Arguments are used to pass data between methods. This may be used to pass a local variable from one method to another within a class, or to pass data from one class to another.

```
public int addEmUp(int x, int y) {
    int value = x + y;
    return value;
}
```

The addEmUp() method takes two arguments of type int and also returns an int. here is an example of how to call this method from elsewhere in the class.

```
int val = addEmUp(12, 4);
```

When passing primitive types as arguments, such as numbers and Boolean values, the arguments become copies of the original variables. Therefore the variable x within the addEmUp() method is distinct from the number that was passed. Consider this code fragment.

```
public int muckEmUp(int x, int y) {
    x = x * 2;
    y = y + 5;
    return x + y;
}

int a = 12;
int b = 4;
int val = muckEmUp(a, b);
```

The muckEmUp() method changes the value of x and y but the values of a and b are not effected. This is because primitive types in Java are passed by copy. This means that the value is cloned into two distinct values before one copy is passed to the method.

All Java objects (including arrays and strings) that are passed as arguments to methods are passed by reference. This means that the variable inside the method that refers to the argument is a reference to the original object passed to it. So any changes made to the argument effect the original object passed. Consider this example.

```
public void effectEm (Note n, Phrase phr) {
    n.setPitch(34);
    phr.addNote(n);
}

Note myNote = new Note(60, 1.5);
Phrase myPhrase = new Phrase(0.0);
effectEm(myNote, myPhrase);
```

The note myNote and phrase myPhrase are declared outside the effectEm() method and passed to it as arguments. Because they are non-primitive types, n and phr become references to myNote and myPhrase respectively. This means that both the name n and the name myNote point to the same Note object as depicted in figure 5.2. Therefore any changes made to n is reflected as a change in myNote, similarly with phr and myPhrase.

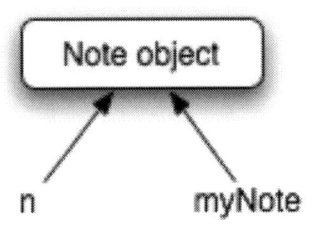

Figure 5.2. One java object referenced by two variables.

While data are often passed to methods in the way just described, methods can also operate on instance and class variables that are visible to all methods of a class.

Access modifiers

Access to methods and variables can be specified using the keywords `private`, `public` or `protected` when declaring them. This changes the visibility of the method or variable from other parts of your program or other programs. By default, that is if no modifier is specified, the variables and methods are accessible to the class itself or other classes in the same package (more on packages later). The `private` modifier restricts access so that the variables or methods are only visible within the class. Private variables and methods can only be used by other methods in the same class. The `public` modifier makes class members accessible from any class. The `protected` modifier makes methods and variables visible within the class, to classes in the same package, and to sucbclasses that extend the current class. Protected access is slightly wider than the default access if no modifier was specified. Here is a table summarizing the four access modifiers.

Modifier	Visibility
private	Only visible within the class
(none)	Visible within the class and other classes in the same package
protected	Visible within the class, the package, and any subclasses
public	Visible from any other class

It is good programming practice to keep access to members as restricted as possible to avoid possible confusion between similarly named classes, methods and variables, and to protect against modification of variables in a haphazard way.

Accessor methods

A safe and convenient way to access the variables within a class from outside of it, is to provide methods that get (retrieve) and set (assign) its value. For example, in the Note class there are methods for accessing the note's pitch variable, Note.getPitch() and Note.setPitch(int newValue).

Get and set methods are required when an instance variable is declared private because, as a result, access from outside the class is prohibited. They are optional, but it is still good practice to define them, when the instance variables are declared public. It is good practice to declare variables private and enable access to them with accessor methods because the get and set methods can do additional tasks that may be required when the values are accessed. Such tasks may include checking that the new value is within range, doing a conversion from an internal data type to an externally required one, updating other values in the class that depend on the variable, or as a convenience method that saves the programmer some time by doing a couple of steps in one call.

For example, in jMusic the Note.setLength() method is a convenience method that changes both the Note's rhythmValue and duration in concert. By default in jMusic when a note is created, the duration is set to 90% of the rhythmValue. To achieve different articulation—staccato or legato performance—the duration can be changed independently from the rhythmValue. It is a common oversight to change the rhythmValue of the Note without changing its duration. The setLength() method does both, and so using it avoids this common error. For a Note n, n.setLength(2.0) is the same as n.setRhythmValue(2.0) and n.setDuration(2.0 * 0.9).

Method overloading

It is often the case that you want the same process to be applied to different types, for example, it is likely that you want to transpose a phrase or a part or a score. Java allows a class to contain methods with the same name if they each have a unique set of arguments. So, these transpose methods in jMusic's Mod class are each unique because they accept different arguments.

```
Mod.transpose(Phrase phr, amount) {}
Mod.transpose(Part p, amount) {}
Mod.transpose(Score s, amount) {}
```

This ability to have several methods of the same name in a class, is called method *overloading*.

Concept Quiz

1. What is a method in Java?
2. Where in a method declaration is the return type indicated?
3. Values passed to a method are called what?
4. What are some differences between a local and an instance variable?
5. If object A is a reference to object B and A is changed, what happens to B?
6. What is the difference in scope between a private and public method?
7. A private variable x may have method `getX()` and `setX()` what are these methods known as?
8. What is method overloading?

TheGrid: Playing several parts

In this chapter, TheGrid application will be extended to include snare and kick drum parts. In addition we will save the score as a standard MIDI file.

TheGrid2

The structure of this application is identical to *TheGrid1* where the `main()` method called the constructor, then calls the compose method.

```
hats = new Phrase(0.0);
snare = new Phrase(0.0);
kick = new Phrase(0.0);
```

This code fragment from the constructor method shows that phrases are created for each drum, and each phrase is set to start at the beginning of the part, at `beat 0.0`. Later in the method each phrase is added to the same part called drums. This means they will share the instrument and channel attributes of that part.

```
int[] snareHits = {REST, REST, REST, REST, D2, REST, REST, REST,
    REST, REST, REST, REST, D2, REST, D2, REST};
snare.addNoteList(snareHits, SIXTEENTH_NOTE);
```

In the `compose()` method, arrays containing the pitches for each drum are added to a phrase.

```
Write.midi(drums, "DrumPattern2.mid");
```

The part is written out to a standard MIDI file, which can be played in any MIDI file player or imported into another MIDI application. The first argument to the `Write.midi()` method is the part to be saved, and the second argument is the name for the saved file. It is conventional for MIDI files to have the `.mid` suffix.

```
    Play.midi(drums);
```

Lastly, the music is played back using Java's internal synthesizer. Here is the complete code.

```
import jm.JMC;
import jm.music.data.*;
import jm.util.*;
public class TheGrid2 implements JMC {
    private Phrase hats, snare, kick;
    private Part drums;
    public static void main(String[] args) {
        TheGrid2 grid = new TheGrid2();
          grid.compose();
          grid.output();
    }
    public TheGrid2() {
        hats = new Phrase(0.0);
        snare = new Phrase(0.0);
        kick = new Phrase(0.0);
        drums = new Part("Drums", 25, 9);
        drums.addPhrase(hats);
        drums.addPhrase(snare);
        drums.addPhrase(kick);
    }
    public void compose() {
         int[] hatsHits = {REST, REST, FS2, REST, REST, REST, FS2, REST,
              REST, REST, FS2, REST, REST, REST, FS2, REST,};
        hats.addNoteList(hatsHits, SIXTEENTH_NOTE);
        int[] snareHits = {REST, REST, REST, REST, D2, REST, REST, REST,
              REST, REST, REST, REST, D2, REST, D2, REST};
        snare.addNoteList(snareHits, SIXTEENTH_NOTE);
        int[] kickHits = {C2, REST, REST, REST, REST, REST, REST, C2, C2,
              REST, REST, REST, REST, REST, REST, REST};
        kick.addNoteList(kickHits, SIXTEENTH_NOTE);
    }
    public void output() {
        Write.midi(drums, "DrumPattern2.mid");
        Play.midi(drums);
    }
}
```

6: Design and Layout

Creating music is not just about making a single phrase, nor is writing Java programs just about defining one method. Sophisticated compositions and programs are made of many parts that fit together in a design that creates a working whole. In this chapter we begin to look at issues and techniques of arrangement and design of both music and code.

Viewing and Arranging Music

The arrangement of a musical work concerns its structure and texture, the organization of and relationships between musical events. When considering the arrangement of musical elements it is useful to consider their organization over time and space.

Musical structure over time is the most obvious aspect of arrangement. When considering this we think about when musical events start and stop, when they might reappear, how we might consider groups of events as a coherent block (such as phrase, sections, verses, choruses, and movements). In this chapter, we will explore techniques for placing musical sections in time.

Musical space is multi-dimensional, and we will explore techniques that control some of the dimensions now, and others in later chapters. A good place to start is to consider sounds in physical space. Their location can be organized from left to right in the stereo spectrum controlled by panning, and from front to back in an imaginary depth perspective controlled, largely, by loudness. Another consideration is texture; the number of concurrent parts and their interaction. As parts are added to the music the texture becomes thicker, but it need not be cluttered if attention is played to each parts timbre (sound quality), pitch range, and independence (or synchrony), to name some important considerations. As we proceed through this chapter techniques allowing the control of these features in Java will be introduced, as well as some tools to assist to judge the monitor the musical arrangement by seeing it, hearing it, and manipulating it.

We will see with the jMusic `HelperGUI` interface how the computer can be a useful tool for speeding up the processes of testing out compositional ideas. As we move through the rest of this chapter we will see how the computer can also start to act like a compositional *partner*. It will do this by taking on some of the responsibility for musical decision making.

HelperGUI

The `HelperGUI` is a jMusic class that provides a graphical user interface (GUI) for your programs that can speed up the trialing of different values without the need to go through the complete cycle of writing, saving, compiling, and running the program. The `HelperGUI` is part of the jMusic package and it's availability means that you can have a visual interface to your composition without having to write new interface code for each new work. The `HelperGUI` is designed using the Java Advanced Windowing Toolkit (AWT) package - more on this later - and will take on the appearance of your operating system. In Mac OS X it appears as in figure 6.1.

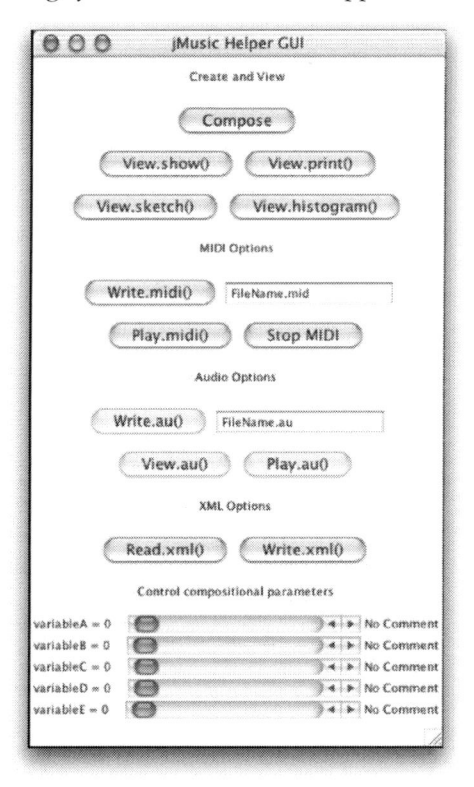

Figure 6.1. The HelperGUI interface

For the `HelperGUI` class to be available, visible, to your program make sure to import it.

```
import jm.gui.helper.HelperGUI;
```

You use the `HelperGUI` class by writing a program that *extends* it. This way your class gets all the features of the `HelperGUI` class, including this visual appearance. Here is an example class declaration that extends `HelperGUI`.

```
public final class HelperTest extends HelperGUI implements JMC {
```

As the *HelperTest* example shows, a class that extends the `HelperGUI` class must have a more sophisticated structure than simply having one main method. It will include a short `main` method that simply calls the constructor.

```
public static void main(String[] args){
    new HelperTest();
}
```

The constructor makes a call to the `HelperGUI` class; its *super* class, the one it extends, as part of the class instantiation process. This makes sure the `HelperGUI` class does its necessary set up procedures, and does any initializing the class requires. In this example, a variable (used for the initial pitch) is set in the constructor.

```
public HelperTest() {
    super();
    setVariableA(60);
}
```

Importantly, your class needs to have a `compose()` method, which will be run each time the compose button on the interface is clicked. It is in this method that all of your musical logic will go.

```
public Score compose() { ...
```

Notice that the `compose()` method declaration indicates that it will return a `Score` object. This means that within the method you must declare a score, fill it with whatever data you want, then return the score as a last line in the method using the code,

```
return score;
```

As well as providing button to trigger composition of your score, the `HelperGUI` interface has buttons for starting and stopping playback of the score using JavaSound's General MIDI soundbank, so you can audition the composition. If you like what you hear, the score can be saved as a standard MIDI file using the `Write.midi()` button, with any name you specify in the filename field. The interface has buttons for viewing the score, which we'll explore later in this chapter, and there is an option to save as an audio file of the composition, which we will see more about later in this book.

Finally, the interface has five sliders labeled `variableA – E`. These can use used to set variables within your composition to change values of any parameter. Once values are changed on the interface, the compose button can be clicked to recalculate your composition with the new values, then you can audition and re-view the result. In our example program *HelperTest*, we have used `vari-`

ableA to specify the beginning pitch of a scale. The composer method simply creates a chromatic scale of one octave starting on the pitch indicated by `variableA`. The other variable sliders could be used in the same way to adjust other features. The values of the sliders are always integers between 0 and 127, so some remapping may need to be done in the program to achieve an appropriate range of values.

Here is the complete code of a the *HelperTest* program that extends the `HelperGUI` class.

```
import jm.JMC;
import jm.music.data.*;
import jm.gui.helper.HelperGUI;

public final class HelperTest extends HelperGUI implements JMC {
    public static void main(String[] args){
        HelperTest ht = new HelperTest();
    }

    public HelperTest() {
        super();
        setVariableA(60);
    }

    public Score compose() {
        Score score = new Score("Test");
        Part xylophonePart = new Part("Xylophone", XYLOPHONE, 0);
        Phrase scale = new Phrase(0.0);
        for (int i=0;i<12;i++){
            Note n = new Note(variableA + i, DEMI_SEMI_QUAVER);
            scale.addNote(n);
        }
        xylophonePart.addPhrase(scale);
        score.addPart(xylophonePart);
        return score;
    }
}
```

Random notes

A random number generator is a function whose result cannot be determined in advance, since every outcome has equal likelihood, probability, of occurring. The random element in the *RandomNotes* program is in the selection of pitches from a pitch set. An array of pitches is declared and for each note a pitch is randomly selected from that array. A call to the random method of Java's static Math class, Math.random(), results in a double value between 0.0 and 1.0. However, in this program we require an int between 0 and 4 so the random number needs to be scaled. We multiply by the number of pitches in the array (the array length) and cast to an integer so it is the correct type for the pitch value of the note constructor. Each time the piece is 'composed' a different melody is likely to be generated.

```
pitches[(int)(Math.random() * pitches.length)
```

This line is quite compact and could be rewritten with each step more explicit as,

```
int numberOfPitches = pitches.length;
double randomNumber = Math.random();
int pitchNumberToUse = (int)(randomNumber * numberOfPitches);
pitches[pitchNumberToUse];
```

Only the compose method of *RandomNotes* is printed here because otherwise the program is similar to the *HelperTest* program above.

```
public Score compose() {
    Score score = new Score("Random Notes", 140);
    Part xylophonePart1 = new Part("Xylophone",XYLOPHONE, 0);
    Phrase melody1 = new Phrase(0.0);
    int[] pitches = {C4,D4,E4,F4,G4};
    double[] rhythm = {EN,EN,SN,EN,EN,EN,EN,SN,EN};

    for (int i=0; i<rhythm.length; i++) {
        Note n = new Note(pitches[(int)(Math.random()*
            pitches.length)], rhythm[i]);
        melody1.addNote(n);
    }

    Mod.repeat(melody1, 8);
    xylophonePart1.addPhrase(melody1);
    score.addPart(xylophonePart1);
    return score;
}
```

Start times

Phrases can be positioned anywhere in the score by setting their start time variable, either when declaring the phrase,

```
Phrase melody1 = new Phrase(0.0);
```

or at any other time by setting a new value.

```
melody1.setStartTime(24.0);
```

A phrase can only have one start time, and so can only be in one location. However, it is easy to copy a phrase and then set a new start time for the copy when a restatement of a phrase is required in another section of a piece.

```
Phrase melody2 = melody1.copy();
melody2.setStartTime(9.0);
```

In the *StartTimes* example below, one of the phrases starts at beat 0.0 while a second phrase has a start time that is dependent upon `variableA` of the `HelperGUI` interface. In order to keep some sense of musicality the start time change is quantized to be in thirty-second note increments.

```
melody2.setStartTime(variableA * TN);
```

Different values of the start time, cause the two phrases to be out of synchronization, resulting in a variety of musical effects from interlocking counterpoint at short distances to echo or delay at larger differences.

The compose method of *StartTimes* is an elaboration of the *RandomNotes* program above. There is an additional xylophone part which is on a separate channel. A second melodic phrase is made as a copy of the first and added to the second part. The start time of the second phrase is set based on the `variableA` value. Below is the critical `compose` method of the *StartTimes* example.

```
public Score compose() {
    Score score = new Score("Test", 140);
    Part xylophonePart1 = new Part("Xylophone",XYLOPHONE, 0);
    Part xylophonePart2 = new Part("Xylophone",XYLOPHONE, 1);
    Phrase melody1 = new Phrase(0.0);
    int[] pitches = {C4,D4,E4,F4,G4};
    double[] rhythm = {EN,EN,SN,EN,EN,EN,EN,SN,EN};
    for (int i=0; i<rhythm.length; i++) {
        Note n = new Note(pitches[(int)(Math.random() *
            pitches.length)], rhythm[i]);
        melody1.addNote(n);
    }
    Mod.repeat(melody1, 8);
    Phrase melody2 = melody1.copy();
    melody2.setStartTime(variableA * TN);
```

```
        xylophonePart1.addPhrase(melody1);
        xylophonePart2.addPhrase(melody2);
        score.addPart(xylophonePart1);
        score.addPart(xylophonePart2);
        return score;
    }
```

Also the line below is added to the constructor to set `variableA` to 4.

```
        setVariableA(4);
```

Variables can also have an associated label that appears on the `HelperGUI` interface to remind you what that variable does.

```
        setVariableA(4, "Phrase 2 start");
```

Automatically appending phrases

In the same way that notes in a phrase follow one another in the order added, it is common that phrases follow one another without a break. Rather than having to calculate the new start times for each phrase in these situations, phrases can be declared without any start time at all. When such a phrase is added to a part it will automatically be placed at the end of the part. In the code fragment below, eight phrases will be added to the part end on end.

```
        Part part1 = new Part("Melody", FLUTE, 0);
        for (int i=0; i<8; i++) {
            Phrase phr1 = new Phrase();
            //... add notes to the phrase ...
            part1.addPhrase(phr1);
        }
```

Panning

The position of notes across the stereo field can be specified by their pan value. A pan value of 0.0 will have the sound out the left speaker only, a value of 1.0 will have the sound out the right speaker only. While a value of 0.5 (the default) will sound in the centre, equal volume from left and right speakers.

The *StartTimes* program can be modified to have the `melody1` phrase play to the left and the `melody2` phrase play to the right by using the phrase's `setPan()` method. This will effect all notes in the phrase at the time the method is called.

```
melody1.setPan(0.0);
melody2.setPan(1.0);
```

In order to have the pan positions controlled by variable sliders on the `HelperGUI` interface, we declare the initial values in the constructor,

```
setVariableB(0);
setVariableC(127);
```

Then we replace the fixed pan settings with ones based on the variables, using appropriate rescaling math to keep the values as floats between 0.0 and 1.0. Be aware of the Java convention that when an `int` and a `double` are multiplied, the result is a `double`.

```
melody1.setPan(variableB / 127.0);
melody2.setPan(variableC / 127.0);
```

Programming Practice

> Try modifying the *StartTimes* program to randomly set the panning location of each note individually. Because the both the pan value and `Math.random()` output is a double between 0.0 and 1.0, no scaling of the random values are required. The line below can be placed in the compose method, after the note declaration which is inside the for-loop.
>
> ```
> n.setPan(Math.random());
> ```
>
> Remember that later pan settings will override earlier ones, so the phrase and note level panning above make no sense to be simultaneously added the *StartTimes* program. Try each individually to hear the different effects.

Dynamics and mixing

An important aspect of getting the music to sound right is to have an appropriate balance between the parts and phrases. So that the bass is not too loud for the drums, or the flute is able to be heard over the saxophone, for example. As well, musical performances rarely have a completely even dynamic on every note so it is natural to allow each note to have its own dynamic level. A jMusic `Note` can take a third constructor value specifying its dynamic, either as a number or as a JMC constant.

```
Note n = new Note(C4, QUARTER_NOTE, FORTE);
```

The volume of a note in jMusic is controlled by its dynamic value, an `int` with a value between 1 (softest) and 127 (loudest). For convenience, there are methods to change the dynamic of all notes in a phrase, part or score in one step. To change the dynamic values within a part so that all notes are at a specific level use the `phrase.setDynamic()` method and pass an integer value. Each note can have a separate dynamic value which can add richness and life to the music. If we wish to adjust the overall dynamic level of a part that has notes with varying dynamic levels, we an use the `Mod.increaseDynamic()` method, and pass the object to be modified (the part) and an `int` value for the amount of increase (a negative value for a decrease) to apply to each note. Use the `Mod.shake()` method to randomly adjusts all Notes' dynamic value to create uneven loudness. An `int` that specifies the degree of randomization is one argument to the `shake()` method.

The *MixingParts* program adds dynamic control to the *PanningPhrases* program. Variables D and E are used to control the volume of the two parts. These lines are added to the constructor to set the initial values.

```
setVariableD(100);
setVariableE(50);
```

These lines are added towards the end of the compose method to set the dynamic level of each part.

```
xylophonePart1.setDynamic(variableD);
xylophonePart2.setDynamic(variableE);
```

Viewing as a piano roll

Earlier we saw how phrases can be viewed as CPN. Another useful view of music is the piano roll view, named after the paper scrolls used on old pianolas; player pianos that played automatically powered by the energy of pumped air. In these scrolls the music was represented as holes in the paper, whose position on one axis was the pitch and whose length on the other was the note duration. As air was let through the holes the notes were played on the pianola. These piano roll displays are now common on many MIDI sequencing programs.

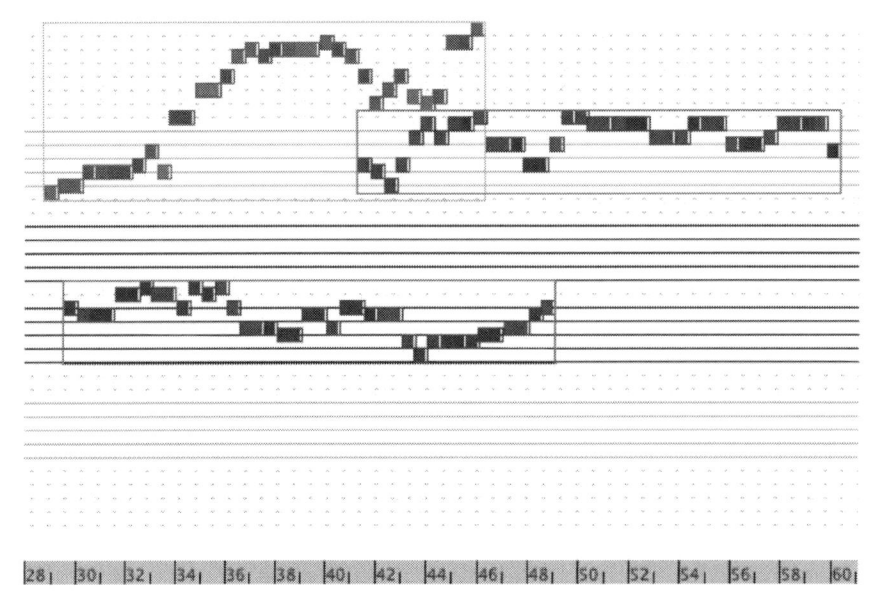

Figure 6.2. Show view.

The Show view, figure 6.2, displays the jMusic score in a piano roll view. At this stage the viewer does not allow editing of the displayed score. Unlike a traditional piano roll view, the pitch scale is shown on a grand stave (rather than the more usual linear chromatic scale) and notes are shown as rectangles using the piano-roll-like note bars. The horizontal black lines indicate lines in a standard treble and bass staves, while the grey staves indicate more extreme pitches, and can be read as treble (upper) and bass (lower) staves two octaves away. Chromatic notes (black notes on the piano) are shown with a sharp (#) sign in front, as per a CPN display. Phrase boundaries are drawn as rectangles on the display, and notes from different parts are shown in different colors. The depth of color indicates the dynamic level of the note, darker shades are higher in dynamic value. The ruler along the bottom displays a line for each beat and larger lines every two beats. The horizontal scale of the score can be adjusted by dragging on the ruler bar. Beat numbers are displayed when ruler size permits. There is a Show menu, that contains options to change the notation size, save the displayed score as a MIDI file, or to quite from the current application.

Scores, parts and phrases can be displayed using the View.show() method and passing the music data object to be displayed. When using the HelperGUI interface there is a View.display() button that performs this task.

Viewing as printed data

While a visual display of the score provides a useful overview of the score, some times it is useful to see the precise data values. The print view is used for this. It provides a list of the important values in the score, displaying each part, phrase and note in turn. You can see this display of any music data object by passing it to the `View.print()` method. The display will be similar to figure 6.3.

```
******* SCORE: Scatter Piece. Contains 8 parts. *******
Tempo = 140.0 bpm
———————— PART: Part 0. Contains 2 phrases. ————————
Channel = 0
Instrument = 6
———————— PHRASE: Untitled Phrase. Contains 30 notes.  Start time: 88.9580309758615 ————————
Note: [Pitch = 81][RhythmValue = 0.5][Dynamic = 90][Pan = 0.8039950782602798][Duration = 0.45]
Note: [Pitch = 84][RhythmValue = 0.5][Dynamic = 54][Pan = 0.8039950782602798][Duration = 0.45]
Note: [Pitch = 86][RhythmValue = 0.5][Dynamic = 93][Pan = 0.8039950782602798][Duration = 0.45]
Note: [Pitch = 88][RhythmValue = 0.5][Dynamic = 34][Pan = 0.8039950782602798][Duration = 0.45]
Note: [Pitch = 86][RhythmValue = 0.5][Dynamic = 95][Pan = 0.8039950782602798][Duration = 0.45]
Note: [Pitch = 91][RhythmValue = 0.5][Dynamic = 35][Pan = 0.8039950782602798][Duration = 0.45]
Note: [Pitch = 81][RhythmValue = 0.5][Dynamic = 34][Pan = 0.8039950782602798][Duration = 0.45]
Note: [Pitch = 81][RhythmValue = 0.5][Dynamic = 34][Pan = 0.8039950782602798][Duration = 0.45]
Note: [Pitch = 79][RhythmValue = 0.5][Dynamic = 58][Pan = 0.8039950782602798][Duration = 0.45]
Note: [Pitch = 76][RhythmValue = 0.5][Dynamic = 68][Pan = 0.8039950782602798][Duration = 0.45]
Note: [Pitch = 76][RhythmValue = 0.5][Dynamic = 89][Pan = 0.8039950782602798][Duration = 0.45]
Note: [Pitch = 76][RhythmValue = 1.0][Dynamic = 71][Pan = 0.8039950782602798][Duration = 0.9]
```

Figure 6.3. Print view.

The `HelperGUI` interface has a button to provide a print list display of the current score.

Viewing as music notation

In addition to hearing your music played it can be useful to see a visual representation of it as well. jMusic supports a number of visualization displays which are accessed with the static `View` class. A frequently used music representation is common practice notation (CPN). The `View` class has a limited CPN facility that currently supports viewing a single phrase at a time. The code for calling this method is, `View.notate(phraseName);`.

To see the notation of the phrase used as a motif in the *PianoPhase* program, add a call to the `View` class after the phrase is created, as shown in this code sample.

```
Phrase phrase1 = new Phrase("Piano Phase Motif", 0.0);
int[] pitchArray = {E4,FS4,B4,CS5,D5,FS4,E4,CS5,B4,FS4,D5,CS5};
phrase1.addNoteList(pitchArray, SN);
View.notate(phrase1);
```

The result will appear similar to figure 6.4.

Figure 6.4: The jMusic common practice notation (CPN) view.

Scattered phrases

This program *Scatter* generates a piece that employs all of the arrangement variables we have discussed in this chapter and has random functions on almost every parameter. Each time this program is run a different piece results. Clearly the computer has a strong partnership role in this piece through its 'choice' of random numbers. The choice of melodic pitch it selected by a random walk algorithm.

Random walk

Earlier we saw how to select random note pitches from an array when creating a phrase. This will produce a scatter of pitches across the range of the pitch set. This worked in previous examples because the pitch set was very small, when choosing notes from a wide range a random melody can be less coherent. This is because some intervals between successive notes are very wide, which is uncommon in conventional melodies. A random walk algorithm solves this problem by keeping intervals between notes within a reasonable range but allowing the overall melodic contour to drift quite widely.

The *Scatter* program uses a random walk algorithm to generate note pitches within a phrase. The 'walk' aspect of the algorithm is based upon the fact that the next pitch is relative to the previous pitch; in this case within five semitones.

```
pitch += (int)(Math.random()*10-5);
```

Further, it constrains the pitches to a pentatonic (five note) scale to maintain harmonic coherence. This constraint of note pitches to a scale is achieved using the `isScale()` method from the `Note` class, which accepts a JMC scale constant as an argument. This method returns a Boolean, true or false, result about weather a particular note is a member of the specified scale. Here is a simplified version of the method showing the workings of the random walk process.

```java
private Phrase makePhrase() {
    Phrase phr = new Phrase();
    int pitch = 60;
    double[] rhythm = {EN,EN,SN,EN,EN,EN,EN,SN,EN};

    for (int i = 0; i < rhythm.length; i++) {
        Note note;
        do {
            pitch += (int)(Math.random()*10-5);
            note = new Note(pitch, rhythm[i]);
        } while (!note.isScale(PENTATONIC_SCALE));
        phr.addNote(note);
    }
    return phr;
}
```

The *Scatter* example uses all five `HelperGUI` variables to allow the exploration of different tempo and textual densities. The variables are often scaled to an appropriate amount. For example, `variableA` controls the tempo - but the tempo in beats per minute (BPM) is twice the variable readout. For example, a `variableA` value of 70 equals a tempo of 140 bpm. Below is the complete code for the *Scatter* example.

```java
import jm.JMC;
import jm.util.*;
import jm.music.data.*;
import jm.music.tools.*;
import jm.gui.helper.HelperGUI;

public final class Scatter extends HelperGUI implements JMC{
    public static void main(String[] args){
        new Scatter();
    }

    public Scatter() {
        super();
        setVariableA(70, "Tempo");
        setVariableB(60, "# of parts");
        setVariableC(2, "Phrases per part");
```

```java
            setVariableD(80, "Score length");
            setVariableE(30, "Note in phrases");
    }

    public Score compose() {
        Score score = new Score("Scatter Piece", variableA * 2);
        for (int i=0;i<(int)((variableB + 1) / 8) + 1;i++) {
            Part part = new Part("Part", (int)(Math.random() * 113),i);
            for (int j=0; j<variableC;j++) {
                Phrase phrase = new Phrase();
                phrase = makePhrase();
                part.addPhrase(phrase);
            }
            score.addPart(part);
        }
        return(score);
    }
    private Phrase makePhrase() {
        Phrase phr = new Phrase((Math.random()*variableD) * HALF_NOTE);
        double phrasePanLocation = Math.random();
        int pitch = (int)(Math.random()*60+40);
        for (int i=0;i<variableE;i++) {
            Note note;
            do {
                pitch += (int)(Math.random()*10-5);
                if (pitch<0) pitch = 0 {
                    if (pitch>127) pitch = 127;
                        double rv;
                    if (Math.random() < 0.2);
                        rv = QUARTER_NOTE;
                } else rv = EIGHTH_NOTE;
                note = new Note(pitch, rv,
                    (int)(Math.random()*70+30));
            } while (!note.isScale(PENTATONIC_SCALE));
            note.setPan(phrasePanLocation);
            phr.addNote(note);
        }
        return phr;
    }
}
```

Math Moment

Algorithms and Heuristics: An algorithm, to be precise, is a process that is guaranteed to produce a specified outcome. Many times, particularly where aesthetic judgments are involved, an answer which is mostly true or close to optimal will be fine. A rule of thumb that almost always gives a 'resonable' answer is called a heuristic. In many cases it is quite acceptable to use a heuristic, rather than an algorithm, and sometimes it may make no practical difference. Because algorithms are guaranteed to give the correct answer they may be quite slow to execute as they search through all possible answers to make sure they provide the best one. For example, in computer chess programs, an algorithm to find the best move would need to search every possible end game of every possible combination of moves available. Because this is a ridiculously large number and would (at best) make the game very slow and boring, chess programs use heuristics which may provide the best answer on occasion but provide a very good one in most cases. Many of the 'limitations' of computers turn out to be the limitations of algorithms and, consequently, our ability to adequately describe a process.

Structure

The importance of structure can be heard in the next example program, *MelodicStructure*. The form of this piece is a simple nursery rhythm structure with four sections A, B, C and D where the A and C sections are reused (copied) to add a sense of familiarity through repetition. Each section is four beats long except section D which is eight beats long. The form is A, B, A, C, D, A, C. This example uses a random walk melody in the `makePhrase()` method very similar to the *Scatter* program, the argument passed is the length of the generated phase, in beats. The strength of the example is to hear how this simple structure can add cohesion to a random series of notes. The format of the *MelodicStructure* program is similar to the others in this chapter, therefore only the critical compose method is listed below.

```java
public Score compose() {
    Phrase a = makePhrase(4.0);
    Phrase b = makePhrase(4.0);
    Phrase c = makePhrase(4.0);
    Phrase d = makePhrase(8.0);
    Phrase a1 = a.copy();
    Phrase a2 = a.copy();
    Phrase c1 = c.copy();
    Part part = new Part();
    Score score = new Score (130);

    part.addPhrase(a);
```

```
        part.addPhrase(b);
        part.addPhrase(a1);
        part.addPhrase(c);
        part.addPhrase(d);
        part.addPhrase(a2);
        part.addPhrase(c1);
        score.addPart(part);

        return score;
    }
```

Concept Quiz

1. What makes a scale "pentatonic"?
2. Is the oder in which phases are added to a part related to their playback order?
3. What is an algorithm?
4. Tempi can be written in bpm; what does BPM stand for?
5. What is a random walk?
6. Name three built in music viewing classes in jMusic.

Program Structure – Arranging code into two classes

In this program we create a composition by making a polyphonic texture from themes derived from the same melodic material. The piece is in two small classes and provides a good example of programming as well as musical structuring processes. Below is the source code for both the *Journey.java* file and the *NPart.java* file (both are required to run the program). Let's have a closer look at sections of the *Journey* class first:

```
import jm.JMC;
import jm.music.data.*;
import jm.util.View;
import jm.util.Play;

/**
 * This class creates a collage of similar parts, each
 * of which may overlap and be rhythmically juxtaposed.
 * The phrase repetition is in a minimalist style.
 * The creation of parts is handled by the NPart class.
 */
public class Journey implements JMC {
    private Score score = new Score();
```

```java
public static void main(String[] args) {
    new Journey();
}
```

The first few lines import the required jMusic packages and classes. After a comment to describe the piece, the class is declared. First, a `Score` object is created at the class level. This means that this object will be 'visible' to all methods in this class. Because it is `private` it can't be seen outside this class.

The first method is `main()` in which all we do is create a new instance of the `Journey` class. In effect the `main()` method simply calls the constructor of this class. The `new` keyword is important in these lines of code. It is used to create an instance of the `Score` class, then used to create an instance of the `Journey` class.

```java
public Journey() {
    for (int i=0; i<8; i++) {
        new NPart(newPart());
    }
    View.print(score);
    Play.midi(score);
}
```

The code above shows the constructor method for the `Journey` class. Remember that the constructor method has the same name as the class (`Journey` in this case) and does not have a return type specified in the first line like all other methods do.

This method provides an overview of our compositional process. First, eight new parts are created in a loop. Next, the `View` class is used to print out the music as text so we can see what was generated visually. Thirdly, the `Play` class is called upon to playback the composition.

The for-loop iterates over one line. This line uses the `new` keyword to create instances of the `NPart` class (we'll see more of it below). The `NPart` class takes a `Part` as an argument. This is created by the `newPart()` method because we want to set some values of the part before giving it over to the `NPart` class.

```java
private Part newPart() {
    Part p = new Part();
    p.setChannel(score.size());
    score.addPart(p);
    return p;
}
```

This `newPart()` method saves us some typing because we want to do things to each part we create. By making it a separate method we write it once and call it many times.

"What does it do?" I hear you ask. First, it creates a standard jMusic `Part` object. Next, it sets the channel depending on how many parts already exist. Using the `size()` method of the score it looks to see how many parts there are and uses that to set the channel. That way each new part is on a new channel. (Remember that if you save jMusic scores as MIDI files you are limited to 16 channels (0-15)).

The part is added to the score and then passed back to the calling method and, in this case, on to the `NPart` class for further computation. A final curly bracket closes the class.

Well, that's the `Journey` class dealt with. Now let's look at the `NPart` class in detail:

```java
import jm.JMC;
import jm.music.data.*;
import jm.music.tools.Mod;
import jm.util.*;

public class NPart implements JMC {
    private Part part;
    private int[] pitches = {C4, E4, G4, A4, D4, F4, E4};
    private double[] rhythms = {Q, Q, Q, Q, Q, Q, C};
    private double partLength = 40.0;
    private double fadeInLength = 12.0;
    private double fadeOutLength = 12.0;
    private double nPartStartTime;
    private int panPosition = (int)(Math.random() * 127);
```

The `import` statements provide access to the classes we need for this program.

The class is defined and some variables are declared for use in this class. Instance variables are used because many aspects of the class are going to vary from instance to instance. This localized variation is how we add musical variety to the piece. So let's examine each class variable.

The `part` variable provides a local holder for the `Part` passed to this class by `Journey`.

The `pitches` and `rhythms` arrays hold the data to make up the notes. Changing these will change the stylistic character of the piece - you may want to give that a shot. The `partLength` variable holds the duration of the part in beats (quarter notes). Other variables `fadeInLength` and `fadeOutLength` specify how long it takes to ramp up and down the loudness of notes at the beginning and ending of the part. Compositionally this has the effect of crossfading the parts which makes the piece more interesting. The variable `nPartStartTime` contains the time (in beats) when the music of this part should begin. The variable `panPosition` holds the information about where in the stereo spectrum notes from this part should emerge.

Java Moment

> The breaking up of this program into classes and methods makes the code easier to read and edit, and multiple method calls save repetitive typing. The division of the program into more than one class file also keeps each file manageable in size, and provides a physical division where there is a logical (compositional) one. In this case the operations on parts is kept separate from working on the score structure of those parts.

Let's examine the NPart class.

```java
public NPart(Part p) {
    this.part = p;
    p.setInstrument((int)(Math.random()*60));
    nPartStartTime = (int)(Math.random() * 200) * SN;
    p.addPhrase(makePhrase());
}
```

There are two methods in this class, the first (above) is the constructor. Remembering that constructor methods have the same name as the class. The constructor is run (called) when a new instance of the class is made (constructed). Within the constructor the part passed from the Journey class is assigned to the local variable part. Next, a General MIDI instrument number for this Part is selected at random between 0 and 59. Then a start time for this Part is calculated using a random value somewhere within the first 200 semiquaver (sixteenth- note) steps of the piece.

Each part in this piece has just one Phrase and the last line calls the makePhrase() method to make it and adds it to the part, all in one fell swoop.

```java
private Phrase makePhrase() {
    Phrase phr = new Phrase( nPartStartTime);
    phr.addNoteList(pitches, rhythms);
    phr.setPan(Math.random());
    Mod.shuffle(phr);
    Mod.cycle(phr, partLength);
    Mod.fadeIn(phr, fadeInLength);
    Mod.fadeOut(phr, fadeOutLength);
    return phr;
}
```

This method generates a phrase based on notes attributes (pitch and rhythm) specified earlier as class variables.

First, it makes an empty phrase and sets the start time. Second, it uses the `Phrase.addNoteList()` method to generate notes based on the pitches and rhythm values provided as arrays earlier. Thirdly, it sets the pan position for each note in the phrase. The pan position is calculated at random. In jMusic pan positions range between 0.0 and 1.0 in the stereo field, with 0.0 being extreme left, and 1.0 being extreme right, therefore 0.5 positions the sound in the middle. By default the `Math.random()` method generates double values between 0 and 1 so no scaling or offsetting is required.

At this stage the notes in the phrase are set. But we want each phrase to be somewhat different so we modify the phase to add variety. To do this we make use of the `Mod` class in `jm.music.tools` directory. We imported this class at the top of the code - have a look to check.

The first modification is `shuffle()` which randomly mixes up the note order of the phrase. The second modification is `cycle()` which loops the phrase until it fills the required number of beats. This makes the phrase the length we specified with the variable `partLength`. The third and fourth modifications fade the dynamic values of notes in and out over a specified length. Finally we pass back the generated and modified phrase to the calling method (above).

Programming Practice

You should try changing the variables to see how they effect the music, and then try some more significant changes, perhaps adding different modifications to the phrase, or being more 'careful' about the choice of instrument or start time by replacing the simple (and dumb) random choices made so far.

Concept Quiz

1. What are some advantages of using instance variables?
2. What keyword is used to define a new Java class?
3. If there is more than one class in a program, which one is run first?
4. What is the difference between a class and a method?
5. What effect does the `shuffle()` method of jMusic's Mod class have an notes in a `Phrase`?
6. What are some reasons or benefits of breaking a program into several classes?

Java GUI Classes

One of the advantages of programming applications in Java is that they can be cross platform. The same program can run on the Macintosh, Windows and Linux operating systems and beyond. This is facilitated for end-user software by Java packages that describe its own graphical user interface classes for drawing windows, buttons, and more and for the handling mouse and keyboard interactions and the like. The disadvantage of providing platform-independent interface libraries is that Java applications often look like, well, Java applications that may not always look the same as native applications. In many cases this is a small price to pay for the universality, and if you write your own interface components (like many music applications have a tendency to do) them this "unofficial" appearance is of no concern. In this section we will introduce some of Java's user interface classes, but a comprehensive coverage is well beyond the current scope and the interested reader is directed to seek one some of many good reference sources on Java GUI programing.

Introducing the AWT package

The abstract windowing toolkit (AWT) is Java's original graphical user interface library. It handles many of the basic interface attributes for Java and many aspects of it are still widely used. The AWT package has elements relating to four aspects of interaction:

1. Graphics - colors, drawing, images and so on.

2. Components - windows, buttons, sliders and so on.

3. Layout Managers - component positioning on screen

4. Event Handlers - tracking and handling mouse, keyboard and other interaction events

To access these features a program imports the `java.awt.*` classes.

Listeners

One of the important features of the AWT package are `ActionListeners` that receive ObjecEvents generated by components or interaction with components. Typically, this includes the monitoring of and responding to mouse clicks, slider movements, button clicks, and so on.

Interactions with components can generate events. For example a `Button` object, when clicked, generates a ActionEvent. All events have a corresponding event handling method call a listener. For example, `ActionEvents` are sent to an `actionPerformed()` method. There are other event-listener pairings provided by a range of AWT interfaces. A commonly used one is the `MouseListener` interface that responds to `MouseEvents` and has a number of handler methods such as `mouseClicked()`, `mousePressed()` and `mouseRelease()`. In your program you would use this infrastructure in this way;

1. Implement the appropriate listener interface

```
public class MyClass implements ActionListener {
    ...
}
```

2. Create a component and add a listener to it. The use of 'this' as an argument indicates that the even handling method will be in the current class (in 'this' class).

```
...
playBtn = new Button("Play");
playBtn.addActionListener(this);
...
```

3. Override the event handling method. `ActionEvent` objects contain information about what generated them, current status or value, and so on.

```
public void actionPerformed(ActionEvent e) {
    // code to process the event
}
```

To access AWT listeners a program needs to import the `java.awt.event.*` classes.

Introducing the Swing package

The Swing interface toolkit was introduced in Java 1.2 and provides a new set of graphical interface component classes, while using much of the other aspects of the AWT package. Also introduced with Swing (but not covered here) were accessibility support for non-standard input and output devices, the 2D API for higher quality drawing, and support for drag and drop functionality.

To differentiate the Swing graphical interface classes from those of the AWT is is common for their names to have a "J" suffix. For example the AWT has a `Button` class, and Swing has a `JButton` class. (It should be noted that jMusic was named well prior to the introduction of the Swing class convention of "J" suffices, and has no particular relationship to Swing.) Given that the Swing user interface classes are more modern than the AWT ones (and look and function more nicely, too) we will deal with them for the rest of the chapter.

To access the Swing package features, a program imports the `javax.swing.*` classes.

Components

Many user interface classes are "components" like buttons, sliders, scrollbars and so on. The JComponent class is fundamental to Swing and the other component classes extend JComponent. The JComponent has attributes and behaviors such as setting its size, noticing mouse clicks on itself, setting its color, making itself visible or invisible, and many others.

Frames

Graphical interfaces need a main window and this is provided by the JWindow or JFrame classes. A JFrame is a JWindow with a title bar, resize tab and other niceties, so it's the one we tend to use for applications. The JFrame constructor accepts, as an argument, a name to display in the title bar. Here is a simple application that displays an empty window.

```
import javax.swing.*;

public class DemoWindow {
    public static void main(String[] args) {
        String name = "My App Name";
        JFrame f = new JFrame(name);
        f.setSize(600, 400);
        f.setVisible(true);
    }
}
```

Containers such as JFrames implement a layout manager that controls the organization of other components added to it. We will not discuss layout managers in detail here but be aware that the default layout manager is called FlowLayout and simply arranges components one after the other side by side within the container.

Buttons

JButton objects create a GUI button with name and/or icon that when clicked by the user generates an ActionEvent. As mentioned above, ActionEvents are handled by the actionPerformed() method which is part of the ActionListener interface. Let's add a button to out demo application that prints to the console when clicked.

```
import javax.swing.*;
import java.awt.event.*;

public class DemoWindow2 implements ActionListener {
```

```
    public static void main(String[] args) {
        new DemoWindow2();
    }
    public DemoWindow2() {
        String name = "My App name";
        JFrame f = new JFrame(name);
        JPanel panel = new JPanel();
        f.add(panel);
        JButton btn = new JButton("Play");
        btn.addActionListener(this);
        panel.add(btn);
        f.setSize(600, 400);
        f.setVisible(true);
    }
    public void actionPerformed(ActionEvent e) {
        System.out.println("play button clicked");
    }
}
```

A `JPanel` object was inserted between the `JFrame` and the `JButton` so that the `JButton`'s size is minimized to fit the text. Otherwise the button would default to occupy the entire space of the `JFrame`.

CheckBoxes

CheckBoxes provide a visible toggle, that appears as a box that can be selected (checked) or unselected. In other respects `JCheckBox` objects behavior similarly to buttons and utilize the `ActionListener` interface. Below is the code to add a JCheckBox to the application. Note that the components were declared as instance variables so they can be accessed in more than one method, and that the status of the check box determines what statement to print to the console.

```
import javax.swing.*;
import java.awt.event.*;

public class DemoWindow3 implements ActionListener {
    String name = "My App name";
    JFrame f;
    JCheckBox box1;

    public static void main(String[] args) {
```

```
            new DemoWindow3();
    }
    public DemoWindow3() {
        f = new JFrame(name);
        JPanel panel = new JPanel();
        f.add(panel);
        box1 = new JCheckBox("Mute");
        box1.addActionListener(this);
        panel.add(box1);
        f.setSize(600, 400);
        f.setVisible(true);
    }
    public void actionPerformed(ActionEvent e) {
        if (e.getSource() == box1) {
            if (box1.isSelected()) {
                System.out.println("Playback muted");
            } else System.out.println("Playbck unmuted");
        }
    }
}
```

Sliders

Sliders allow users to control variables within the program. The `JSlider` objects are typically established with an orientation, minimum, maximum, and starting values. Slider movements generate `ChangeEvents` that can be handled by the `stateChanged()` method of the `ChangeListener` interface. The `ChangeListener` interface was introduced as part of swing so you need to import the `javax.swing.event.*` classes to access it. Below is code that implements a volume slider.

```
import javax.swing.*;
import javax.swing.event.*;

public class DemoWindow4 implements ChangeListener {
    JSlider slider1;

    public static void main(String[] args) {
        new DemoWindow4();
    }
    public DemoWindow4() {
        String name = "My App name";
```

```java
            JFrame f = new JFrame(name);
            JPanel panel = new JPanel();
            f.add(panel);
            slider1 = new JSlider(JSlider.HORIZONTAL, 0, 127, 100);
            slider1.addChangeListener(this);
            panel.add(slider1);
            f.setSize(600, 400);
            f.setVisible(true);
        }
        public void stateChanged(ChangeEvent e) {
            System.out.println("Volume = " + slider1.getValue());
        }
    }
```

Programming Practice

In each of the recent examples components were added independently to the application frame. You can try to combine all these components into the one program so they are all displayed at once in the fame. Don't forget to include all relevant imports. You will need to add logic to the listeners to differentiate between action events generated by each component.

Concept Quiz

1. What does AWT stand for?
2. What are the four aspects of interaction that the AWT toolkit provides for?
3. Name some of the Java Swing GUI components.
4. What is the relationship between events and listeners?
5. Do all components generate the same events?

TheGrid: Adding a Visual Appearance

It is now time to add a graphical user interface (GUI) to the *TheGrid* application. We'll do this in two stages, the first contained the *TheGrid3* application and the second in *TheGrid4*. We're dividing this GUI implementation in two stages because the graphical user interface code will significantly increase the complexity of the program and the *TheGrid3* shows the process for the hi hats which is then replicated for the snare and kick drum in *TheGrid4*. In this chapter the visual appearance will be created for the application, but it will not be functional. The GUI will act as a display of the underlying music – a form of music notation. In the next chapter we'll make changes to the interface effect the music.

TheGrid3

This program will add a display showing hi-hat rhythm as a series of check boxes, where crosses or ticks represent sounding notes. The result will appear similar to figure 6.5.

Figure 6.5: TheGrid3 appearance.

Structurally there are three new methods in this version of TheGrid. The GUI code is in the `makeInterface()` method, and we've separated the MIDI file writing and playback each to their own methods. The constructor method will call each of these methods in turn. Here is a code fragment from the constructor method where this occurs.

```
compose();
makeInterface();
saveFile();
play();
```

The compose method is unchanged from *TheGrid2* and the `saveFile()` and `play()` methods simply have the one line of code required to do their job. Therefore, we will concentrate on the new code in the `makeInterface()` method.

Here is the complete method.

```
private void makeInterface() {
    JFrame window = new JFrame("Drum pattern");
    JPanel grid = new JPanel(new GridLayout(1,16));
    for (int i=0; i<16; i++) {
        JCheckBox tick = new JCheckBox();
        if (hats.getNote(i).getPitch() != REST) {
            tick.setSelected(true);
        }
        grid.add(tick);
    }
    window.getContentPane().add(grid);
    window.pack();
    window.setVisible(true);
}
```

A frame named 'window' is created first with a title passed as an argument. The `JFrame` class from Java's Swing library is used. In fact, we will always use Swing components – identified by starting with the letter J – where they are available for TheGrid.

A panel call 'grid' is then created with a `GridLayout` structure. The arguments to `GridLayout` indicate that its format will be a lattice 1 row deep and 16 columns across.

The for-loop creates a check box each time it cycles, the if-statement checks that the corresponding note in the hats phrase is not (!=) a `REST` and sets the box as selected (showing a cross or tick) if note and, finally, adds the check box to the next cell in the panel.

To finish up the display task the panel is added to the frame, the frame is 'packed,' to ensure all components take up as little space as possible, then displayed.

TheGrid4

In this version of TheGrid we will add panels of check boxes for the snare and kick drums, and create buttons for saving and playing the music. The visual appearance will be similar to figure 6.6.

Figure 6.6: The appearance of TheGrid4.

The addition of the snare and kick drum check boxes repeats the process used to create the hats appearance, so that code will not require much explanation. Once change required to accommodate the additional components is the layout of the frame.

```
window.getContentPane().setLayout(new GridLayout(4,1));
```

In *TheGrid3* the frame used the `FlowLayout`, which is the default and did not need to be set. With *TheGrid4* the frame uses a `GridLayout` with 4 rows and 1 column. These cells are filled with the three panels of check boxes and a panel containing the buttons. Elements are positioned in the `GridLayout` in the order they are added, from the top down. The really new information in this version of TheGrid is the buttons.

```java
playBtn = new JButton("Play");
btnPanel.add(playBtn);
saveBtn = new JButton("Save MIDI file");
btnPanel.add(saveBtn);
window.getContentPane().add(btnPanel);
```

The code fragment above shows the instantiation and addition of the buttons. A `JButton` constructor takes the button name to be displayed as an argument. Each button is added to a (previously created) panel called `btnPanel`. The `btnPanel` uses the default `FlowLayout` so each component is displayed aligned to the center and from left to right and top to bottom as space allows. Finally, the `btnPanel` is added to the frame.

Below is the complete source code for *TheGrid4* application.

```java
import jm.JMC;
import jm.music.data.*;
import jm.util.*;
import java.awt.*;
import javax.swing.*;

public class TheGrid4 implements JMC {
    private Phrase hats, snare, kick;
    private Part drums;
    private JCheckBox[] hatTicks, snareTicks, kickTicks;
    private JButton playBtn, saveBtn;

    public static void main(String[] args) {
        new TheGrid4();
    }

    public TheGrid4() {
        hats = new Phrase(0.0);
        snare = new Phrase(0.0);
        kick = new Phrase(0.0);
        drums = new Part("Drums", 25, 9);
        drums.addPhrase(hats);
        drums.addPhrase(snare);
        drums.addPhrase(kick);
```

```java
        // set look and feel
        String local = javax.swing.UIManager.getSystemLookAndFeelClassName();
        String metal = javax.swing.UIManager.
                    getCrossPlatformLookAndFeelClassName();
        try {
            UIManager.setLookAndFeel(local); // use local or metal
        } catch (Exception e) {}
        // set graphic data
        hatTicks = new JCheckBox[16];
        snareTicks = new JCheckBox[16];
        kickTicks = new JCheckBox[16];
        // call other methods
        compose();
        makeInterface();
        saveFile();
        play();
    }
    public void compose() {
         int[] hatsHits =
            {REST, REST, FS2, REST, REST, REST, FS2, REST, REST, REST, FS2,
                REST, REST, REST, FS2, REST,};
        hats.addNoteList(hatsHits, SIXTEENTH_NOTE);
        int[] snareHits =
            {REST, REST, REST, REST, D2, REST, REST, REST, REST, REST, REST,
                REST, D2, REST, D2, REST};
        snare.addNoteList(snareHits, SIXTEENTH_NOTE);
        int[] kickHits =
            {C2, REST, REST, REST, REST, REST, REST, C2, C2, REST, REST, REST,
                REST, REST, REST, REST};
        kick.addNoteList(kickHits, SIXTEENTH_NOTE);
    }

    private void makeInterface() {
        JFrame window = new JFrame("Drum pattern");
        window.getContentPane().setLayout(new GridLayout(4,1));
        // hats
        JPanel grid = new JPanel(new GridLayout(1,16));
        for (int i=0; i<16; i++) {
            JCheckBox tick = new JCheckBox();
            if (hats.getNote(i).getPitch() != REST) tick.setSelected(true);
```

```java
            grid.add(tick);
            hatTicks[i] = tick;
        }
        window.getContentPane().add(grid);
        // snare
        JPanel grid2 = new JPanel(new GridLayout(1,16));
        for (int i=0; i<16; i++) {
            JCheckBox tick = new JCheckBox();
            if (snare.getNote(i).getPitch() != REST) tick.setSelected(true);
            grid2.add(tick);
            snareTicks[i] = tick;
        }
        window.getContentPane().add(grid2);
        // kick
        JPanel grid3 = new JPanel(new GridLayout(1,16));
        for (int i=0; i<16; i++) {
            JCheckBox tick = new JCheckBox();
            if (kick.getNote(i).getPitch() != REST) tick.setSelected(true);
            grid3.add(tick);
            kickTicks[i] = tick;
        }
        window.getContentPane().add(grid3);
        JPanel btnPanel = new JPanel();
        //   buttons
        playBtn = new JButton("Play");
        btnPanel.add(playBtn);
        saveBtn = new JButton("Save MIDI file");
        btnPanel.add(saveBtn);
        window.getContentPane().add(btnPanel);

        window.pack();
        window.setVisible(true);
    }
    private void saveFile() {
        Write.midi(drums, "DrumPattern4.mid");
    }
    private void play() {
        Play.midi(drums, false);
    }
}
```

7: Building Interfaces

Having in previous chapters created classes using the HelperGUI and making graphical user interfaces for *TheGrid* application, and with your experience using many other software applications, you will be well aware of how much a graphical interface can assist the use of software. In this chapter we will walk you through the process of creating your own music applications with a GUI.

Graphical User Interfaces

Let's have a close look at the code first.

```java
import java.awt.*;
import java.awt.event.*;
import javax.swing.*;

import jm.JMC;
import jm.music.data.*;
import jm.util.*;

public class SimpleGUI extends JFrame implements ActionListener, JMC {
    private JButton composeBtn;

    public static void main(String[] args) {
        SimpleGUI gui = new SimpleGUI();
    }

    public SimpleGUI() {
        composeBtn = new JButton("Compose");
        composeBtn.addActionListener(this);
        this.getContentPane().add(composeBtn);
        this.pack();
        this.setVisible(true);
    }

    public void actionPerformed(ActionEvent ae){
        if (ae.getSource() == composeBtn) compose();
```

```
        }

        public void compose() {
            System.out.println("Button pressed.");
            // rest of music code here....
        }
    }
```

The import statements include packages that we need to use in the program. The `javax.swing` package contains the GUI objects such as `JFrame`. The `java.awt.event` packages has classes for handling user events such as detecting when a button has been clicked.

After the import statements, the next line declares the class. Because we are going to need a GUI window we need to extend the `JFrame` class. The `JFrame` class is the 'super class' of `SimpleGUI` because the `SimpleGUI` class 'extends' the `JFrame` class when declaring the `SimpleGUI` class. Handling the window and its contents is the main thing the `JFrame` class does for us.

The `main()` method follows. It is very short and just calls the `SimpleGUI` constructor. This architecture with a constructor and main methods allows this class to be run either directly - which uses the main method which runs the constructor - or indirectly from another class - where the instantiation bypasses the `main()` method.

The `SimpleGUI()` constructor passes a window title to the frame. The program then adds one button to the frame. This is done in these next four lines. A `JButton` is declared, and is registered with an `ActionListener` that notifies us when the button is clicked. Finally, the button is added to the content pane of frame.

The `pack()` statement makes all components as small as possible, and the `setVisible()` method displays the frame on the screen. When the program is run is appears similar to figure 7.1.

Figure 7.1. A simple graphical user interface.

When a user clicks the button the `actionPerfomed()` method is called automatically by the `actionListener`. Within this method we check that the action was generated by the appropriate button object by getting the 'source' of the `actionEvent`. Then, if the comparison is true, the `compose()` method is called and a short statement printed to the terminal.

Adding GUI details

The *SimpleGUI* application, was a minimal implementation and you may have noticed some behavior inconsistencies with other applications. For example, when the frame was resized, by dragging it from the bottom right corner, the button continued to expand to fill the entire window. Also, when the close or exit button was clicked the window may have closed, but the application was still running. In this section we'll fix these details. All the changes take place in the constructor. Assuming you copy the previous class and rename it *SimpleGUI2*, here is a our new constructor.

```java
public SimpleGUI2() {
    composeBtn = new JButton("Compose");
    composeBtn.addActionListener(this);
    JPanel panel = new JPanel();
    panel.add(composeBtn);
    this.getContentPane().add(panel);
    this.setSize(200, 100);
    this.setDefaultCloseOperation(JFrame.EXIT_ON_CLOSE);
    this.setVisible(true);
}
```

In order to prevent the button expanding when we resize the frame we will first add the button to a `JPanel` object, then insert the panel into the frame. One line creates a new `JPanel` called panel, and a second adds the `composeBtn` object to the panel. The panel is then added to the frame.

The previous program's appearance was somewhat crowded because we used the `pack()` method to keep everything as small as possible. This time we'll specify a dimension for our frame using the `setSize()` method, that takes pixel values for width and height as arguments.

In order to ensure that the program exits when we close the window we use this self explanatory method that takes a constant from the `JFrame` class as an argument.

```java
setDefaultCloseOperation(JFrame.EXIT_ON_CLOSE);
```

The results should appear similar to figure 7.2.

Figure 7.2. A more elegant simple GUI window.

Adding music

Now that we have our simple interface under control we'll add some music code to the compose method. The *SimpleGUI3* application will create an arpeggio pattern where the notes are selected above a root note at specified intervals. These intervals will be stored in an array called `pattern`. The pitch order will be randomly determined. All notes will be half a beat long.

Because the phrase is to be repeated eight times we need to import the Mod class.

```
import jm.music.tools.Mod;
```

All the instance variables we require are created near the top of the class.

```
int rootNote = C2;
int[] pattern = {0,0,4,7};
Part arpPart;
private int counter = 0;
```

The compose method makes an arpeggio of notes in a random order. Repeats the phrase, sets the tempo, and calls the `saveAs()` method.

```
public void compose() {
    Phrase phr = new Phrase();
    arpPart = new Part("Apreggio", SYNTH_BASS, 0);
    for (int i=0; i<pattern.length; i++ ) {
        phr.addNote(new Note(rootNote + pattern[(int)(Math.random() *
            pattern.length)], EIGHTH_NOTE));
    }
    Mod.repeat(phr, 8);
    arpPart.addPhrase(phr);
    arpPart.setTempo(130.0);
    saveAndPlay();
}
```

The `saveAndPlay()` method saves the music as a MIDI file and plays it back. So that multiple versions of the music can be saved one after another, each MIDI file is give a unique name using the counter variable that increments each time.

```
public void saveAndPlay() {
    Write.midi(arpPart, "RandomArp" + counter++ + ".mid");
    Play.midi(arpPart, false);
}
```

This class can save multiple MIDI files of the score, and each is numbered using the counter variable. The counter variable is used to keep track of how many MIDI files have been created and it increments each time a file is written. The maintenance of the counter value is possible because it is an instance that persists as long as the class lives. The `Play.midi()` method takes a second `Boolean` argument, false, to indicate that the program should not exit after playing back the music.

Changing variables via the interface

In this final elaboration of the *SimpleGUI* applications, we'll add a slider to the interface that will control the length of the arpeggio. The *SimpleGUI4* program will look similar to figure 7.3 when run.

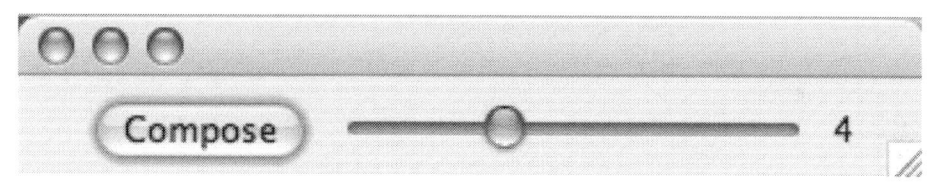

Figure 7.3. Interface of the SimpleGUI4 program.

The implementation of GUI slider components was outlined in Chapter 6, and a review of the process is outlined below. Here is the complete code for *SimpleGUI4*.

```
import java.awt.*;
import java.awt.event.*;
import javax.swing.*;
import javax.swing.event.*;
import jm.JMC;
import jm.music.data.*;
import jm.util.*;
import jm.music.tools.Mod;

public class SimpleGUI4 extends JFrame
```

```java
        implements ActionListener, ChangeListener, JMC {

    private JButton composeBtn;
    private JSlider slider;
    private JLabel label;
    private int rootNote = C2;
    private int[] pattern = {0,0,4,7};
    private Part arpPart;
    private int counter = 0;
    private int arpLength = 4;

    public static void main(String[] args) {
        SimpleGUI4 gui = new SimpleGUI4();
    }

    public SimpleGUI4() {
        composeBtn = new JButton("Compose");
        composeBtn.addActionListener(this);
        JPanel panel = new JPanel();
        panel.add(composeBtn);
        slider = new JSlider(2, 8, 4);
        slider.addChangeListener(this);
        panel.add(slider);
        label = new JLabel("4");
        panel.add(label);
        this.getContentPane().add(panel);
        this.setSize(350, 60);
        this.setDefaultCloseOperation(JFrame.EXIT_ON_CLOSE);
        this.setVisible(true);
    }

    public void actionPerformed(ActionEvent ae){
        if (ae.getSource() == composeBtn) compose();
    }

    public void stateChanged(ChangeEvent ce) {
        if (ce.getSource() == slider) {
            arpLength = slider.getValue();
            label.setText("" + slider.getValue());
        }
```

```
        }

        public void compose() {
            Phrase phr = new Phrase();
            arpPart = new Part("Apreggio", SYNTH_BASS, 0);
            for (int i=0; i<arpLength; i++ ) {
                phr.addNote(new Note(rootNote +
                    pattern[(int)(Math.random() * pattern.length)],
                        EIGHTH_NOTE));
            }
            Mod.repeat(phr, 8);
            arpPart.addPhrase(phr);
            arpPart.setTempo(130.0);
            saveAndPlay();
        }

        public void saveAndPlay() {
            Write.midi(arpPart, "RandomArp" + counter++ + ".mid");
            Play.midi(arpPart, false);
        }
    }
```

Adding the slider involves a few steps. The addition of the slider component itself, a label component to display the slider value, and implementation of the ChangeListener interface to detect slider movements.

In order to access the ChangeListener interface the javax.swing.event.* package is imported. The class declaration includes the implementation of the ChangeListener interface that will detect slider movements. The JSlider and Jlabel classes from the Swing library are used. The slider and label instance variables are declared near the top of the file and instantiated in the constructor. These are each added to the panel object and the size of the frame is altered to allow the three components to fit. In order that movements of the slider are monitored, the slider object is registered with the ChangeListener using the addChangeListener() method. This method (like all listener registering methods) takes as an argument the class that will handle the slider changes, in our case it is this class itself; 'this'. The ChangeListener implementation requires the stateChanged method to be overridden. This method is called when the slider is moved. Inside that method the new slider value is assigned to the arpLength variable (controlling the length of the arpeggio pattern created by the compose method), and the label display is updated. The final change is to vary the number of notes added to the phrase by setting the for-loop in the compose method to iterate `arpLength` times.

Reading MIDI Files

The *SimpleGUI* applications wrote out MIDI files. It is also possible for jMusic applications to read standard MIDI files which are translated into a jMusic Score format. `Read.midi(score, "filename.mid");` will import the named MIDI file into the score object. The file name may need to include the directory path information as well, such as "Volumes/HardDrive/My_music/filename.mid". The score will have a part for each track in the MIDI file (sometimes more than one if the music is very polyphonic). MIDI files contain information about the tempo, program changes (instruments used for parts) which are added to the score. The jMusic MIDI file importer does not support less commonly used elements of MIDI files such as meta events, controller events, or system exclusive messages. Once the MIDI file has been imported as a score it can be used in the same as we have been doing with locally defined jMusic scores.

Java Details

In recent code examples we have introduced some Java keywords with only a passing description of their meaning. Here we outline some more details about the 'this' and 'static' keywords.

The 'this' keyword

Throughout the example code some variables have been preceded by the keyword this, as in `this.myValue = 40;`. Although it seems quite straight forward to say that `this` refers to the current instance of the class, in practice it can take a bit of getting used to the syntax and the usage of the keyword may appear somewhat convoluted at times.

The keyword `this` refers to the current instance of an object. Any variable preceded by `this.` refers to the instance variable. As in `this.pitch = pitch;` where an instance variable named pitch is assigned the value of a local variable named pitch. The use of the keyword can help distinguish between a instance variable and a class variable of the same name, or between an instance variable and a local variable of the same name passed as a method argument, or between a method of the current class and one in a super class of the same name.

The keyword this is also used at times as an argument to a method. As is the case for registering listeners, for example, `slider.addChangeListener(this);` where the current class instance is passed to the listener.

The 'static' keyword

Variables and methods within a class that are declared static are shared by each instance of the class. This contrasts with instance variables and methods where each instance of the class has a unique copy of the variable or method. Static variables should to be used sparingly because they 'break' data encapsulation which is a strong aspect of object-oriented design, but they are useful because they can hold data that can be shared amongst all instances of the class, they only take up memory in the class and not in each instance of the class, and static variables and methods may be accessed by other classes even when no instance of the class has been created.

Static variables

The data in a static variable resides with the class and is accessible from all instances of the class. Use the static keyword to declare a variable as static.

```
public static tempo = 120.0;
```

If this tempo variable were in a class named `Voice`, then each instance of the class would share the same tempo.

```
Voice soprano = new Voice();
Voice alto = new Voice();
Voice tenor = new Voice();
Voice baritone = new Voice();
```

When a change to the tempo was made, `Voice.tempo = 85.0;` then all voice instances would be effected.

Static methods

A method is declared static using the static modifier.

```
public static myMethod()
```

Static methods are used quite frequently in jMusic. For example the `midi()` method in the `Play` class is static, as are most methods in the `Mod` class such as `repeat()`. They are used less frequently in Java itself, however, a notable example is the `Math` class which has many static methods including `Math.random()`.

The most common use of a static method is Java's `main()` method which must be declared static. This is because it would be very confusing for Java to decide where to start executing a program if there could be more than one `main()` method.

TheGrid: Connecting Music and Vision

In this version of *TheGrid* application we'll add a few visual niceties to the interface such as labels and, importantly, add the glue code to connect the graphical interface with the music data structure so that changes to the interface are reflected in what we hear. This process is achieved by adding Java listeners to the interface components so that when they are changed the data structure is notified of the change. These changes are part of *TheGrid5*. In *TheGrid6* we'll add some missing features, including tempo and repeat options and show how these changes can be reflected in the music data structure.

TheGrid5

In order to help the user TheGrid5 adds some labels to the rows of check boxes, and in order to help the programmer we'll add some comments to the source code. After this we'll look at implementing listeners for the check boxes and buttons.

Labels

To make it clear which sixteenth-note each check box column aligns with a panel with a grid of numbers is added at the top of the application. In order to avoid squashing the numbers together the size of the panel (called numGrid) is set using the setPreferredSize() method which takes a Dimension object (width and height) as its argument.

```
JPanel numbGrid = new JPanel(new GridLayout(1,16));
numbGrid.setPreferredSize(new Dimension(400, 20));

for (int i=1; i<17; i++) {
    numbGrid.add(new JLabel(""+i, SwingConstants.CENTER));
}

window.getContentPane().add(numbGrid);
```

We are using the JLabel constructor with two arguments. The first is a text string to be displayed, in this case the number 1 to 16. The second argument is the alignment of the text within its grid space. The default is to left align, so to position the numbers in the center of the grid box the SwingConstants.CENTER constant is used.

Java Moment

In Java, a `listener` is a class or interface that monitors events in your program, for example when the user clicks a button, and sends a notification when the event occurs to all classes that have registered with the listener. All listeners extend the `java.util.EventListener` class which sets up a thread in the background to regularly check of events, a process called polling. Most `listeners` in the Java libraries are interfaces, so a class that want to use a listener must implement the interface. It must also register the objects that it wants the listener to monitor and pass the class to notify as an argument – usually the class to be notified is the current class, so the this keyword is used to mean 'this class'.

Listeners

This code fragment shows how a particular area (panel) within the GUI can respond to mouse clicks within it. By implementing the `MouseListener` interface and registering a panel with the listener.

```
public class MyInterfaceClass implements MouseListener {
    // other class code here.
    Panel displayArea = new Panel();
    displayArea.addMouseListener(this);
    // other class code here..
}
```

When an event is 'heard' by the listener it 'tells' the registered classes by calling a specified method that all registering classes must implements. In the case of a mouse clicking on an button the `MouseListener` it calls a `mouseClicked()` method in each of the registered classes. Each listener responds to specific types of events. The `MouseListener` responds to `MouseEvents`. The methods that are called by the listener when an event occurs as passed the event. So the `mouseClicked()` method takes one argument with an is `MouseEvent` object, often named e by convention. Below is a simple implementation of the `mouseClicked()` method that might be used when monitoring a GUI button named `startBtn`.

```
public void mouseClicked(MouseEvent e) {
    if (e.getSource() == startBtn) startMusic();
    ...
}
```

There are a number of listeners in the Java `AWT` and `Swing` libraries. The two required for this application are the `ItemListener`, which can handle check box changes, and the `ActionListener`, which handles button clicks.

```java
public class TheGrid5 implements JMC, ItemListener, ActionListener {
```

The listeners are Java *interfaces*, a special type of class, and all interfaces employed by a class are implemented as part of the class declaration.

```java
tick.addItemListener(this);
playBtn.addActionListener(this);
```

In order that only the relevant interface changes are listened too, each component needs to register itself with the listener. This is done using the `addItemListener` and `addActionListener` method calls. These methods take one argument which indicates the class that will handle the events. In this case the class within which they are implement, this class.

Listeners typically require at least one method to be implemented by the class that handles the events it generates. So we need to add `itemStateChanged` method for the `ItemListener` and the `actionPerformed` method for the `ActionListener`.

```java
public void itemStateChanged(ItemEvent e) {
    for (int i=0; i<16; i++) {
        if (e.getSource() == hatTicks[i]) {
            if (hatTicks[i].isSelected()) hats.getNote(i).setPitch(FS2);
            else hats.getNote(i).setPitch(REST);
            return;
        }
    }
}
```

This section of the `itemStateChanged()` method shows how the hi hats data is updated when a check box is clicked. Because we're not sure which checkbox has been clicked there is a for-loop that cycles through an array of each of the 16 check boxes for each drum. The method `e.getSource()` compares the clicked check box to the check box at the current array index. If we find a match the corresponding note set to be a pitch number or to a REST as determined by the check box's `isSelected()` method.

```java
public void actionPerformed(ActionEvent e) {
    if (e.getSource() == playBtn) play();
    if (e.getSource() == saveBtn) saveFile();
}
```

The `actionPerformed()` method handles the button clicks. An if-statement checks each button to see whether it was clicked then calls the appropriate method.

Our application is now interactive! You can switch on or off each drum on any of the 16 subdivisions, and play back or save the drum pattern whenever you like. Below is the full code for *TheGrid5*.

```java
import jm.JMC;
import jm.music.data.*;
import jm.util.*;
import java.awt.*;
import javax.swing.*;
import java.awt.event.*;

public class TheGrid5 implements JMC, ItemListener, ActionListener {
    private Phrase hats, snare, kick;
    private Part drums;
    private JCheckBox[] hatTicks, snareTicks, kickTicks;
    private JButton saveBtn, playBtn;

    public static void main(String[] args) {
        new TheGrid5();
    }
    /**
    * Constructor. Sets up the parameters.
    */
    public TheGrid5() {
        hats = new Phrase(0.0);
        snare = new Phrase(0.0);
        kick = new Phrase(0.0);
        drums = new Part("Drums", 25, 9);
        drums.addPhrase(hats);
        drums.addPhrase(snare);
        drums.addPhrase(kick);
        // set look and feel
        String local = javax.swing.UIManager.getSystemLookAndFeelClassName();
        String metal =
                javax.swing.UIManager.getCrossPlatformLookAndFeelClassName();
        try {
            UIManager.setLookAndFeel(local); // use local or metal
        } catch (Exception e) {}
        hatTicks = new JCheckBox[16];
        snareTicks = new JCheckBox[16];
        kickTicks = new JCheckBox[16];
```

```java
        compose();
        makeInterface();
    }
    /**
     * Do the real musical work
     */
    public void compose() {
        int[] hatsHits = {REST, REST, FS2, REST, REST, REST, FS2, REST, REST,
            REST,FS2, REST, REST, REST, FS2, REST,};
        hats.addNoteList(hatsHits, SIXTEENTH_NOTE);
        int[] snareHits = {REST, REST, REST, REST, D2, REST, REST, REST, REST,
            REST, REST, REST, D2, REST, D2, REST};
        snare.addNoteList(snareHits, SIXTEENTH_NOTE);
        int[] kickHits = {C2, REST, REST, REST, REST, REST, REST, C2, C2,
            REST, REST, REST, REST, REST, REST, REST};
        kick.addNoteList(kickHits, SIXTEENTH_NOTE);
    }
    /**
     * GUI code
     */
    private void makeInterface() {
        JFrame window = new JFrame("Drum pattern");
        window.getContentPane().setLayout(new GridLayout(5,1));
        // numbers
        JPanel numbGrid = new JPanel(new GridLayout(1,16));
        numbGrid.setPreferredSize(new Dimension(400, 20));
        for (int i=1; i<17; i++) {
            numbGrid.add(new JLabel(""+i, SwingConstants.CENTER));
        }
        window.getContentPane().add(numbGrid);
        // hats
        JPanel grid = new JPanel(new GridLayout(1,16));
        for (int i=0; i<16; i++) {
            JCheckBox tick = new JCheckBox();
            tick.addItemListener(this);
            tick.setHorizontalAlignment(SwingConstants.CENTER);
            if (hats.getNote(i).getPitch() != REST) tick.setSelected(true);
            grid.add(tick);
            hatTicks[i] = tick;
        }
```

```java
            window.getContentPane().add(grid);
            // snare
            JPanel grid2 = new JPanel(new GridLayout(1,16));
            for (int i=0; i<16; i++) {
                JCheckBox tick = new JCheckBox();
                tick.addItemListener(this);
                tick.setHorizontalAlignment(SwingConstants.CENTER);
                if (snare.getNote(i).getPitch() != REST) tick.setSelected(true);
                grid2.add(tick);
                snareTicks[i] = tick;
            }
            window.getContentPane().add(grid2);
            // kick
            JPanel grid3 = new JPanel(new GridLayout(1,16));
            for (int i=0; i<16; i++) {
                JCheckBox tick = new JCheckBox();
                tick.addItemListener(this);
                tick.setHorizontalAlignment(SwingConstants.CENTER);
                if (kick.getNote(i).getPitch() != REST) tick.setSelected(true);
                grid3.add(tick);
                kickTicks[i] = tick;
            }
            window.getContentPane().add(grid3);
            JPanel btnPanel = new JPanel();
            //  buttons
            playBtn = new JButton("Play");
            playBtn.addActionListener(this);
            btnPanel.add(playBtn);
            saveBtn = new JButton("Save MIDI file");
            saveBtn.addActionListener(this);
            btnPanel.add(saveBtn);
            window.getContentPane().add(btnPanel);
            window.pack();
            window.setVisible(true);
    }
    /**
     * Handle the checkbox clicks
     */
    public void itemStateChanged(ItemEvent e) {
        for (int i=0; i<16; i++) {
```

```java
            if (e.getSource() == hatTicks[i]) {
                if (hatTicks[i].isSelected()) hats.getNote(i).setPitch(FS2);
                else hats.getNote(i).setPitch(REST);
                return;
            } else
            if (e.getSource() == snareTicks[i]) {
                if (snareTicks[i].isSelected()) snare.getNote(i).setPitch(D2);
                else snare.getNote(i).setPitch(REST);
                return;
            } else
            if (e.getSource() == kickTicks[i]) {
                if (kickTicks[i].isSelected()) kick.getNote(i).setPitch(C2);
                else kick.getNote(i).setPitch(REST);
                return;
            }
        }
    }
    /**
     * Handle the button clicks
     */
    public void actionPerformed(ActionEvent e) {
        if (e.getSource() == playBtn) play();
        if (e.getSource() == saveBtn) saveFile();
    }
    /**
     * Write the music to a MIDI file
     */
     private void saveFile() {
        Write.midi(drums, "DrumPattern5.mid");
    }
    /**
     * Play back the music
     */
    private void play() {
        Play.midi(drums, false);
    }
}
```

TheGrid6

In *TheGrid6* application labels are added to each of the drums and controllers are added to control tempo and repetition.

Labels

So that it is clear which row of checkboxes is for hi hats and which is for snare or kick, we'll add a label to the left of each grid.

```
JPanel grid = new JPanel(new GridLayout(1, 17));
grid.add(new JLabel("Hats"));
```

The grid width is increased to 17, to allow for the label and new `JLabel` is created and added to the first (left most) cell in the grid. This process in repeated for the snare and kick grids also.

JComboBoxes

Up till now, TheGrid application has played only one bar of music and always at the same speed. In *TheGrid6* we remedy this and add a new component type, the `JComboBox`. A `JComboBox` is a control that provides a pop-up menu to select from. This application adds one for selecting the tempo and another for selecting the number of repetitions.

```
private JComboBox repeatMenu, tempoMenu;
```

The new components are declared at the top of the file as private instance variables so they are available to all methods within instances of this class.

```
repeatMenu = new JComboBox();
repeatMenu.addActionListener(this);
repeatMenu.addItem("1");
repeatMenu.addItem("2");
repeatMenu.addItem("4");
repeatMenu.addItem("8");
repeatMenu.addItem("16");
```

This code fragment shows the instantiation of the `repeatMenu` object as a `JComboBox`, its registration with the `ActionListener`, and the adding of items to be displayed in the pop-up menu.

```
btnPanel.add(new JLabel("Repeats = "));
btnPanel.add(repeatMenu);
```

Because the `JComboBox` does not have a label, a `JLabel` is created and added next to the `JComboBox` in the layout.

```
Mod.repeat(temp, Integer.parseInt((String)repeatMenu.getSelectedItem()));
```

Before playback each time a `temp` copy of the drums part is duplicated to repeat the required number of times. Because the items in the menu are text Strings they need to be converted to `int` values for the `Mod.repeat()` method. The code for this looks a little awkward, but is conceptually simple. The work is done by the `Integer.parseInt()` method.

Now *TheGrid* application can play a longer repeated rhythms at various speeds which makes it much more interesting. Here is the full code for *TheGrid6*.

```java
import jm.JMC;
import jm.music.data.*;
import jm.util.*;
import jm.music.tools.Mod;
import java.awt.*;
import javax.swing.*;
import java.awt.event.*;

public class TheGrid6 implements JMC, ItemListener, ActionListener {
    private Phrase hats, snare, kick;
    private Part drums;
    private JCheckBox[] hatTicks, snareTicks, kickTicks;
    private JButton saveBtn, playBtn;
    private JComboBox repeatMenu, tempoMenu;
    
    public static void main(String[] args) {
        new TheGrid6();
    }
    // Constructor. Sets up the parameters.
    public TheGrid6() {
        hats = new Phrase(0.0);
        snare = new Phrase(0.0);
        kick = new Phrase(0.0);
        drums = new Part("Drums", 25, 9);
        drums.addPhrase(hats);
        drums.addPhrase(snare);
        drums.addPhrase(kick);
        String local = javax.swing.UIManager.getSystemLookAndFeelClassName();
```

```java
        String metal =
            javax.swing.UIManager.getCrossPlatformLookAndFeelClassName();
        try {
            UIManager.setLookAndFeel(local); // use local or metal
        } catch (Exception e) {}
        // set graphic data
        hatTicks = new JCheckBox[16];
        snareTicks = new JCheckBox[16];
        kickTicks = new JCheckBox[16];
        // call other methods
        compose();
        makeInterface();
    }
    /**
     * Do the real musical work
     */
    public void compose() {
        int[] hatsHits = {REST, REST, FS2, REST, REST, REST, FS2, REST, REST,
            REST, FS2, REST, REST, REST, FS2, REST,};
        hats.addNoteList(hatsHits, SIXTEENTH_NOTE);
        int[] snareHits = {REST, REST, REST, REST, D2, REST, REST, REST, REST,
            REST, REST, REST, D2, REST, D2, REST};
        snare.addNoteList(snareHits, SIXTEENTH_NOTE);
        int[] kickHits = {C2, REST, REST, REST, REST, REST, REST, C2, C2,
            REST, REST, REST, REST, REST, REST, REST};
        kick.addNoteList(kickHits, SIXTEENTH_NOTE);
    }
    /**
     * GUI code
     */
    private void makeInterface() {
        JFrame window = new JFrame("Drum pattern");
        window.getContentPane().setLayout(new GridLayout(5,1));
        // numbers
        JPanel numbGrid = new JPanel(new GridLayout(1,17));
        numbGrid.setPreferredSize(new Dimension(400, 20));
        numbGrid.add(new JLabel(""));
        for (int i=1; i<17; i++) {
            numbGrid.add(new JLabel(""+i, SwingConstants.CENTER));
        }
```

```java
window.getContentPane().add(numbGrid);
// hats
JPanel grid = new JPanel(new GridLayout(1,17));
grid.add(new JLabel("Hats"));
for (int i=0; i<16; i++) {
    JCheckBox tick = new JCheckBox();
    tick.addItemListener(this);
    tick.setHorizontalAlignment(SwingConstants.CENTER);
    if (hats.getNote(i).getPitch() != REST) tick.setSelected(true);
    grid.add(tick);
    hatTicks[i] = tick;
}
window.getContentPane().add(grid);
// snare
JPanel grid2 = new JPanel(new GridLayout(1,17));
grid2.add(new JLabel("Snare"));
for (int i=0; i<16; i++) {
    JCheckBox tick = new JCheckBox();
    tick.addItemListener(this);
    tick.setHorizontalAlignment(SwingConstants.CENTER);
    if (snare.getNote(i).getPitch() != REST) tick.setSelected(true);
    grid2.add(tick);
    snareTicks[i] = tick;
}
window.getContentPane().add(grid2);
// kick
JPanel grid3 = new JPanel(new GridLayout(1,17));
grid3.add(new JLabel("Kick"));
for (int i=0; i<16; i++) {
    JCheckBox tick = new JCheckBox();
    tick.addItemListener(this);
    tick.setHorizontalAlignment(SwingConstants.CENTER);
    if (kick.getNote(i).getPitch() != REST) tick.setSelected(true);
    grid3.add(tick);
    kickTicks[i] = tick;
}
window.getContentPane().add(grid3);

JPanel btnPanel = new JPanel();
//  buttons
```

```java
            playBtn = new JButton("Play");
            playBtn.addActionListener(this);
            btnPanel.add(playBtn);
            saveBtn = new JButton("Save as MIDI file");
            saveBtn.addActionListener(this);
            btnPanel.add(saveBtn);
            // repeats
            repeatMenu = new JComboBox();
            repeatMenu.addItem("1");
            repeatMenu.addItem("2");
            repeatMenu.addItem("4");
            repeatMenu.addItem("8");
            repeatMenu.addItem("16");
            btnPanel.add(new JLabel("Repeats = "));
            btnPanel.add(repeatMenu);
            // tempo
            tempoMenu = new JComboBox();
            tempoMenu.addActionListener(this);
            tempoMenu.addItem("60");
            tempoMenu.addItem("80");
            tempoMenu.addItem("100");
            tempoMenu.addItem("120");
            tempoMenu.addItem("140");
            tempoMenu.addItem("180");
            btnPanel.add(new JLabel("Tempo = "));
            btnPanel.add(tempoMenu);
            btnPanel.add(new JLabel("bpm"));
            window.getContentPane().add(btnPanel);
            window.pack();
            window.setVisible(true);
    }
    /**
    * Handle the checkbox clicks
    */
    public void itemStateChanged(ItemEvent e) {
        for (int i=0; i<16; i++) {
            if (e.getSource() == hatTicks[i]) {
                if (hatTicks[i].isSelected()) hats.getNote(i).setPitch(FS2);
                else hats.getNote(i).setPitch(REST);
                return;
```

```java
                } else
                if (e.getSource() == snareTicks[i]) {
                    if (snareTicks[i].isSelected()) snare.getNote(i).setPitch(D2);
                    else snare.getNote(i).setPitch(REST);
                    return;
                } else
                if (e.getSource() == kickTicks[i]) {
                    if (kickTicks[i].isSelected())
                        kick.getNote(i).setPitch(C2);
                    else kick.getNote(i).setPitch(REST);
                    return;
                }
            }
        }
        /**
         * Handle the interaction events
         */
        public void actionPerformed(ActionEvent e) {
            if (e.getSource() == playBtn) {
                Part temp = drums.copy();
                Mod.repeat(temp,
                        Integer.parseInt((String)repeatMenu.getSelectedItem()));
                Play.midi(temp, false);
            }
            if (e.getSource() == saveBtn) saveFile();
            if (e.getSource() == tempoMenu) {
                drums.setTempo(new Double
                        ((String)tempoMenu.getSelectedItem()).doubleValue());
            }
        }
        /**
         * Write the music to a MIDI file
         */
        private void saveFile() {
            Part temp = drums.copy();
            Mod.repeat(temp,
                        Integer.parseInt((String)repeatMenu.getSelectedItem()));
            Write.midi(temp, "DrumPattern6.mid");
        }
}
```

8: Combination and Recombination

Digital audio processes can produce large scale works, and automation can allow us to create enormous amounts of sound with just a little code. However, matching this ability to scale is the considerable size of digital audio tasks, where each and every digital audio outcome must be specified sample by sample. The ability to control musical structures at all levels of scale is a powerful attribute of computer music. In this chapter we'll examine some processes of structuring music in large and small chunks and examine how, at a micro level, we can even control the sound of our music at the sample-by-sample level, and how, at a macro level, we can organize musical form. This ability to explore music at various levels of granularity is made accessible because we can utilize Java classes to operate on data from sample to score.

Musical Chunks

The jMusic data structure provides levels of granularity with the Note, Phrase, Part and Score objects. It is possible to algorithmically control the structure of your music at any of these levels. We've seen often in this book how this is achieved at the note level, but larger chunks – especially phrases – can be usefully arranged as well. The texture of the music can be altered by turning on or off particular parts, and larger forms (such as rondo or verse-chorus forms) can be modeled by using whole scores as musical sections.

Chords

A chord occurs when several notes sound together. In our exploration thus far, we've concentrated on monophonic and polyphonic music where the musical thinking focuses on horizontal musical lines. Chordal, or homophonic, musical thinking is concerned with the vertical dimension. Notes which play together, like when the six strings of a guitar are strummed, form a chord. jMusic provides a way to add notes as chords to parts using the CPhrase class.

CPhrases

The CPhrase (chord phrase) class allows the composer to construct homophonic musical structures easily. That is, provide a convenient way for jMusic to manage chords. A jMusic chord is a group of notes that share the same onset time and duration but have different pitches. The

`CPhrase` class can be used just like the `Phrase` class but, behind the scenes, `CPhrase` structures are converted into `Phrases`. This becomes important only when you work with relatively complex musical structures in jMusic.

Here is a program that uses a `CPhrase` to play some chords. Three arrays of pitches are created and they are each added one, the first chord is added again at the end to enhance musical resolution.

```java
import jm.JMC;
import jm.music.data.*;
import jm.music.tools.*;
import jm.util.*;

public final class Chords implements JMC{
    public static void main(String[] args){
        CPhrase cphrase1 = new CPhrase("Chords", 0.0);
        int[] notePitches1 = {C4, E4, G4};
        int[] notePitches2 = {C4, F4, A4};
        int[] notePitches3 = {D4, G4, B4};
        cphrase1.addChord(notePitches1, QUARTER_NOTE);
        cphrase1.addChord(notePitches2, QUARTER_NOTE);
        cphrase1.addChord(notePitches3, QUARTER_NOTE);
        cphrase1.addChord(notePitches1, QUARTER_NOTE);
        Part part1 = new Part("Guitar", GUITAR, 0);
        part1.addCPhrase(cphrase1);
        Play.midi(part1);
    }
}
```

A final elaboration to this program is to make the chords sound as though they were strummed. Rather than all notes starting at exactly the same time, as they do by default, we use a special method of the `CPhrase` class to create the effect.

```java
cphrase1.flam();
```

This line should be placed in the code after the point where chords have been added to the `CPhrase` object. The `flam()` method can take a double value as an argument to specify a particular degree of flam. Values between 0.01 and 0.1 are reasonable.

Notice that `Parts` can contain `CPhrases` and/or `Phrases` so a mixture of monophonic, polyphonic and homophonic textures can be used in different `Parts` within the same `Score`.

Recombination

The algorithmic arranging of existing musical chunks in this way is often referred to as recombination or, more formally, musical combinatorics which dates back as far as the ars combinatoria published by the German philosopher and mathematician Gottfried Wilhelm Leibnitz in 1666 (Selfridge-Field 2001). A famous example of recombination is Musikalisches Würfelspiel, a dice game attributed to Mozart where the results of throws choose amongst possible prewritten bars of music.

Musical Moment

Mozart's Dice Music: Mozart's Musikalisches Würfelspiel combines fragments of music into a short two-part waltz. Depending upon the numbers thrown, different, but similar, musical works can result. At each of sixteen rolls of the die there are eleven musical fragments to choose from. At each stage the fragments are interchangeable because they share an underlying harmonic progression and structural function. You can read more about the workings of Musikalisches Würfelspiel in "The Computer Music Tutorial" (Roads 1996:823), and the full score for it can be found in the Appendix of the book "Machine Models of Music" (Schwanauer and Levitt 1993).

The *MozartDiceGame* application is an implementation in Java of this game, and the process is repeated twice to create a thirty-two measure composition, in two distinct halves. The program is in two files. The `MozartDiceGame.java` file has the main method and generates the random numbers and assembles the score. The `MozartPhraseList.java` file has the data, it sets up a matrix (two dimension array) of one-measure-long phrases.

You may like to look at an implementation of the Mozart Dice Game at the tutorials page of the jMusic web site. http://jmusic.ci.qut.edu.au/

Assembling rhythms

In this section we will examine a simple recombinational program that will create rhythmic phrases from individual one-beat rhythm patterns.

All recombinatorial processes have three stages. First, the collection or creation of the musical data available for use. Second, the selection and organization of that data into a whole and, thirdly, the rendering or performing of the completed score.

```
import jm.JMC;
import jm.music.data.*;
```

```java
import jm.util.*;

public class Recombine implements JMC {
    Part structure = new Part(0, 9);
    double[] r1 = {1.0};
    double[] r2 = {0.5, 0.5};
    double[] r3 = {0.25, 0.25, 0.5};
    double[] r4 = {0.25, 0.5, 0.25};
    double[] r5 = {0.25, 0.25, 0.25, 0.25};
    double[][] rhythms = {r1, r2, r3, r4, r5};

    public static void main(String[] args) {
        Recombine rec = new Recombine();
    }

    public Recombine(){
        arrange();
        savePlay();
    }

    public void arrange() {
        for (int i=0; i<16; i++) {
            Phrase phr = new Phrase();
            if (i%4 == 0) phr.addNoteList(36, rhythms[0]);
            else { phr.addNoteList(42,
                rhythms[(int)(Math.random() *rhythms.length)]);
            }
            structure.addPhrase(phr);
        }
    }

    public void savePlay() {
        Play.midi(structure);
        Write.midi(structure, "Recomb2.mid");
    }
}
```

Phrases and form

Phrase-level organization provides a useful method of adding structure to you music. Phrases can be melodies, riffs, beats, or motifs. Groups of notes, as phrases, are a common building block for musical form or structure. In jMusic, notes added to phrases are sequenced one after another, similarly, when phrases are added to parts are similarly added end on end. This behavior can be overridden by specifying a specific start time for a phrase. The program *MelodicStructure* shows how significant phrase-level structure can be by piecing together random notes into a coherent work. The final structure will be in the form A B A C D A C.

The *MelodicStructure* application creates phrases with its `makePhrase()` method. This method chooses pitches as a random walk in C minor and uses recombined rhythmic cells. See the source code below for the full implementation. For now we will examine some relevant code fragments.

```
Phrase a = makePhrase(4.0);
Phrase b = makePhrase(4.0);
Phrase c = makePhrase(4.0);
Phrase d = makePhrase(8.0);
```

Four phrases are constructed by calling this method. `Phrases` a, b, c and d. Each passes an argument to the `makePhrase()` method indicating how long it should be, either 4 or 8 beats.

```
Phrase a1 = a.alias();
Phrase a2 = a.alias();
Phrase c1 = c.alias();
```

Because some phrases a reused in the form, aliases of them are created. Aliases of phrases in jMusic are very similar to copies; they are new objects that are identical to the original but can have their own start time, tempo and other attributes. The difference is that an alias refers to the same note objects as the original, such that any changes made to the notes in the original will be reflected in the alias, while a copy of a phrase makes new objects for all notes therefore changes to one notes in one do not effect the copied notes.

```
Part p = new Part();

p.addPhrase(a);
p.addPhrase(b);
p.addPhrase(a1);
p.addPhrase(c);
p.addPhrase(d);
p.addPhrase(a2);
p.addPhrase(c1);

View.show(p);
```

These phrases are next structured by adding them, in order, to the Part called p. Finally, the part is displayed in the piano roll view. The show view has a menu from which playback can be selected. Here is the full source code for the *MelodicStructure* example.

```java
import jm.JMC;
import jm.music.data.*;
import jm.music.tools.Mod;
import jm.gui.helper.HelperGUI;
/**
* This class demonstrates how even random melodies
* can benefit from higher order structure.
*/
public class MelodicStructure extends HelperGUI implements JMC {;
    Phrase phr;
    int pitch;

    public static void main(String[] args) {;
        new MelodicStructure();
    }

    public MelodicStructure() {}

    public Score compose() {
        Phrase a = makePhrase(4.0);
        Phrase b = makePhrase(4.0);
        Phrase c = makePhrase(4.0);
        Phrase d = makePhrase(8.0);
        Phrase a1 = a.copy();
        Phrase a2 = a.copy();
        Phrase c1 = c.copy();
        Part part = new Part();
        Score score = new Score (130);
        // create the structure
        part.addPhrase(a);
        part.addPhrase(b);
        part.addPhrase(a1);
        part.addPhrase(c);
        part.addPhrase(d);
        part.addPhrase(a2);
        part.addPhrase(c1);
```

```
            score.addPart(part);
            return score;
        }
        // Generate a phrase based on a random walk
        private Phrase makePhrase(double beats) {
            Phrase phr = new Phrase();
            int pitch = (int)(Math.random()* 24 + 48);
            for (int i = 0; i < beats * 2; i++) {
                Note note;
                do {
                    pitch += (int)(Math.random() * 10 - 5);
                    if (pitch < 0) pitch = 0;
                    if (pitch > 127) pitch = 127;
                    note = new Note(pitch, EN, (int)(Math.random()* 70 + 30));
                } while (!note.isScale(PENTATONIC_SCALE));
                phr.addNote(note);
            }
            Mod.accents(phr, 2.0);
            return phr;
        }
    }
```

Macrostructure & microstructure

Creating musical forms at the phrase level, as we did in the previous section, is useful and common place. In this section we'll see how larger data chunks (parts and score) and smaller chunks (notes and sample data) can be manipulated to create musical structures. Larger chunks allow us to manipulate the macrostructure of the work, and organizing the music at the sample level allows us to change the microstructure.

Appending sections

As we have already seen, notes, phrases, parts and scores can be used to structure our work. The *AppendRhythms* program will demonstrate how large sections, even whole scores, can be combined one after another into large-scale musical forms.

Phrases are generated by a `makePattern()` method that returns a rhythmic phrase pitched to a random percussion instrument. These phrases form the basis of larger data constructs. The AppendRhythms class applies the `Mod.append()` method at three levels, phrase, part and score.

```
        Phrase phr = makePattern();
```

```
Phrase phr2 = makePattern();
Mod.append(phr, phr2);
p.addPhrase(phr);
View.show(p);
```

In this code fragment two phrases are created, `phr2` and `phr`. Then, `phr2` is appended to `phr` using the Mod.append() method. The phrase `phr` is added to part p, which is then displayed using the piano-roll view class, show.

```
Part p2 = new Part();
Phrase phr3 = makePattern();
Phrase phr4 = makePattern();
Mod.append(phr3, phr4);
p2.addPhrase(phr3);
Mod.append(p, p2);
s.addPart(p);
View.show(s, 50, 50);
```

A second part `p2` is created in a similar manner and appended to part `p`. The part is added to a score called `s`, created earlier, and the score is displayed at position 50, 50 on the screen.

```
Score s2 = new Score();
s2 = s.copy();
Mod.append(s, s2);
s.setTitle("Appended score");
View.show(s, 100, 100);
```

The third section of this application appends two scores together. A copy of the original score is created and called `s2`. It is then appended to the original score, in this case effectively repeating the score. The title of the score is changed prior to display so that the view of the appended score is easily identifiable. The appended score is shown in a piano-roll display positioned 100 pixels in and down from the top left corner of the screen.

Granular organization

The *Spray* example shows how audio samples can be processed in response to note attributes. In this example note pitch determines sample playback frequency, note duration determines the length of the sample to be played, (usually a very small segment) note pan position and dynamic are mapped as would be expected. A key to this example is that the `sampleStartTime` note attribute specifies the location within the sample to begin reading data. jMusic instruments that use the `SampleIn` audio object, such as `SimpleSampleInst`, can make use of the sample-

StartTime parameter. Below is the full code for the *Spray* example that includes extensive comments. Make sure you substitute your own audio file for processing in place of the "Welcome.au" file name in the code.

```java
import java.io.*;
import jm.JMC;
import jm.music.data.*;
import jm.util.*;
import jm.audio.*;
import jm.audio.io.*;
import jm.audio.synth.*;

public class Spray implements JMC {

        public static void main(String[] args) {
            new Spray();
        }

        public Spray() {
                Score score = new Score();
                Part p = new Part("Spray",0,0);
                Phrase phr = new Phrase();
                String fileName = "Welcome.au";
                // get file size
                int numb = (int)(Math.random()*10)+1;
                File f = new File(fileName);
                double fileSize = (double)(f.length() - 32)/44100/2/2;
                // make instrument stuff
                Instrument[] ensemble = new Instrument[1];
                ensemble[0] = new SimpleSampleInst(fileName, FRQ[C4]);
                // set start time in file
                double st = 0.0;
                // the length of each note (audio segment)
                double dur = 0.1;
                // the start panning position (left)
                double pan = 0.0;
                // sets the number of steps between panning changes
                int panSpeed = 8;
                // iterate through many notes
                for (int i=0; i<100; i++) {
                        // check about updating panning position
```

```java
            if (i%panSpeed == 0) {
                    pan = Math.sin(i/panSpeed)/2+0.5;
            }
            // create a note
            Note n = new Note(C4+(int)(Math.random()*12), dur,
                    (int)(Math.random()*127));
            n.setPan(pan);
            n.setDuration(dur*1.3);
            // set the sample read point for this note
            n.setSampleStartTime(st);
            // add the note to the phrase
            phr.addNote(n);
            // shift the sample read point forward
            st += dur;
            // if sample read point past the end of the sample, reset
            if ((st + dur) > fileSize) st = 0.0;
            panSpeed += (int)(Math.random()*2)-1;
            if (panSpeed < 1) panSpeed = 1;
        }
        // pack the phrase into the jMusic score structure
        p.addPhrase(phr);
        score.addPart(p);
        // display the score on screen
        View.show(score);
        // render the score as an audio file
        Write.au(score, "TestSpray.au", ensemble);
    }
}
```

TheGrid: Organizing Files and Audio Playback

In these versions of *TheGrid* application we break the application up into two classes. One called `TheGrid` and another the `GridMusic`. We do this because the application is getting large and we can divide the functionality between music and graphical sections. This shows that structure applies to code as much as it applies to music. Applying the techniques discussed in this chapter around audio processing, we turn TheGrid application into a drum machine that uses audio samples for playback. There are more detailed discussions of jMusic audio later in the book, and you might like to flip forward to those chapters to better understand the details of jMusic audio classes.

TheGrid7

Functionally, *TheGrid7* is identical to *TheGrid6*. The code has been divided into two classes. The main method and GUI code is in `TheGrid7.java` and the musical logic is in a new class called `GridMusic7.java`.

```
private GridMusic7 musicObject;
...
musicObject = new GridMusic7();
```

The program starts by running `TheGrid7` which uses the line above to declare an instance of `GridMusic7` which it calls `musicObject`. In the constructor of `TheGrid7`, `musicObject` is instantiated. When musical changes are required, for example from clicks on the `JCheckBoxes`, `TheGrid7` makes appropriate calls to `musicObject`.

```
public void setHatsPitch(int arrayIndex, int pitch) {
    hats.getNote(arrayIndex).setPitch(pitch);
}
```

To facilitate communication, *GridMusic7* provides a number of assessor methods for `TheGrid7` to call, such as the `setHatsPitch()` method above.

By now we know that to make changes or additions to the visual appearance of the application we work in the `TheGrid7.java` file, and to make changes to the music aspects of the application we work in the `GridMusic7.java` file.

TheGrid with audio

As we have been focusing on audio playback in this chapter, it is natural that our next version of the *TheGrid* application will add features for audio playback and saving of the music as an audio file. Also, in the chapter, each drum part will get it's own volume control so we can set the mix levels. There are a few other minor changes to the application, including setting the default tempo to 100 bpm.

TheGrid8

In *TheGrid8* we add two new buttons, one for playing the music with synthesized instruments, the other for rendering that output to an audio file.

```
private JButton saveBtn, playBtn, audioSavebtn, audioPlayBtn;
```

The buttons are first declared as instance variables. The `audioSaveBtn` and `audioPlayBtn` are new in the version of the `TheGrid`.

```
audioPlayBtn = new JButton("Play Audio");
audioPlayBtn.addActionListener(this);
btnPanel.add(audioPlayBtn);
audioSavebtn = new JButton("Save Audio");
audioSavebtn.addActionListener(this);
btnPanel.add(audioSavebtn);
```

This code fragment shows how the buttons are instantiated, registered with the action listener and added to the button panel.

```
if (e.getSource() == audioPlayBtn) {
    musicObject.audioPlay();
}
if (e.getSource() == audioSavebtn) {
    musicObject.saveAudioFile("DrumPattern8.au");
}
```

In the `actionPerformed` method, two new if-statements are added to handle the new buttons. Each calls the appropriate method in the `GridMusic8` instance associated with this application, called `musicObject`. Notice that the `saveAudioFile` method takes a `String` as an argument which specifies the file name for the rendered audio.

The `GridMusic8.java` file has the two new methods that do the work of playing and saving.

```
import jm.audio.*;
```

Because the `GridMusic8` class utilizes jMusic's audio features, it needs to import the `jm.audio` package. In particular it will use the `Instrument` class from this package.

```
hats.setInstrument(0);
snare.setInstrument(1);
kick.setInstrument(2);
```

There is an important distinction between the General MIDI drum instrument and the jMusic audio instruments. The General MIDI drumkit is a multi-sample instrument with different drum samples allocated to each note. For jMusic audio processes we specify a different instrument for hi-hats, snare and kick drum. We will create an array of instruments for this purpose, so hi-hats will be the zeroth element of the array, snare the first and kick the second. These instrument allocations are being made to each phrase. In jMusic, the instrument allocated to a phrase will override any instrument allocated to a part. You may notice that the drums part is still set to instrument 26, but this is now redundant.

```
public void audioPlay() {
    Instrument hats = new TR808HatsInst();
    hats.setOutput(Instrument.REALTIME);
    Instrument snare = new TR808SnareInst();
    snare.setOutput(Instrument.REALTIME);
    Instrument kick = new TR808KickInst();
    kick.setOutput(Instrument.REALTIME);
    Instrument[] kit = {hats, snare, kick};
    Part temp = drums.copy();
    Mod.repeat(temp, this.repeats);
    Score score = new Score(temp.getTempo());
    score.addPart(temp);
    Play.audio(score, kit);
}
```

The real time playback of the music is handled by the `audioPlay()` method. Instruments are declared for each drum and set to operate as real time instruments. By default, jMusic Instruments are usually set up for rendering. The `TR808HatsInst` and those for snare and kick have been specially created for this example. In later chapters we'll examine how to create your own jMusic instruments. The instruments use white noise and sine wave oscillators to create synthetic drum sounds in the style of the famous Roland *TR808* drum machine. The instruments are added to an instrument array called kit. The order of their addition is important, because it corresponds to the instrument numbers assigned to each phrase above.

Just as for MIDI playback, we first create a copy of the drums part so as not to effect the original with any changes, and apply the required number of repeats to the pattern with a method from the `Mod` class. A Score, called score, is created and assigned the tempo from the part – as chosen by the user. A copy of the drums part, called `temp`, which holds all the phrases and notes is added to the score. Finally, the score and instrument array are passed as arguments to jMusic's `Play.audio()` method, which plays the music.

```
public void saveAudioFile(String fileName) {
    Instrument hats = new TR808HatsInst(44100);
    Instrument snare = new TR808SnareInst(44100);
    Instrument kick = new TR808KickInst(44100);
    Instrument[] kit = {hats, snare, kick};
    Part temp = drums.copy();
```

```
            Mod.repeat(temp, this.repeats);
            Write.au(temp, fileName, kit);
    }
```

Rendering the music to an audio file is handled by the `saveAudioFile()` method. The procedure is similar to that for audio playback. Instruments are declared, added to an array, repeats are made to a copy of the part, and the `Write.au()` method is called. Notice that the instrument constructor used in this case takes one argument, 44100, which is the sample rate to be used. For the sake of efficiency in playback the default sample rate for the instruments is 22050, but for rendering there is no issue of processor load so the higher sample rate provides better quality but makes the process take a little longer. A higher sample rate allows for higher frequencies, so the result of the rendered output is somewhat brighter than the audio playback. The rendered file is also normalized, and may sound a little louder than the audio playback.

So, we have added audio playback and the MIDI playback has not been effected nor has the music composition process had to change except for the more careful instrument allocation.

TheGrid9

In this version was enhance the musical structure and rhythm patterns.

```
import jm.JMC;
import jm.music.data.*;
import jm.util.*;
import jm.music.tools.Mod;
import jm.audio.*;

public class GridMusic9 implements JMC {
    private Phrase hats, snare, kick;
    private Part drums;
    private int repeats;

    public GridMusic9() {
        hats = new Phrase(0.0);
        hats.setInstrument(0);
        snare = new Phrase(0.0);
        snare.setInstrument(1);
        kick = new Phrase(0.0);
        kick.setInstrument(2);
        drums = new Part("Drums", 26, 9);
        drums.setTempo(60);
```

```java
        drums.addPhrase(hats);
        drums.addPhrase(snare);
        drums.addPhrase(kick);
    }
    /**
    * Create the initial state of the music by filling arrays
    * with notes and rests.
    */
    public void compose() {
        int[] hatsHits =
            {REST, REST, FS2, REST, REST, REST, FS2, REST, REST, REST, FS2,
                REST, REST, REST, FS2, REST,};
        hats.addNoteList(hatsHits, SIXTEENTH_NOTE, 127);
        int[] snareHits =
            {REST, REST, REST, REST, D2, REST, REST, REST, REST, REST, REST,
                REST, D2, REST, D2, REST};
        snare.addNoteList(snareHits, SIXTEENTH_NOTE, 127);
        int[] kickHits =
            {C2, REST, REST, REST, REST, REST, REST, C2, C2, REST, REST, REST,
                REST, REST, REST, REST};
        kick.addNoteList(kickHits, SIXTEENTH_NOTE, 127);
    }
```

A series of accessor methods are declared. Many of these specify and interrogate the pitch of notes within the arrays, particularly to allow or check for changes between sounding notes and rests (notes with a pitch of -1 in jMusic). The last couple of methods set the number of repeats and tempo.

```java
    public void setHatsPitch(int arrayIndex, int pitch) {
        hats.getNote(arrayIndex).setPitch(pitch);
    }
    public void setSnarePitch(int arrayIndex, int pitch) {
        snare.getNote(arrayIndex).setPitch(pitch);
    }
    public void setKickPitch(int arrayIndex, int pitch) {
        kick.getNote(arrayIndex).setPitch(pitch);
    }
    public boolean getHatsState(int arrayIndex) {
        return (!hats.getNote(arrayIndex).isRest());
    }
    public boolean getSnareState(int arrayIndex) {
```

```java
        return (!snare.getNote(arrayIndex).isRest());
    }
    public boolean getKickState(int arrayIndex) {
        return (!kick.getNote(arrayIndex).isRest());
    }
    public void repeatMusic(int times) {
        this.repeats = times;
    }
    public void setTempo(double tempo) {
        drums.setTempo(tempo);
    }
```

Next are playback methods for both MIDI playback to the JavaSound synthesizer and audio playback using jMusic's synthesized instruments.

```java
    public void saveFile(String fileName) {
        Part temp = drums.copy();
        Mod.repeat(temp, this.repeats);
        Write.midi(temp, fileName);
    }
    public void audioPlay() {
        Instrument hats = new TR808HatsInst();
        hats.setOutput(Instrument.REALTIME);
        Instrument snare = new TR808SnareInst();
        snare.setOutput(Instrument.REALTIME);
        Instrument kick = new TR808KickInst();
        kick.setOutput(Instrument.REALTIME);
        Instrument[] kit = {hats, snare, kick};
        Part temp = drums.copy();
        Mod.repeat(temp, this.repeats);
        Play.audio(temp, kit);
    }
```

The use of audio samples is added with the `SamplePlay()` method. This uses a `SampleInst` class which is described in more detail below. Audio samples are passed to new instances of this class. These relate to the various drum kit elements; hi hat, snare drum and kick (or bass) drum.

```java
    public void samplePlay() {
        Instrument hats = new SampleInst("Hats.au");
        hats.setOutput(Instrument.REALTIME);
        Instrument snare = new SampleInst("Snare.au");
```

```java
        snare.setOutput(Instrument.REALTIME);
        Instrument kick = new SampleInst("Kick.au");
        kick.setOutput(Instrument.REALTIME);
        Instrument[] kit = {hats, snare, kick};
        Part temp = drums.copy();
        Mod.repeat(temp, this.repeats);
        Play.audio(temp, kit);
    }
```

Finally, there are two methods that support the rendering of a music as audio files. These are very similar to the playback methods but use the `Write.au()` methods to send the audio to a file rather than the audio output. One method is supplied to support synthesized sounds and the other to support sample-based sounds.

```java
    public void saveAudioFile(String fileName) {
        Instrument hats = new TR808HatsInst(44100);
        Instrument snare = new TR808SnareInst(44100);
        Instrument kick = new TR808KickInst(44100);
        Instrument[] kit = {hats, snare, kick};
        Part temp = drums.copy();
        Mod.repeat(temp, this.repeats);
        Write.au(temp, fileName, kit);
    }
    public void saveSampleFile(String fileName) {
        Instrument hats = new SampleInst("Hats.au");
        Instrument snare = new SampleInst("Snare.au");
        Instrument kick = new SampleInst("Kick.au");
        Instrument[] kit = {hats, snare, kick};
        Part temp = drums.copy();
        Mod.repeat(temp, this.repeats);
        Write.au(temp, fileName, kit);
    }
```

The *SampleInst* class takes an audio file as input and processes it in response to note events by extracting the pitch and dynamic information from the note and applying them to the sample. As well, a simple envelope is provided to avoid clicks at the start and end of sample playback. Below is the full *SampleInst* code.

```java
    import jm.audio.io.*;
    import jm.audio.Instrument;
    import jm.audio.synth.*;
```

```java
import jm.music.data.Note;
import jm.audio.AudioObject;

public final class SampleInst extends jm.audio.Instrument{
    private String fileName;
    private int numOfChannels;
    private double baseFreq;
    private boolean wholeFile;
    private double[] points;
    SampleOut sout;

    public SampleInst(String fileName){
        this(fileName, 440.00);
    }
    public SampleInst(String fileName, double baseFreq){
        this(fileName, baseFreq, new double[]
            {0.0, 0.0, 0.001, 1.0, 0.95, 1.0, 1.0, 0.0});
    }
    public SampleInst(String fileName, double baseFreq, double[] points){
        this.fileName = fileName;
        this.baseFreq = baseFreq;
        this.points = points;
    }
    public void createChain(){
        SampleIn sin = new SampleIn(this, fileName, true);
        Volume vol = new Volume(sin);
        Volume gain = new Volume(vol, 8.0);
        if (output == RENDER) {
            sout = new SampleOut(gain);
            sin.setWholeFile(true);
        } else {
            Envelope env = new Envelope(gain, points);
        }
    }
}
```

9: Following Rules

Control over musical processes at the note-attribute level has been common for many centuries but was taken to extremes in the serialist compositions of Schoenberg, Webern, Boulez and others in the first half of the 20th century. A more accessible form of serialism developed is the later 20th century, notably in the music of Arvo Pärt, where less extreme ranges of music elements were used, such as diatonic harmonies replacing atonal. Rule-based music is a natural candidate for computer-based musical practices given that all music algorithms are codification of rules of some sort. Composers such as Iannis Xenakis and Gottfried Michael Koenig were pioneers in algorithmic computer music, that the electroacoustic music community developed and continues to explore. In this chapter we will investigate some common and historically relevant rule-based music processes.

Music From Text

A simple rule to apply is for the musical structure to follow some existing data. Because langauges have some inherent structures, well described by Noam Chomsky and others, it is reasonable to expect that music based on text might reflect some of this structure. The sonification of text can use simple or complex mappings between the text and sound.

In the *RuleMusic* example we explore a simple mapping from the numerical values of text characters in the computer to MIDI note numbers. So the rule here is that each letter in the text triggers a note of a particular pitch. To make this rule clear in this example, all other variables including rhythmValue, dynamic, instrument, and so on, are kept constant.

```
import jm.JMC;
import jm.music.data.*;
import jm.util.*;

public class RuleMusic implements JMC {
    public static void main(String[] args) {
        new RuleMusic(args[0]);
    }

    public RuleMusic(String sentence) {
```

```
        for (int i = 0; i<sentence.length; i++) {
            for (int j=0; j < sentence[i].length(); j++) {
                int val = Character.getNumericValue(sentence[i].charAt(j));
                System.out.println(val);
                int pitch = val;
                Note n = new Note(pitch, SIXTEENTH_NOTE);
                phr.addNote(n);
            }
        }
        Play.midi(phr);
    }
}
```

Music Moment

One of the oldest known algorithmic music processes is a rule-based algorithm that selects each note based on the letters in a text, credited to Guido d'Arezzo (ca. 1000 A.D.). Originally the intention was that the melody was a sung phrase and the text was the lyric to be sung. Each vowel in the text is allocated a pitch and the number of characters between vowels influences note durations. This implementation is not strict (as the original was designed for modal chants of Latin texts) but has been adapted to Roman languages and modern musical sensibilities.

Guido

The *GuidoWordMusic* program is based on Guido d'Arezzo's lookup chart for generating pitches from syllables. This melody generation tool creates a monophonic phrase by extrapolating from a given text string. A lookup table (see Table 8.2) is the basis for selecting note pitches depending on the vowels found in the text. Although d'Arezzo's original intention was simply to provide an approximate guide from which a composer could make selections to fit his/her taste, our implementation completely automates the process. As well as pitch, the *GuidoWordMusic* program generates a rhythm depending on the number of consonants between each vowel.

```
b3  c4  d4  e4  f4  g4  a4  b4  c5  d5  e5  f5  g5  a5  b5  c6
A   E   I   O   U   A   E   I   O   U   A   E   I   O   U   A
```

Figure 9.1. The note pitch value options assigned by WordMusic to each vowel

When running the program, a number of words are added as arguments to the `java` command. These words are used as the input text (words) on which the music is based. For example, using a command line you would type something like:

```
java GuidoWordMusic "this is some text to make music out of"
```

Here is the code for the *GuidoWordMusic* program.

```java
import jm.JMC;
import jm.music.data.*;
import jm.util.*;

public class GuidoWordMusic implements JMC {
    Phrase phr = new Phrase();
    int[] pitchesA = {b3,g4,e5};
    int[] pitchesE = {c4,a4,f5};
    int[] pitchesI = {d4,b4,g5};
    int[] pitchesO = {e4,c5,a5};
    int[] pitchesU = {f4,d5,c6};
    int consonantCount = 1;
    int prevPitch = 72;

    public static void main(String[] args) {
        new GuidoWordMusic(args);
    }

    public GuidoWordMusic(String[] sentence) {
        for (int i = 0; i<sentence.length; i++) {
            for (int j=0; j < sentence[i].length(); j++) {
                System.out.println(sentence[i].charAt(j));
                if (sentence[i].charAt(j) == 'a') {
                    System.out.println("** A");
                    chooseNote(pitchesA);
                }
                if (sentence[i].charAt(j) == 'e') {
                    System.out.println("** E");
                    chooseNote(pitchesE);
                }
                if (sentence[i].charAt(j) == 'i') {
                    System.out.println("** I");
                    chooseNote(pitchesI);
```

```java
            }
            if (sentence[i].charAt(j) == 'o') {
                System.out.println("** O");
                chooseNote(pitchesO);
            }
            if (sentence[i].charAt(j) == 'u') {
                System.out.println("** U");
                chooseNote(pitchesU);
            }
            consonantCount++;
        }
    }
    phr.setTempo(120.0);
    View.notate(phr);
    Play.midi(phr);
}

private void chooseNote(int[] pitches) {
    int pitch = pitches[(int)(Math.random() * pitchesA.length)];
    while(Math.abs(prevPitch - pitch) > 6) {
        pitch = pitches[(int)(Math.random() * pitchesA.length)];
    }
    Note n = new Note(pitch, EIGHTH_NOTE * consonantCount);
    phr.addNote(n);
    consonantCount = 1;
    prevPitch = pitch;
}
}
```

This melody generation tool, while based on a set of very simple rules, is quite effective in creating musically interesting phrases. Because the music is generated entirely based on a set of rules, it can be said to be taking an algorithmic approach to the generation of music.

Initially, the simplicity of the rules used can be deceiving, however when looked at more closely, they do have some theoretical grounding. Most melodies that are written for specific texts do set notes to every syllable, and the rhythm of the text does in general have some relationship to the length of the words (and the distance between adjacent vowels). Although this is not an exact relationship (and problems occur with words that do not contain vowels, for example "sky"), the results produced by its implementation are very acceptable. It should also be noted that the original rhythm algorithm involved a greater variety of note lengths (ranging from semiquavers to semibrieves), however this was simplified in our implementation as the resulting phrases tended to be somewhat disjointed. The algorithm takes some account of voice leading, and could even be developed to produce polyphonic phrases. However, even in its current form, the melody generation program does provide a good example of the possibilities of algorithmically generating music - even with only the simplest of rules.

Serialism

Serialist music is music composed with strict adherence to rules. In the early 20th century serialism was closely tied to atonal music, that is, music that plays all 12 chromic pitches with equal frequency so as not to create the sense that there is any tonal centre. To achieve this the method developed was to create note rows that included all 12 chromatic pitches then to compose music that used these rows. To provide some variety a number of rules for modifying the rows were developed, these have been included in jMusic's Mod class. The Mod (modification) methods apply rule-based processes to jMusic data classes. For example, the Mod.rotate() method takes a phrase and moves the first note in the phrase to the end.

Arnold Schoenberg and other Atonal serialists composed music by fairly strict adherence to rules of note order. Some of the modifications they regularly employed to vary the tone row (the phrase with all 12 notes of the octave in it) that was the raw material for their works, included playing the row backwards (retrograde) flipping the pitches relative to their intervallic distance from first note in the row (inversion) and the combination of these techniques (retrograde inversion). There are Mod methods for each of these processes with the obvious method names, as follows.

```
Mod.retrograde()
Mod.inversion()
Mod.retrogradeInversion()
```

Programming Practice

Write a program that plays a melody backwards and inverted using the Mod class. Use this program as a the basis of another that composes a multi-part composition using a tone row as its basic material and including the simple variations on the row described here.

Music Moment

The composer Arvo Pärt was trained in the atonal serialist tradition and wrote for many years in this style. In the 1970s he developed a new tonal serial style he called Tintinnabuli, a process that featured small intervallic

> leaps in melodic movement and arpeggiated triadic accompaniment. This style blended the formulaic serialist processes with harmonic and melodic rules reminiscent of mediaeval tonal music. His works are often slow in tempo and vary gently in texture and intensity, resulting in an overall effect that is both meditative and majestic.
>
> One of the earliest works in the Tintinnabuli style was the piano piece Für Alina (1976). This simple piece is a good example of the raw elements of the style and how musically powerful they can be in combination. Many of Pärt's works composed since developing the process are set to Latin liturgical texts and orchestrated for voices, pipe organ and chamber ensemble for performance in the ambient acoustics of Christian cathedrals.

Arvoish

Below is an program called *Arvoish*, which is a jMusic implementation based on the Tintinabuli rules.

The first step is to set up the class and initialize all the variables required.

```java
import jm.JMC;
import jm.music.data.*;
import jm.util.*;

public final class Arvoish implements JMC{
    Score theWork = new Score("Tintinabuli", 84);
    Part melody = new Part("Melody",VOICE, 1);
    Part harmony = new Part("Harmony",PIPE_ORGAN, 2);
    Part bass = new Part("Bass",PIPE_ORGAN, 3);
    Part sub = new Part("Sub",PIPE_ORGAN, 4);
    Phrase voice1 = new Phrase();
    Phrase voice2 = new Phrase();
    Phrase voice3 = new Phrase();
    Phrase voice4 = new Phrase();
    // create a mode for constraining the notes
    int[] mode = {9, 11, 0, 2, 4, 5, 7}; //Aeolean scale degrees
    int[] triadic = {9, 0, 4}; //A minor triad
    //create the set of rhythmic durations to use
    double[] rhythms = {1.0, 1.0, 1.0, 2.0, 2.0, 4.0, 8.0};
```

The main method calls the constructor which, in turn, calls each of the private methods. The first of these creates the melody and the next few create accompanying parts, while the final method collates, writes and plays the music.

```java
public static void main(String[] args){
    new Arvoish();
}

public Arvoish() {
    createMelody();
    createAccompaniment1();
    createAccompaniment2();
    createAccompaniment3();
    saveAndPlay();
}
```

The melody is created as a random walk, starting on pitch 72 and wandering up to one octave from that starting point. Pitches are restricted to an Aeolian mode and rhythm values are randomized but triadic notes are reinforced by having longer note lengths.

```java
private void createMelody() {
    int phraseLength = 47;
    //start on the C above middle C
    int pitch = 72;
    int dynamic = 100;
    //Create the melody as a random walk
    int offset = 0;
    int previousOffset = 0;
    for (int i=0;i<phraseLength;){
        // next note within a couple of actaves and
        // don't allow three repeated notes.
        if (pitch < 84 && pitch > 60) {
            offset = (int)(Math.random() * 8 - 4);
        } else {
            if (pitch <= 60) offset =(int)(Math.random() * 6);
            if (pitch >= 84) offset =(int)(Math.random()*6-6);
        }
        //check that it is a note in the mode
        Note note = new Note(pitch + offset,
            rhythms[(int)(Math.random()*rhythms.length)], dynamic);
        if (note.isScale(mode) && (offset != 0 || previousOffset != 0)) {
```

```
                voice1.addNote(note);
                i++;
                pitch += offset;
                previousOffset = offset;
                dynamic += (int)(Math.random() * 10 - 5);
                // adjust rhythms
                if (note.isScale(new int[] {9,4}) &&
                        note.getRhythmValue()<8.0) {
                    note.setLength(note.getRhythmValue() * 2);
                } else if (note.getRhythmValue() > 1.0)
                    note.setLength(note.getRhythmValue() / 2);
                if (i == phraseLength) note.setLength(8.0);
            }
        }
    }
```

The first accompaniment section harmonizes the melody by locating the closest triadic note below the melody.

```
    private void createAccompaniment1() {
        for (int i=0;i<voice1.size(); i++) {
            Note nn = voice1.getNote(i);
            //find closest harmony pitch
            Note note = new Note(nn.getPitch() - 1, nn.getRhythmValue(),
                (int)(nn.getDynamic() * 0.5));
            while (!note.isScale(triadic)) {
                note.setPitch(note.getPitch() - 1);
            }
            voice2.addNote(note);
        }
    }
```

The second accompaniment section adds to the triadic harmonization by finding another lower triadic note.

```
private void createAccompaniment2() {
    for (int i=0;i<voice1.size(); i++) {
        Note nn = voice1.getNote(i);
        Note note = new Note(nn.getPitch() - (int)(Math.random() * 7 + 7),
            nn.getRhythmValue(), (int)(nn.getDynamic() * 0.5));
        while(!note.isScale(triadic)&&note.getPitch()%12 != nn.getPitch()%12){
            note.setPitch(note.getPitch() - 1);
```

```
        }
        voice3.addNote(note);
    }
}
```

The final accompaniment section plays some tonic notes when long tonic or dominant notes occur in the melody.

```
    private void createAccompaniment3() {
        for (int i=0;i<voice1.size(); i++) {
            Note nn = voice1.getNote(i);
            if ((nn.getPitch()%12 == 9 || nn.getPitch()%12 == 4)
                    && nn.getRhythmValue() >= 4.0) {
                Rest r = new Rest(nn.getRhythmValue() * 0.5);
                voice4.addRest(r);
                Note note = new Note(A2, nn.getRhythmValue() * 0.5,
                    (int)(nn.getDynamic() * 0.5));
                voice4.addNote(note);
            } else voice4.addRest(new Rest(nn.getRhythmValue()));
        }
    }
```

Finally the score is assembled, displayed, saved and played.

```
    private void saveAndPlay() {
        //add a rest to allow reverb to end
        Rest end = new Rest(8.0);
        voice1.addRest(new Rest(8.0));
        // add the phrase to an instrument and that to a score
        melody.addPhrase(voice1);
        theWork.addPart(melody);
        harmony.addPhrase(voice2);
        theWork.addPart(harmony);
        bass.addPhrase(voice3);
        theWork.addPart(bass);
        sub.addPhrase(voice4);
        theWork.addPart(sub);
        // create a MIDI file of the score
        Write.midi(theWork, "Arvoish.mid");
        // display score
        View.show(theWork);
        // playback
```

```
        Play.midi(theWork);
    }
```

Java Details

When writing music based on rules, the algorithms rely on the programming language being able to represent decisions. Because such decision making logic is so common, Java and other computer languages support a number of conditional statements.

if then else

The basis for implementing rules in Java is the `if` statement. Rules are usually specified as 'if x then y else z'. Statements take the form:

```
if (condition) {
    statement
} else {
    alternative statement
}
```

We have used this many times in this book already, for example:

```
for (int i=0;i<voice1.size(); i++) {
    Note nn = voice1.getNote(i);
} else {
    voice4.addRest(new Rest(nn.getRhythmValue()));
}
```

while and do

Variations of the `if-then` statement are the `while` and `do` statements which can sometimes be a more convenient form of setting up a condition. These take the form:

```
while (condition) {
    statement
}
```

and

```
do {
    statement
} while (condition)
```

The difference between these is that do always executes the statement at least once before the conditional check, whereas while checks the condition first and so may never execute the statement. Here's an example from one of the book's recent programs.

```
while (!note.isScale(triadic) && note.getPitch()%12 != nn.getPitch()%12) {
    note.setPitch(note.getPitch() - 1);
}
```

switch statements

Switch statements are useful when there is a condition check that may have several outcomes that require different action taken in each case. For example, when checking someone's age you may want to provide different responses if they are a baby, a child, a teenager, a young adult, middle-aged person, or older person. The switch statement takes the form:

```
switch ( check ) {
    case outcome1:
        statements
        break;
    case outcome2:
        statements
        break;
    default:
        statements
        break;
```

TheGrid: Controlling Parameters

This version of TheGrid application adds a volume slider and other visual appearance improvements.

TheGrid10

In *TheGrid10*, we'll add some functionality by way of a volume slider for each drum part. Sliders are a new component type for this application so there are a few details about their implementation that we need to review.

```
import javax.swing.event.*;

public class TheGrid10 implements JMC, ItemListener, ActionListener,
                                  ChangeListener {
```

The `JSlider` class we are using is from Java's swing library. The associated listener for the `JSlider` is the `ChangeListener`. The `ChangeListener` interface is in the `javax.swing.event` package so we need to import that package. The previous listeners we have used were in the `java.awt.event` package. The `ChangeListener` is implemented, along with the other listeners, with the class declaration as shown above.

```
private JSlider hatVolumeSlider,
   snareVolumeSlider, kickVolumeSlider;
```

Each `JSlider` is declared to be an instance variable so they are accessible from all methods within the class.

```
hatVolumeSlider = new JSlider(JSlider.VERTICAL, 0, 127, 85);
snareVolumeSlider = new JSlider(JSlider.VERTICAL, 0, 127, 85);
kickVolumeSlider = new JSlider(JSlider.VERTICAL, 0, 127, 85);
```

In the constructor each `JSlider` is instantiated. The arguments passed are the orientation, the minimum value, maximum value, and initial value.

```
private void createGrid(String title,
JCheckBox[] boxes, JSlider vol) {
JPanel grid = new JPanel(new GridLayout(1,18));
grid.add(new JLabel(title));
vol.addChangeListener(this);
vol.setPreferredSize(new Dimension(25, 60));
grid.add(vol);
```

The slider objects are passed to the `createGrid()` method with the name `vol`. The number of cells in the grid expands to 18 to fit the slider. The slider, `vol`, is registered with the `ChangeListener` and its size is set to include a reasonable height, then it is added to the grid.

```
JPanel windowPanel = new JPanel(new BorderLayout());
windowPanel.add(numbGrid, "North");
```

There is a subtle change to the layout for this version of the application. There are two reasons for this, the drum grid height with the slider is greater than that required for the number labels that run along the top, and the components in the frame butt up against the edges which looks untidy. The overall design is modified to include two nested panels each with a `BorderLayout`. A new `JPanel`, called `windowPanel`, is created with a `BorderLayout` and the number grid, called `numbGrid`, is added separately to the "North" part of `windowPanel`'s layout, while the drum grids are added to a separate panel with a `GridLayout` which is placed inside the "Centre" section of `windowPanel`'s layout. The button panel is added to the "South". To create some space between the side of the frame and the components, this whole `windowPanel` is placed in the "Center" of the frame and empty `JPanel`s are added to the "North", "South", "East" and "West' sides of frame's layout.

```java
public void stateChanged(ChangeEvent e) {
    if (e.getSource() == hatVolumeSlider)
        musicObject.setHatVolume(hatVolumeSlider.getValue());
    if (e.getSource() == snareVolumeSlider)
        musicObject.setSnareVolume(snareVolumeSlider.getValue());
    if (e.getSource() == kickVolumeSlider)
        musicObject.setKickVolume(kickVolumeSlider.getValue());
}
```

The `ChangeListener` interface requires the implementation the `stateChanged()` method which is called whenever a registered slider is moved. Changes in each slider result in setting of the volume in the *GridMusic9* class, called `musicObject`. The current value of the slider is retrieved using `hatVolumeSlider.getValue()`, or similar, and passed as an argument to the `setHatVolume()`, or similar, method.

```java
public void setHatVolume(int val) {
    hats.setVolume(val);
}
```

In the `GridMusic10` class the `setHatVolume()` method is implemented along with those for snare and kick drums. These set methods are simple accessor methods that pass the new volume value to the `setVolume()` method of the phrase. The volume changes are applied just prior to playback, along with the other GUI settings for repeat and tempo in the `updatedPart()` method.

```java
private Part updatedPart() {
    Part temp = drums.copy();
    Mod.repeat(temp, this.repeats);
    for (int i=0; i<temp.size();i++) {
        Phrase phr = temp.getPhrase(i);
        phr.setDynamic(phr.getVolume());
    }
    return temp;
}
```

The code for these changes is consolidated in the `updatedPart()` method so that it is only written once and used many times. It is used to create a modified drum part by each of the four play and save methods. A copy of the part is created and the selected number of repeats applied. The for-loop iterates through each phrase in the part and sets the dynamic of each note in the phrase to the phrases current volume setting. (There is a subtle difference between musical dynamic and volume, which we'll overlook for the time being.) The updated part, named `temp`, is returned to the calling method.

Below is the complete source code for `TheGrid10` and `GridMusic10` classes.

TheGrid10

```java
import jm.JMC;
import jm.music.data.*;
import jm.util.*;
import jm.music.tools.Mod;

import java.awt.*;
import javax.swing.*;
import java.awt.event.*;
import javax.swing.event.*;
// In this version of TheGrid:
// Add a volume control top each instrument in the grid.
// Add change listener to deal with slider events
// Add an additional JPanel top the layout for the grid.
// Change default tempo to 100
public class TheGrid10 implements JMC, ItemListener, ActionListener, ChangeListener {
    private JCheckBox[] hatTicks, snareTicks, kickTicks;
    private JButton saveBtn, playBtn, audioSavebtn, audioPlayBtn, sampleSaveBtn, samplePlayBtn;
    private JComboBox repeatMenu, tempoMenu;
    // declare a music class
    private GridMusic10 musicObject;
    // declare the GUI window frame
    private JFrame window;
    // declare the faders
    private JSlider hatVolumeSlider, snareVolumeSlider, kickVolumeSlider;
    // A panel for all the instrument grids
    private JPanel gridPanel;
    /**
    * The main method, where it all begins.
    */
```

```java
public static void main(String[] args) {
    new TheGrid10();
}
/**
 * Constructor. Sets up the parameters.
 */
public TheGrid10() {
    // set look and feel
    String local = javax.swing.UIManager.getSystemLookAndFeelClassName();
    String metal = javax.swing.UIManager.
        getCrossPlatformLookAndFeelClassName();
    try {
        UIManager.setLookAndFeel(local); // use local or metal for OS X
    } catch (Exception e) {}
    // set graphic data
    hatTicks = new JCheckBox[16];
    snareTicks = new JCheckBox[16];
    kickTicks = new JCheckBox[16];
    hatVolumeSlider = new JSlider(JSlider.VERTICAL, 0, 127, 85);
    snareVolumeSlider = new JSlider(JSlider.VERTICAL, 0, 127, 85);
    kickVolumeSlider = new JSlider(JSlider.VERTICAL, 0, 127, 85);
    // call other methods
    musicObject = new GridMusic10();
    musicObject.compose();
    makeInterface();
}
/**
 * GUI code
 */
private void makeInterface() {
    window = new JFrame("Drum Pattern");
    window.getContentPane().setLayout(new BorderLayout());
    JPanel windowPanel = new JPanel(new BorderLayout());
    // numbers
    JPanel numbGrid = new JPanel(new GridLayout(1,18));
    numbGrid.add(new JLabel("")); // fill label
    numbGrid.add(new JLabel("Vol", SwingConstants.CENTER));
    for (int i=1; i<17; i++) {
        numbGrid.add(new JLabel(""+i, SwingConstants.CENTER));
    }
```

```java
        windowPanel.add(numbGrid, "North");
        // create a grid for each instrument
        gridPanel = new JPanel(new GridLayout(3,1));
        createGrid("Hats", hatTicks, hatVolumeSlider);
        createGrid("Snare", snareTicks, snareVolumeSlider);
        createGrid("Kick", kickTicks, kickVolumeSlider);
        windowPanel.add(gridPanel, "Center");
        // initialise the grid values
        for (int i=0; i<16; i++) {
            hatTicks[i].setSelected(musicObject.getHatsState(i));
            snareTicks[i].setSelected(musicObject.getSnareState(i));
            kickTicks[i].setSelected(musicObject.getKickState(i));
        }
        // Add the button controls
        windowPanel.add(addControlPanel(), "South");
        window.getContentPane().add(windowPanel, "Center");
        // provide some padding
        window.getContentPane().add(new JPanel(), "North");
        window.getContentPane().add(new JPanel(), "South");
        window.getContentPane().add(new JPanel(), "East");
        window.getContentPane().add(new JPanel(), "West");
        window.pack();
        window.setVisible(true);
    }
    // Makes a single new grid row
    private void createGrid(String title, JCheckBox[] boxes, JSlider vol) {
        JPanel grid = new JPanel(new GridLayout(1,18));
        grid.add(new JLabel(title));
        vol.addChangeListener(this);
        vol.setMinimumSize(new Dimension(25, 40));
        vol.setPreferredSize(new Dimension(25, 60));
        grid.add(vol);
        for (int i=0; i<16; i++) {
            JCheckBox tick = new JCheckBox();
            tick.setHorizontalAlignment(SwingConstants.CENTER);
            tick.addItemListener(this);
            grid.add(tick);
            boxes[i] = tick;
        }
        gridPanel.add(grid);
```

```java
}
// Makes the GUI button and pop controller area
private JPanel addControlPanel() {
    JPanel btnPanel = new JPanel(); //new GridLayout(2,1)
    //   buttons
    JPanel midiPanel = new JPanel(new GridLayout(2,1));
    playBtn = new JButton("Play MIDI");
    playBtn.addActionListener(this);
    midiPanel.add(playBtn);
    saveBtn = new JButton("Save MIDI");
    saveBtn.addActionListener(this);
    midiPanel.add(saveBtn);
    btnPanel.add(midiPanel);
    JPanel audioPanel = new JPanel(new GridLayout(2,1));
    audioPlayBtn = new JButton("Play Audio");
    audioPlayBtn.addActionListener(this);
    audioPanel.add(audioPlayBtn);
    audioSavebtn = new JButton("Save Audio");
    audioSavebtn.addActionListener(this);
    audioPanel.add(audioSavebtn);
    btnPanel.add(audioPanel);
    JPanel samplePanel = new JPanel(new GridLayout(2,1));
    samplePlayBtn = new JButton("Play Samples");
    samplePlayBtn.addActionListener(this);
    samplePanel.add(samplePlayBtn);
    sampleSaveBtn = new JButton("Save Samples");
    sampleSaveBtn.addActionListener(this);
    samplePanel.add(sampleSaveBtn);
    btnPanel.add(samplePanel);
    // repeats
    repeatMenu = new JComboBox();
    repeatMenu.addActionListener(this);
    repeatMenu.addItem("1");
    repeatMenu.addItem("2");
    repeatMenu.addItem("4");
    repeatMenu.addItem("8");
    repeatMenu.addItem("16");
    btnPanel.add(new JLabel("Repeats = "));
    btnPanel.add(repeatMenu);
    // tempo
```

```java
            tempoMenu = new JComboBox();
            tempoMenu.addActionListener(this);
            tempoMenu.addItem("60");
            tempoMenu.addItem("80");
            tempoMenu.addItem("100");
            tempoMenu.addItem("120");
            tempoMenu.addItem("140");
            tempoMenu.addItem("180");
            tempoMenu.setSelectedIndex(2);
            btnPanel.add(new JLabel("Tempo = "));
            btnPanel.add(tempoMenu);
            btnPanel.add(new JLabel("bpm"));
            //
            return btnPanel;
    }
    /**
    * Handle the checkbox clicks
    */
    public void itemStateChanged(ItemEvent e) {
        for (int i=0; i<16; i++) {
            if (e.getSource() == hatTicks[i]) {
                if (hatTicks[i].isSelected()) musicObject.setHatsPitch(i, FS2);
                else musicObject.setHatsPitch(i, REST);
                return;
            } else
            if (e.getSource() == snareTicks[i]) {
                if (snareTicks[i].isSelected())musicObject.setSnarePitch(i,D2);
                else musicObject.setSnarePitch(i, REST);
                return;
            } else
            if (e.getSource() == kickTicks[i]) {
                if (kickTicks[i].isSelected()) musicObject.setKickPitch(i, C2);
                else musicObject.setKickPitch(i, REST);
                return;
            }
        }
    }
```

```java
/**
 * Handle the button clicks
 */
public void actionPerformed(ActionEvent e) {
    if (e.getSource() == playBtn) {
        musicObject.play();
    }
    if (e.getSource() == audioPlayBtn) {
        musicObject.audioPlay();
    }
    if (e.getSource() == samplePlayBtn) {
        musicObject.samplePlay();
    }
    if (e.getSource() == saveBtn) {
        musicObject.saveFile("DrumPattern10.mid");
    }
    if (e.getSource() == audioSavebtn) {
        musicObject.saveAudioFile("DrumPattern10.au");
    }
    if (e.getSource() == sampleSaveBtn) {
        musicObject.saveSampleFile("DrumSamplePattern10.au");
    }
    if (e.getSource() == tempoMenu) {
        musicObject.setTempo(new Double((String)tempoMenu.
            getSelectedItem()).doubleValue());
    }
    if (e.getSource() == repeatMenu) {
        musicObject.repeatMusic(Integer.parseInt(
            (String)repeatMenu.getSelectedItem()));
    }
}
/**
 * Handle slider movements
 */
public void stateChanged(ChangeEvent e) {
    if (e.getSource() == hatVolumeSlider)
        musicObject.setHatVolume(hatVolumeSlider.getValue());
    if (e.getSource() == snareVolumeSlider)
        musicObject.setSnareVolume(snareVolumeSlider.getValue());
    if (e.getSource() == kickVolumeSlider)
```

```
            musicObject.setKickVolume(kickVolumeSlider.getValue());
    }
}
```

GridMusic10

```java
import jm.JMC;
import jm.music.data.*;
import jm.util.*;
import jm.music.tools.Mod;
import jm.audio.*;
// Added setHatVolume etc. fields and method, and change default tempo to 100
// Extend notes on sample playback with Mod.fillRests
public class GridMusic10 implements JMC {
    private Phrase hats, snare, kick;
    private Part drums;
    private int repeats;

    public GridMusic10() {
        hats = new Phrase(0.0);
        hats.setInstrument(0);
        snare = new Phrase(0.0);
        snare.setInstrument(1);
        kick = new Phrase(0.0);
        kick.setInstrument(2);
        drums = new Part("Drums", 26, 9);
        drums.setTempo(100);
        drums.addPhrase(hats);
        drums.addPhrase(snare);
        drums.addPhrase(kick);
    }
    /**
     * Create initial state of music by filling arrays with notes and rests.
     */
    public void compose() {
        int[] hatsHits =
            {REST, REST, FS2, REST, REST, REST, FS2, REST, REST, REST, FS2,
                REST, REST, REST, FS2, REST,};
        hats.addNoteList(hatsHits, SIXTEENTH_NOTE);
        int[] snareHits =
            {REST, REST, REST, REST, D2, REST, REST, REST, REST, REST, REST,
```

```java
              REST, D2, REST, D2, REST};
    snare.addNoteList(snareHits, SIXTEENTH_NOTE);
    int[] kickHits =
        {C2, REST, REST, REST, REST, REST, REST, C2, C2, REST, REST, REST,
                REST, REST, REST, REST};
    kick.addNoteList(kickHits, SIXTEENTH_NOTE);
}
/**
 * Specify the pitch (including as a REST) of a note in the hats array.
 * @param arrayIndex The note to be changed.
 * @param pitch The value to change it's pitch to.
 */
public void setHatsPitch(int arrayIndex, int pitch) {
    hats.getNote(arrayIndex).setPitch(pitch);
}
/**
 * Specify the pitch (including as a REST) of a note in the snare array.
 * @param arrayIndex The note to be changed.
 * @param pitch The value to change it's pitch to.
 */
public void setSnarePitch(int arrayIndex, int pitch) {
    snare.getNote(arrayIndex).setPitch(pitch);
}
/**
 * Specify the pitch (including as a REST) of a note in the kick array.
 * @param arrayIndex The note to be changed.
 * @param pitch The value to change it's pitch to.
 */
public void setKickPitch(int arrayIndex, int pitch) {
    kick.getNote(arrayIndex).setPitch(pitch);
}
/**
 * Pass back weather or not the specified hat note is a rest or not.
 * @return boolean True if it is a pitched note, false if it is a rest.
 */
public boolean getHatsState(int arrayIndex) {
    return (!hats.getNote(arrayIndex).isRest());
}
/**
 * Pass back weather or not the specified snare note is a rest or not.
```

```java
 * @return boolean True if it is a pitched note, false if it is a rest.
 */
public boolean getSnareState(int arrayIndex) {
    return (!snare.getNote(arrayIndex).isRest());
}
/**
 * Pass back weather or not the specified kick note is a rest or not.
 * @return boolean True if it is a pitched note, false if it is a rest.
 */
public boolean getKickState(int arrayIndex) {
    return (!kick.getNote(arrayIndex).isRest());
}
public void repeatMusic(int times) {
    this.repeats = times;
}
public void setTempo(double tempo) {
    drums.setTempo(tempo);
}
/**
 * Save the music as a standard MIDI file.
 * @param fileName The name of the MIDI file, usually ending in .mid
 */
public void saveFile(String fileName) {
    Write.midi(updatedPart(), fileName);
}
/**
 * Playback the music using JavaSound internal synth sounds.
 */
public void play() {
    Play.midi(updatedPart(), false);
}
/**
 * Specify the new volume for the hats
 */
public void setHatVolume(int val) {
    hats.setVolume(val);
}
 /**
 * Specify the new volume for the snare drum
 */
```

```java
public void setSnareVolume(int val) {
    snare.setVolume(val);
}
/**
* Specify the new volume for the kick drum
*/
public void setKickVolume(int val) {
    kick.setVolume(val);
}
/**
* Return a part with the necessary modification ready for playback.
*/
private Part updatedPart() {
    Part temp = drums.copy();
    Mod.repeat(temp, this.repeats);
    // apply volume to note dynamic for each phrase
    for (int i=0; i<temp.size();i++) {
        Phrase phr = temp.getPhrase(i);
        phr.setDynamic(phr.getVolume());
    }
    return temp;
}
/**
* Playback the music using jMusic audio.
*/
public void audioPlay() {
    // set up instruments
    Instrument hats = new TR808HatsInst();
    hats.setOutput(Instrument.REALTIME);
    Instrument snare = new TR808SnareInst();
    snare.setOutput(Instrument.REALTIME);
    Instrument kick = new TR808KickInst();
    kick.setOutput(Instrument.REALTIME);
    Instrument[] kit = {hats, snare, kick};
    Play.audio(updatedPart(), kit);
}
/**
* Save the music as an au file.
* @param fileName The name of the  file, usually ending in .au
*/
```

```java
    public void saveAudioFile(String fileName) {
        // set up instruments
        Instrument hats = new TR808HatsInst(44100);
        Instrument snare = new TR808SnareInst(44100);
        Instrument kick = new TR808KickInst(44100);
        Instrument[] kit = {hats, snare, kick};

        Write.au(updatedPart(), fileName, kit);
    }
    /**
     * Playback the music using jMusic audio with sampled sounds.
     */
    public void samplePlay() {
        // set up instruments
        Instrument hats = new SampleInst("blah.aif"); //Hats.au");
        hats.setOutput(Instrument.REALTIME);
        Instrument snare = new SampleInst("Snare.au");
        snare.setOutput(Instrument.REALTIME);
        Instrument kick = new SampleInst("Kick.au");
        kick.setOutput(Instrument.REALTIME);
        Instrument[] kit = {hats, snare, kick};
        // extend notes to occupy rests
        Part p = updatedPart();
        Mod.fillRests(p);
        Play.audio(p, kit);
    }
     /**
      * Save the music as an au file using sampled sounds.
      * @param fileName - The name of the  file, usually ending in .au
      */
    public void saveSampleFile(String fileName) {
        // set up instruments
        Instrument hats = new SampleInst("Hats.au");
        Instrument snare = new SampleInst("Snare.au");
        Instrument kick = new SampleInst("Kick.au");
        Instrument[] kit = {hats, snare, kick};

        Write.au(updatedPart(), fileName, kit);
    }
}
```

10: Uncertainty

An important consideration when composing music is achieving an appropriate balance between predictability and surprise. Too much predictability leads to boredom, while too much uncertainly leads to confusion. When writing music with a computer, we can pass some of the responsibility for musical choices to the computer. The computer might fill in detail, leaving us free to think about higher level structure, or the computer might be given choices between equally acceptable alternatives. But, how can a computer make musical choices? Essentially it cannot, however, the computer can select between options based on weighted probability, in the simplest case as pseudo-randomness. The result is that the outcome is uncertain to some degree, and it is up to the composer/programmer to decide the nature of the uncertainties and their boundaries.

Aleatoric and Stochastic Music

Music that relies on chance is referred to as aleatoric music. Composers have been interested in the use of chance for some time. A famous example is Mozart's musical dice game Musikalisches Würfelspiel, mentioned previously, where numbered fragments of music are recombined according to the outcome of rolling the dice. But, more specifically, aleatoric music relies on chance in the execution, rather than composition; although at times these are one and the same. John Cage was a twentieth century American composer noted for promoting aleatoric music. In his works chance elements included selecting cards from a shuffled deck, calling phone numbers at random, rolling dice, and relying on the chance actions of an unsuspecting audience.

Music that uses mathematical probability is often referred to as stochastic music. There are historical examples of stochastic music where the calculations were done manually, but since the availability of the computer in the middle of last century the capacity to create stochastic music has increased dramatically. Iannis Xenakis was a composer very interested in stochastic music. He wrote pieces with stochastic elements both using manual calculations and with computers. These works were for both acoustic instruments and for computer generated output, and focused on probabilistic control of almost every aspect of a musical work, from the macro structure to the micro structure. Aspects determined this way included the overall duration and structure of a work, individual note attributes, and sound generation and spatial positioning.

Math Moment

There is an important distinction between systems that always produce the same result and those that produce unpredictable results. Stochastic systems are *indeterminate*, or unpredictable, as are all systems that make use of random number generators. Rule based systems are often *determinate* because although there may be alternative paths, the system is determinate if when given particular starting conditions the same result is returned. There are systems that fall unintuitively into one these two categories so it is useful to consider carefully whether or not your algorithm in deterministic or indeterminate. For example, systems that follow the rules of chaos theory are deterministic, while those using fractals are indeterminate. Systems using fuzzy logic are deterministic, while those using probability are indeterminate.

Music from randomness

The *WindChimes* program is an example of unpredictable music generation. It uses random rhythm values and dynamics with a small pitch set to mimic the uncertain collisions of wind chimes blowing in the breeze. There is a nested loop that creates 24 notes in each of 4 phrases. Each phrase has notes of a particular pitch, but chooses note lengths and volumes using the `Math.random()` method and an appropriate multiplier. Here is the heart of the *WindChimes* program.

```
Part part = new Part("All Chimes", BELLS, 0);
int[] pitchSet = {C6, F6, G5, D7};
for (int i=0; i<pitchSet.length; i++){
    Phrase phr = new Phrase((double)i);
    for (int j=0; j<24; j++) {
        Note note = new Note(pitchSet[i], Math.random() * 8,
            (int)(Math.random() * 80 + 20));
        phr.addNote(note);
    }
    part.addPhrase(phr);
}
```

Probability and music

For matters of chance and uncertainly we can usually calculate a probability. That is, a likelihood of occurrence. In the case of a coin toss the probabilities of a heads or tails result are each 50 percent. Likewise, the probability of a 6 on a dice is 1 in 6, or 15 percent. Importantly, the result of one roll of the dice does not influence the outcome of the next. The probabilities and levels of unpredictability remain the same at each roll or toss. When, as in these cases, there is an equal chance of each outcome, the probability distribution is said to be linear. The java method,

`Math.random()`, produces a linear distribution of its possible outcomes, any double value from 0.0 to less than 1.0. So we will use it when we want to simulate the roll of a dice, spin of the roulette wheel, or unpredictable musical accent.

The *CloudX* program uses randomness in the selection of note pitch, rhythmValue, dynamic, panning position and beat location. In jMusic, position in time is an attribute of Phrases, so in order to position each note at a random location they are each added to a separate phrase. The note lengths are very short and the sound specified is a breathy chiff, so the result is a cluster of short sound bursts that create a cloud-like texture. This program is inspired by one of Xenakis' stochastic compositions, *Concert PH*, which has similar sonic properties.

```
double cloudDensity = 0.1;
Phrase phr = new Phrase()
for (int i = 0; i < 1500; i++) {
    int pitch = (int)(Math.random()*127);
    double rv = Math.random() * cloudDensity;
    int dyn = (int)(Math.random()*127);
    Note n = new Note(pitch, rv, dyn);
    n.setPan(Math.random());
    phr.addNote(n);
}
Mod.fadeOut(phr, 20);
Part p = new Part("Cloud", BREATHNOISE, 0);
p.addPhrase(phr);
Score s = new Score(p);
View.show(s);
```

The `Math.random()` method provides a linear distribution of values. That is, each result has the same probability. This can be seen, and heard, in the *CloudX* program where the notes are evenly distributed across the entire range of pitch values. In many musical situations a linear distribution is not always what we want. Rather, we often want some events to occur more often than others, for example, the occurrence of tonic and dominant notes in a diatonic melody. We will now explore processes that create uneven, or weighted, probabilities.

Gaussian distribution

The Gaussian distribution provides an uneven randomness where values are more likely around a centre value and become less likely to occur the further away from that value. A diagram showing a linear distribution is a flat line, whereas the Gaussian distribution looks like a hill or a hump, which is why it is often called the 'bell curve'. The Gaussian distribution is named after the mathematician

K. F. Gauss and his work in the early 1800s. It is sometimes called the 'normal' distribution, because the probability of many occurrences in the natural world fit this distribution. Musical occurrences are no exception. For example, when a musician plays an instrument the loudness of the notes are generally similar although somewhat uneven when closely inspected. That is, they have a tendency to be around-about a certain level, but can vary above or below that, but do not often deviate widely from the norm.

The *GaussianCloud* program is a variation on the *CloudX* program that uses the `Prob` class from the `jm.music.data` package to determine note pitch. All other values are as for *CloudX*. The `Prob.gaussianPitch()` method is used, which takes two arguments. The first is the pitch value at the centre of the gaussian distribution, or bell curve, this will be the most common value returned. The second is the standard deviation, in semitones from that pitch. The vast majority of values will fall within the range of the centre pitch plus or minus the standard deviation. There is, however, a small chance that pitches outside this range will occur. In the case of *GaussianCloud*, the centre pitch is middle C (C4 or 60) and the standard deviation is one octave (12 half-steps or semitones). As a result most pitches will be in the two octave range from C3 to C5.

```
int pitch = Prob.gaussianPitch(C4, 12);
```

Random walk

A random walk algorithm generates a series where the distance between each value is specified at random within a specific range. For example, a random walk melody is a series of notes where the interval between each note pitch is randomized within a certain range; say, plus or minus a perfect fifth (seven half-steps or semitones). As a result the melodic contour of a random walk melody is quite smooth (it never makes any particularly large leaps) but is otherwise unpredictable.

A random walk melody is created by the *RandomWalk* program. A code fragment of this program is shown below. First, an initial value is set for the pitch and the standard deviation, that is the largest possible interval. A for-loop generates 24 notes each with a rhythm value equal to an eighth note, which are added to the one phrase, called `melody`. The pitch is then updated relative to itself, with a value plus or minus the deviation amount. Lastly, checks are carried out to ensure that the new pitch value does not exceed the minimum and maximum allowable pitch values.

```
int pitch = C4;
int deviation = 12;
for (int i=0; i<24; i++) {
    Note note = new Note(pitch, EIGHTH_NOTE);
    melody.addNote(note);
    pitch += (int)(Math.random()* (2*deviation) - deviation);
```

```
        if (pitch < 0) pitch = 0;
        if (pitch > 127) pitch= 127;
    }
```

The similar *GuassianWalk* program uses the `Prob.gaussianPitch()` method in place of the `Math.random()` method of the *RandomWalk* program.

```
    pitch = Prob.gaussianPitch(pitch, deviation);
```

The melodies that result tend to have a greater number of small intervals but also feature occasional large leaps greater than an octave. Comparing the melodies from the *RandomWalk* and *GuassianWalk* programs provides a good comparison of the linear and Gaussian distributions in a music context.

There are numerous probability distributions that can be applied to music, each has its own characteristics. Some common ones include binomial, poisson, and Cauchy, however, in most musical situations linear and Gaussian options should provide a sufficient degree of control. For a detailed exploration of the musical applications of these probability distributions see the book, *Formalized Music: Thought and mathematics in Music*, by Iannis Xenakis (1971).

Markov process

Andrei Andreevich Markov was a Russian mathematician who discovered a technique for recording the dependencies between items in series. This technique has been named the Markov process in honor of its inventor. At the heart of the Markov process is the creation of a Markov Chain, a series of values that follow one another with a certain degree of probability. Markov Chains have a long and successful history in computer music research, and for good reason. Markov Chains provide an effective mechanism for creating and using stochastic matrices in musically satisfying ways.

Markov Chains are created by analyzing the chance of any given value going directly to any other value. For example, within a melody, the probability that a note of pitch C4 will be followed by a note of pitch G4. Because C4 might also be followed by D4 with a different likelihood, a Markov Chain is derived by creating first a Markov Matrix of all possibilities. We can calculate the probabilities for the matrix by checking a particular pitch every time it occurs, seeing which notes do follow it, and counting how many times it is followed by each one. If we do this for every pitch value we build a stochastic matrix which resembles the composition that it is based on.

Let's take a look at an example of a melodic series (a melody).

{64,62,60,62,64,64,64,62,62,62,64,67,67,64,62,60,62,64,64,64,64,62,64,62,60}

This pitch array is the start of a very well known nursery rhyme and provides us with a perfect vehicle for investigating Markov Chains. The first step is to identify each individual pitch in this array.

60	62	64	67

If we now mark out all the notes that could precede these few notes we can make a proper two dimensional matrix.

	60	62	64	67
60				
62				
64				
67				

Values in the left column are known as the current *state* or the *seed*. Values along the top row are known as the *transition* or *output* values. We now need to fill in the matrix with probabilities of each note following another. To do this we just count up all the times that a pitch in the left column is followed by any pitch in the top column.

	60	62	64	67
60	0	2	0	0
62	3	3	4	0
64	0	5	5	1
67	0	0	1	1

To turn this table into a working Markov matrix we need to weight the totals in each row so that their sum is equal to 1.0, that is, give the totals a percentage rather than absolute probability weighting.

	60	62	64	67
60	0.0	1.0	0.0	0.0
62	0.3	0.3	0.4	0.0
64	0.0	0.4545	0.4545	0.0909
67	0.0	0.0	0.5	0.5

In the example above we can deduce that provided a seed pitch of 67 (A4) there is 50% likelihood that the pitch of the next note will be 64 (E4) and a 50% likelihood that it will be 67 (A4). Following this one step further, we use the output of this choice as the seed of the next choice, and so on, to create a melody of any length. This new melody will have a similar character to the original melody used to create the matrix.

The *BasicMarkov* program implements the Markov process we've been examining. You can run it several times to hear how the musical results are different each time, but maintain a stylistic consistency.

This matrix defines links between one note and the next. When constructing the matrix we looked a single step ahead in the melody, so we say the matrix is a single state matrix and that it has a depth of one. If Markov matrices were limited to a single state per seed then their musical usefulness would be limited. Luckily, there are no such limit and seeds can in fact be any length you like up to the length of the original melody. Typically, a depth of more that four is unnecessary.

To produce a Markov matrix of a depth of more than one we use seeds of more than one element. For example, we analyze the original melody to see when C4 is followed by G4 how many times the next note is A4? We calculate a matrix with a depth of 2 in the same way we calculate a matrix with a depth of 1. The only difference is that all our calculations are based upon any two numbers being followed by another number. Only pairs of pitches that are in the original melody are included in the matrix. Although our seed is now two pitches in a row, the output is always one pitch. This is true regardless of the Markov depth. Our primary matrix now looks like this.

	60	62	64	67
64,62	0.6	0.4	0.0	0.0
62.60	0.0	1.0	0.0	0.0
60,62	0.0	0.0	1.0	0.0
62,64	0.0	0.25	0.5	0.25
64,64	0.0	0.4	0.6	0.0
62,62	0.0	0.3333	0.6666	0.0
67,67	0.0	0.0	1.0	0.0
67,64	0.0	1.0	0.0	0.0
64,67	0.0	0.0	0.0	1.0

Changes from the previous matrix include that the far left hand column now contains two numbers (prior states) as the seed rather than one, there are more rows than there were previously, and there are more 1.0 (100%) weightings than there were before. The last two points seem obvious, but they point to the most important feature of Markov chains; the ability to maintain local context and provide for more discriminatory, therefore musically coherent, output. Where there is a 1.0 probability it is a forced move for the melody, there is no other choice. This the resulting three note motive from the original will appear unchanged in the generated melody, and will likely be a recognizable link between them. We might say the Markov matrix stores a sense of style.

A Markov chain can be of any depth (any seed length) but there are a number of important considerations when regarding depth. As the depth of the Markov chain approaches the length of the original melody the probability of variation in output decreases. This presents a tradeoff when using Markov chains. The guarantee of a particular sequence introduces stability and thematic coherence, however, it also introduces the chance of a very similar, even identical, outcome. If the depth of the matrix is high the resulting melody might be too close to the original to be valuable in a creative sense.

To test this matrix we will look at the *MarkovTest* program that make use of jMusic's in built `Markov` classes. The main jMusic `Markov` class is called `PhraseMatrix` and it calculates a matrix from a phrase and also generates a new phrase of any length based on the calculated matrix. It will do this at any depth level and can calculates matrices for pitch, rhythm and volume. Here is a code fragment from the *MarkovTest* program showing the use of the `PhraseMatrix` constructor and the `generate()` method.

```
Phrase marysLamb = new Phrase();
marysLamb.addNoteList(pitches, rhythms, dynamics);
int markovDepth = variableA;
PhraseMatrix matrix = new PhraseMatrix(marysLamb, markovDepth);
Phrase myLamb = matrix.generate(true, false, false, 20);
```

The *MarkovTest* application uses the same nursery rhyme as the *BasicMarkov* program to construct the matrix. Be aware that while matrices are built for pitch, rhythm and dynamic, only the pitch will change in the *MarkovTest* program at this stage. The slider `variableA` on the `HelperGUI` interface specifies the depth level for the matrix. You will notice that as this is increased the generated melody is more like the original nursery rhyme. Below is the complete code for the *MarkovTest* application.

```
import jm.JMC;
import jm.music.data.*;
import jm.music.tools.*;
import jm.util.*;
import jm.gui.helper.HelperGUI;

/*
* An elementary use of the PhraseMatrix class that
* enables a markov process.
```

```
*/

public class MarkovTest extends HelperGUI implements JMC{

    public static void main(String[] args){
        new MarkovTest();
    }

    public MarkovTest() {
        setVariableA(2, "Seed depth");
    }

    public Score compose() {
        int[] pitches = {64,62,60,62,64,64,64,62,62,62,64,67,67,64,62,
            60,62,64,64,64,64,62,62,64,62,60};
        double[] rhythms = {QN,QN,QN,QN,QN,QN,HN,QN,QN,HN,QN,QN,HN,QN,
            QN,QN,QN,QN,QN,QN,QN,QN,QN,QN,QN,HN};
        int[] dynamics = {80,70,60,70,80,80,80,70,70,70,80,100,100,80,
            70,60,70,80,80,80,80,70,70,80,70,60};
        Phrase marysLamb = new Phrase();
        marysLamb.addNoteList(pitches, rhythms, dynamics);
        int markovDepth = variableA;
        PhraseMatrix matrix = new PhraseMatrix(marysLamb, markovDepth);
        Phrase myLamb = matrix.generate(true, false, false, 20);
        Score scr = new Score("MarysLamb", 120);
        Part part = new Part();
        part.addPhrase(myLamb);
        scr.addPart(part);
        return scr;
    }
}
```

Programming Practice

Here are some enhancements to the *MarkovTest* program that you can try.

1. Turning on the Markov generation process for the rhythm and dynamic values.

```
Phrase myLamb = matrix.generate(true, true, true, 20);
```

2. Using different Markov depths for each of pitch, duration and dynamics;

```
int pitchDepth = 2;
int rhythmDepth = 4;
int dynamicDepth = 1;
PhraseMatrix matrix = new PhraseMatrix(marysLamb, pitchDepth,
      rhythmDepth, dynamicDepth);
```

3. Assign the Markov depth of each note attribute using the `HelperGUI` sliders.

```
setVariableA(2, "Pitch depth");
setVariableB(3, "Rhythm depth");
setVariableC(1, "Dynamic depth");
...
int pitchDepth = variableA;
int rhythmDepth = variableB;
int dynamicDepth = variableC;
```

Viewing histograms

A histogram is a bar graph showing the number of occurrences of each element in a group. A common usage in music is to show the pitch distribution within a work. In this way it can be quickly seen which notes occur most frequently and which do not occur at all. A histogram can show such a graph of any data, however, the histogram in jMusic displays the note attributes; pitch, rhythm value, dynamics, and pan. It can display the results from a phrase, part, or score. When combined with jMusic's ability to read a MIDI file into a score, the histogram class can be a very useful musical analysis tool.

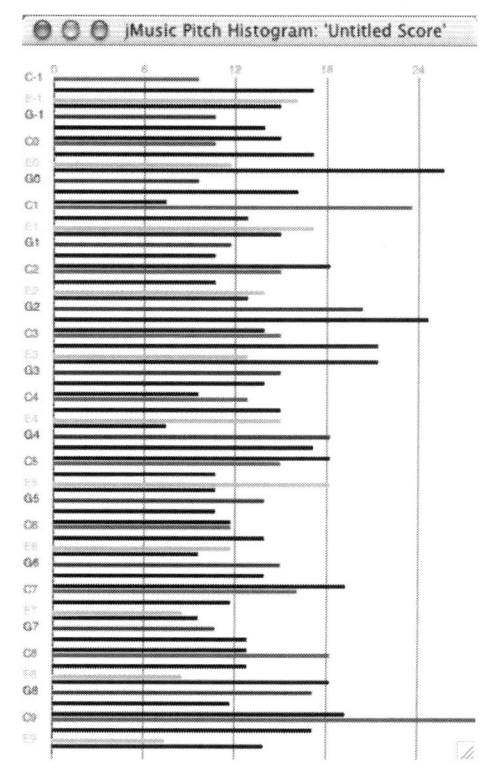

Figure 10.1. Histogram Viewer

To instantiate a histogram viewer use the static method of the jMusic View class View.histogram(Score s); passing a music data object, typically a score, as an argument. The display shows all the possible values down the left hand side, with bars from left to right indicating the number of each value present in the score, for example the number of each note pitch from 0 to 127. The color-coding is to aid readability. All similar values are the same color; for example, all C pitches are yellow. The histogram menu allows you to s switch between viewing the pitch, rhythm, dynamic and pan values in the histogram. There are options to open a MIDI or jMusic XML file for viewing, and so to save the analysis data as a tab delimited text file, for further viewing or treatment in another program such as a spread sheet, word processor, or data base.

A demonstration of the histogram can be seen with the *HistogramAnalysis* program. This program creates a score of notes with random pitch, rhythm, duration and pan values. Histograms of each are opened, then lastly a dialog box appears enabling you to select a MIDI file for analysis and display.

The HelperGUI interface has a View.histogram() button which brings up the histogram display showing an analysis of the current composition. Below is the code the HistogramAnalysis program.

```java
import jm.music.data.*;
import jm.JMC;
import jm.util.View;
import java.awt.*;

public class HistogramAnalysis implements JMC {
    public static void main(String[] args) {
        Phrase phr = new Phrase();
        for (int i=0; i<1000; ) {
            Note n = new Note((int)(Math.random() * 127),
                        (int)(Math.random() * 20) * 0.25,
                        (int)(Math.random() * 127));
            n.setPan(Math.random());
            if (n.isScale(MAJOR_SCALE)) {
                phr.addNote(n);
                i++;
            }
        }
        Score score = new Score (new Part(phr));
        View.histogram(score);
        View.histogram(score, RHYTHM, 40, 30);
        View.histogram(score, DYNAMIC, 80, 60);
        View.histogram(score, PAN, 120, 90);
        View.histogram();
    }
}
```

Noise

Randomess in an audio waveform results in noise. Although noise may seem undesirable, there are many musical sounds that require it. These include many percussion sounds, the breath noise of wind instruments, and the scraping of bows on stringed instruments. Noise timbres can be widely varied depending upon the distribution of frequencies in the spectrum and the granularity of amplitude changes. A linear distribution of values across will produce white noise, with a bright timbre not unlike waves crashing on the sea. In jMusic there are a variety of noise generators including one for white noise.

The noise audio object in jMusic is different from the oscillator object (that produces sine, triangle, square and other periodic waveforms) because it is not cyclic. Oscillators create repeated, periodic sounds, but noise is made up of random and unpredictable sample values and so any repetition from cycling through a wavetable undermines the unpredictability of pure noise. Therefore, the noise audio objects continually calculate random sample values as required.

The *WhiteNoiseNote* program creates an audio file of white noise from a single note score, and displays it in a wave viewer window. It uses the `NoiseInst` instrument that defaults to a monophonic white noise output. The `NoiseInst` instrument adds a percussive envelope to the sound which is clearly audible and visible in the wave viewer.

```
Instrument wave = new NoiseInst(44100);
```

The *AllNoiseTypes* program is similar but creates an audio file in each of the noise types supported by jMusic. It allows you to compare the sound and appearance of each of the noise types. It uses the `NoiseInst` constructor that accepts three arguments, the sample rate, the number of channels, and the noise type. The noise type argument is an integer but, for convenience, there are constants in the `jm.audio.synth.Noise` class for each of them.

```
WHITE_NOISE = 0
STEP_NOISE = 1
SMOOTH_NOISE = 2
BROWN_NOISE = 3
FRACTAL_NOISE = 4
GAUSSIAN_NOISE = 5
WALK_NOISE = 6
GENDYN_NOISE = 7;
```

Below is the instantiation of the *NoiseInst* instrument in the *AllNoiseTypes* program.

```
Instrument wave = new NoiseInst(44100, 1, noiseType);
```

The differences between each noise type derive from variations in the amplitude distribution and granularity of change – some noise type change value at each sample, others less frequently. To clearly see the differences in the wave viewer zoom in to the wave form to a 1:1 viewing ratio so that each sample can be seen. Below is the source code for the *AllNoiseTypes* example.

```
import jm.music.data.*;
import jm.JMC;
import jm.audio.*;
import jm.util.*;

/*
* This class shows each jMusic noise type
*/
```

```
public class AllNoiseTypes implements JMC {

    public static void main(String[] args) {
        new AllNoiseTypes();
    }

    public AllNoiseTypes() {
        Score score = new Score(new Part(new Phrase(new Note(60, 4.0))));
        // loop through each noise types in jMusic
        for (int i=0; i<6; i++ ) {
            Instrument wave = new NoiseInst(44100, 1, i);
            Write.au(score, "NoiseType" + i + ".au", wave);
            View.au("NoiseType" + i + ".au", i*20, i*20);
        }
    }
}
```

Java Randomness and Determinism

Despite our heavy use of randomness in this chapter, it is quite difficult for computers to be entirely random given their very precise nature. However, for all of our purposes they can have pseudo-random number generators that are quite unpredictable.

Math.random()

The Java Math class includes an extensive range of functions including one for generating pseudo-random numbers. The Math.random() methods produces a pseudorandom double greater than or equal to 0.0 and less than 1.0. Values within this range are equally likely; that is they have a linear distribution. As you will have noticed from example code in this book these values can be scaled and cast to meet most of your programming needs.

The Random class

Java includes a Random class that is more fully featured than Math.random(). It allows for a constructor that takes a seed value, the advantage of which is that a pseudo-random series from the same seed will be identical each time. This may prove useful for some musical situations. Also an instance of the Random class can use the nextInt(), nextDouble(), nextLong() and nextFloat() methods to get a random number of the appropriate type and in the desired range without having to scale and cast. The class includes a `nextGaussian()` method so the one instance can create linear and gaussian distributions as required.

The `Random` class only returns floats from the `nextGaussian()` method, so jMusic provides the `jm.music.tools.Prob` class as a wrapper for getting Gaussian values from the `Random` class to make it easier to get jMusic pitch, frequency, rhythmValue, and panning data in the appropriate ranges and types.

TheGrid: Random Velocities

Human performers play each note slightly differently giving a subtly and variation to the performance that we appreciate. Often computer performances can be overly mechanical which does not suite all musical styles. In this version of *TheGrid* application we will add randomness to the loudness of notes that introduces some human quality to the playback.

TheGrid11

One useful application of randomness is to vary the dynamic of each note to add 'feel' to the music. This is sometimes referred to as 'humanizing' the performance because it is impossible for a human performer to play each note exactly the same. To achieve a similar effect for computer playback a small deviation of the existing dynamic value is added to each note.

The code for *TheGrid11* will be identical to *TheGrid10*, and GridMusic11 will require a small change to *GridMusic10* where the following code is substituted for the `updatePart()` method.

```
private Part updatedPart() {
    Part temp = drums.copy();
    Mod.repeat(temp, this.repeats);
    // apply randomness to note dynamic for each phrase
    for (int i=0; i<temp.size();i++) {
        Phrase phr = temp.getPhrase(i);
        for (int j=0; j<phr.size(); j++) {
            Note n = phr.getNote(j);
            n.setDynamic(phr.getVolume() + (int)(Math.random() * 40) - 20);
        }
    }
    return temp;
}
```

11: Emergence

While all algorithmic compositional processes result in music of some kind or another, there can be difference between processes that directly specify a musical outcome and those that are more indirect. Emergent process achieve their results indirectly, the outcomes arise from the interaction between elements within the process and often the outcome is quite unexpected or difficult to predict precisely. The surprising outcomes from emergent processes are somewhat different to stochastic processes, even though chance elements are often used in emergent algorithms. The classic case of emergence is evolution. In nature, the rules of natural selection give rise to the myriad of life forms that inhabit the earth. The rules of evolution don't specify what those life forms should be like but they do describe the process by which they will evolve. The life forms emerge from the evolutionary process.

Other examples of emergent systems include the behavior of an ant colony, where the rules that govern the actions of an individual ant in its foraging and building seem quite unlike the well organized community of ants that somehow manage to build coherent social structures and survive repeated disruption by predators and natural disasters. The existence of human consciousness is often cited as an emergent entity. The rules of life encoded in human beings do not directly describe consciousness, rather they describe how the human body and in particular the human brain should be built and operate. Consciousness emerges as a result of the brain functioning according to this design. A final example of an emergent system is a human constructed one, traffic flow in busy cities. Viewed on a large scale the behavior of traffic is particularly complex, especially when it is disrupted by accidents, traffic lights, and vehicles traveling at different speeds. Traffic flow patterns as a system are difficult to predict based on the 'rules' that control individual vehicles. The larger-scale traffic patterns emerge from the interactions between vehicles.

There seems to be a lot of potential for interesting musical structures from emergent systems. One difficulty is that the emergent behavior is often difficult to predict based upon the rules of individual elements within the system, and therefore considerable trial and error, and at times some luck, are often required to produce successful emergent systems for music. In this chapter we will look at some musical applications of well understood emergent processes.

Inspired by Nature

In recent years there has been a return to using biological processes as inspiration for art and computer science. In centuries past, there have been many artists and scientists inspired by nature, but generally speaking this inspiration came in the form or external appearance of landscapes, plants, animals, weather conditions and so on. The more recent biological inspiration comes from natural processes and applying these as elegant solutions in human endeavors – technologies. In this section we will examine a few of these natural processes and how they can be used to make music.

A Life

Artificial Life is the name given to the computational simulation of biological processes. One interesting example of this is the flocking algorithm.

The flocking behavior of birds is an emergent property of their individual actions. A flock of birds will stay together as a group despite the fact that there is no leader. Similar behavior can be observed in schools of fish, herds of cattle, and swarms of bees or insects. There are just a few rules required to simulate flocking behavior; 1) move forward in an intended direction (alignment), 2) avoid collisions with other birds or other objects (separation), 3) stay close to the other birds (cohesion). With each bird obeying these rules a robust flocking behavior emerges. Craig Reynolds (1987) famously implemented a computational implementation of this flocking process, he called it the Boids algorithm.

In our musical implementation, alignment is maintained by having notes of equal rhythm value for each phrase, separation is ensured by having concurrent notes in each phrase be of different pitches. Cohesion is implemented as a tendency for the notes to converge on the average pitch and are constrained to notes of the pentatonic scale. The result is a modal sequence of tight chord clusters that vary in range and direction in a random-walk. Figure 11.1 is an example of the output viewed in the jMusic show window.

Figure 11.1. Output from the Swarm program.

Let's examine the source code for the *Swarm* program:

```java
import jm.JMC;
import jm.music.data.*;
import jm.util.*;
import jm.music.tools.Mod;

public class Swarm implements JMC {
    private Note[] notes = {new Note(60, 0.5), new Note(60, 0.5),
        new Note(60, 0.5), new Note(60, 0.5)};
    private Phrase[] phrases = new Phrase[notes.length];
    private Part pianoPart = new Part(PIANO, 0);

    public static void main(String[] args) {
        Swarm noteCluster = new Swarm();
    }

    private Swarm() {
        for (int i=0; i<phrases.length; i++ ) {
            phrases[i] = new Phrase(0.0);
            phrases[i].addNote(notes[i]);
        }
        for (int i=0; i<16; i++) {
            step();
            System.out.println("Completed step " + i);
        }
        for (int i=0; i<phrases.length; i++) {
            pianoPart.addPhrase(phrases[i]);
        }
        Mod.shake(pianoPart, 40);
        View.show(pianoPart);
        Play.midi(pianoPart);
    }
}
```

The constructor method (shown above) outlines the general structure of the *Swarm* program. First, an array of notes is created, each with a pitch of middle C (MIDI pitch 60). This array will be used to store and update notes for the phrases. Four phrases are instantiated, they will be filled with notes as the program proceeds. Next, the `step()` method is called sixteen times (but it could be called any number of times). At each iteration this method adds a note to each of the phrases with the pitches varying according to the flocking rules. Once created these phases are added to the `pianoPart` object. Finally, the part is parsed by jMusic's `Mod.shake()` method that adds variation to the note dynamics, the part is displayed using the `View.show()` method and then played back using Java's inbuilt synthesizer.

```java
private void step() {
    int averagePitch = avPitch();
    for (int i=0; i<notes.length; i++) {
        notes[i].setPitch(nextPitch(notes[i].getPitch(),
            averagePitch, i));
        phrases[i].addNote(notes[i].copy());
    }
}

private int avPitch() {
    int av = 0;
    for (int i=0; i<phrases.length; i++) {
        av += notes[i].getPitch();
    }
    av /= notes.length;
    return av;
}
```

In the `step()` method the first task is to get the average pitch of those in the previous step, this is calculated by a call to the `avPitch()` method. The average pitch value provides the target toward which the notes should head. The pitches of each note in the notes array are updated within a for-loop. The `nextPitch()` method does most of the hard work (see below). Once updated, copies of the notes are added to phrases. Copies are required to create independent note objects, rather than references to the ones in the notes array. This is necessary because the pitches of notes in the notes array are continually changed and so any references would vary with them.

```java
private int nextPitch(int currentPitch, int averagePitch, int noteIndex) {
    // add jitter
    currentPitch += (int)(Math.random() * 12 - 6);
    // converge
    int choiceScope = 1;
    while (Math.abs(averagePitch - currentPitch) > 5 ||
            notInScale(currentPitch)) {
        if (currentPitch > averagePitch) currentPitch -= choiceScope++;
        else currentPitch += choiceScope++;
    }
    // avoid collision
    for (int i=0; i<notes.length; i++) {
```

```java
            if (i== noteIndex) continue;
            choiceScope = 2;
            while (inChord(currentPitch, i) || notInScale(currentPitch)) {
                if (currentPitch > averagePitch)
                    currentPitch -= (int)(Math.random() * choiceScope++);
                else currentPitch += (int)(Math.random() * choiceScope++);
            }
        }
        return currentPitch;
    }
```

The `nextStep()` method implements the cohesion and separation rules. The starting point for the next pitch value is a random walk step from the previous pitch. This starting point may be a jump above or below the previous pitch. The first while-loop reels in the pitch. It executes until the pitch is as close to the average as possible while still being a pitch in the C pentatonic scale. The next while-loop moves the pitch around if required so that it is not the same pitch as any other note sounding at the same time. The `choiceScope` variable controls the amount of pitch variation on each iteration of the while loop. It is incremented on each loop so that an ever increasing pitch range is explored for a solution. Without this increasing search space it is possible that the options were so limited that no solution would be found or that it was so wide that the cohesion rule would be negated. The `nextStep()` method is supported by these two private methods.

```java
    // check if the pitch is the same as any other pitch this beat
    private boolean inChord(int currentPitch, int counter) {
        boolean result = false;
        for (int i=0; i<counter; i++) {
            if (currentPitch == notes[i].getPitch()) result = true;
        }
        return result;
    }

    // check if the pitch is not within the scale
    private boolean notInScale(int currentPitch) {
        int[] scale = JMC.PENTATONIC_SCALE;
        boolean result = true;
        for (int i=0; i<scale.length; i++) {
            if (currentPitch%12 == scale[i]) result = false;
        }
        return result;
    }
```

The `inChord()` and `notInScale()` methods check that the proposed next pitch, stored in the variable `currentPitch`, conforms to the constraints that it is a) not the same as a previous note, and b) is a pitch in the pentatonic scale. While these routines could be inside the `nextStep()` method the code is clearer and more readable with them separated out, and the `notInScale()` method is called twice so unnecessary duplication of code is avoided.

Evolution

One of the most prominent biological processes that can be computationally mimicked is evolution. Darwinian evolution, also called natural section or survival of the fittest, is a process made up on several components; reproduction, mutation, crossover, and selection. Computation processes that model these processes are referred to as Genetic Algorithms or simple GA's. Any or all of these processes can be the basis for interesting algorithmic music.

Reproduction, by itself, can be likened to repetition as a musical strategy. However, in evolutionary reproduction the next generation is usually a variation of the original, rather than a clone. There are two common processes for creating variation in evolutionary biology. Mutation involves the simple random change to some component. In a musical phrase this might be the change of one note's pitch or rhythm value, for example. Crossover involves the combination of components from more than one (usually two) original sources (parents). This could include combining the first half of one phrase and the second half of another, or combining the pitches from one phrase with the rhythm values of a second. Using these methods a enormous variety of variations can be created, choosing between these involves the process of selection. In biological evolution, selection occurs through a process of fitness and luck. In musical selection, a fitness function can be created that scores the phrases according to a criteria and the highest scoring phases are chosen. Evolutionary process are useful for generating variation and novelty and for searching the possibilities in musical space for 'fit' musical sections.

In the program, *BassMutation*, the processes of reproduction and variation are employed, but no selection is undertaken. A short phrase is reproduced with small variations, such that as these are played one after another the music evolves or changes over time. Two versions of *BassMutation* are provided, first a simple one that uses only random mutation then, second, an example that uses crossover between 'parent' phrases and mutation.

Here is the code for the simple version that iteratively mutates a phrase.

```
import jm.JMC;
import jm.music.data.*;
import jm.util.*;
```

```java
public class BassMutate1 implements JMC {
    public static void main(String[] args) {
        new BassMutate1();
    }

    public BassMutate1() {
        Part bassPart = new Part();
        Phrase bassLine = new Phrase(0.0);
        for (int i = 0; i<16; i++) {
            bassLine.addNote(new Note(48, 0.25));
        }
        bassPart.addPhrase(bassLine.copy());

        for (int i=1; i<8; i++){
            Note n = bassLine.getNote((int)(Math.random() *
                bassLine.size()));
            n.setPitch((int)(Math.random() * 12 + 48));
            bassLine.setStartTime(4.0 * i);
            bassPart.addPhrase(bassLine.copy());
        }

        View.print(bassPart);
        Play.midi(bassPart);
    }
}
```

Below is a version of *BassMutate* that iterates through generations of phrase pairs using each pair as parents for the next generation. Both crossover and mutation techniques are applied to create new child phrases.

```java
import jm.JMC;
import jm.music.data.*;
import jm.util.*;

public class BassMutate2 implements JMC {
    Phrase bassLine1 = new Phrase(0.0);
    Phrase bassLine2 = new Phrase(0.0);
    int phraseSize = 16;
    int[] availablePitches = {36, 36, 40, 43, 45, 48, 48, 52, 55,
        REST, REST, REST};
```

Making Music with Java

```
        public static void main(String[] args) {
            new BassMutate2();
        }

        public BassMutate2() {
            Part bassPart = new Part(SYNTH_BASS);
            bassPart.setTempo(130.0);
```

This code fragment (above) sets up the class.

```
        // create parent phrase 1
        for (int i = 0; i<phraseSize; i++) {
            int pitch = availablePitches[(int)(Math.random() *
                availablePitches.length)];
            bassLine1.addNote(new Note(pitch, 0.25));
        }
        // create parent phrase 2
        for (int i = 0; i<phraseSize; i++) {
            int pitch = availablePitches[(int)(Math.random() *
                availablePitches.length)];
            bassLine2.addNote(new Note(pitch, 0.25));
        }
```

This code fragment generates the starting phrases, two bass lines that will be the parents for the next generation of phrases.

```
        for (int i=0; i < 8; i++) {
            Phrase childBassLine1 = createChild();
            Phrase childBassLine2 = createChild();

            childBassLine1.setStartTime(8.0 * i);
            childBassLine2.setStartTime(8.0 * i + 4.0);
            bassPart.addPhrase(childBassLine1);
            bassPart.addPhrase(childBassLine2);

            bassLine1 = childBassLine1;
            bassLine2 = childBassLine2;
        }
```

This loop creates new phrases based on the current parent phrases, then adds them one after the other to the bass part. This loop calls the createChild() method – see below. The final step in the loop is to assign the children to be the parents for the next iteration.

```java
        View.show(bassPart);
        Play.midi(bassPart);
    }
```

Once the iterations are complete, the bass part is displayed on screen and played back via the in-built JavaSound synthesizer.

```java
    private Phrase createChild() {
        Phrase tempPhrase = new Phrase();
        // crossover
        int crossOverPoint = (int)(Math.random() * phraseSize);
        for (int j=0; j<crossOverPoint; j++) {
            tempPhrase.addNote(bassLine1.getNote(j).copy());
        }
        for (int j=crossOverPoint; j<phraseSize; j++) {
            tempPhrase.addNote(bassLine2.getNote(j).copy());
        }
        // mutate
        Note n = tempPhrase.getNote((int)(Math.random() * phraseSize));
        int pitch = availablePitches[(int)(Math.random()
            * availablePitches.length)];
        n.setPitch(pitch);

        return tempPhrase;
    }
}
```

This `createChild()` method creates a child phrase by crossover between the parent phrases and a simple mutation of one of the note pitches.

Programming Practice

Assign variables in the *BassMutation* program to the `HelperGUI` variables. For example, replace the tempo value in the Score declaration with `variableA * 2`, and the number of iterations with `variableB`. Try varying the pitch set to see what different results you get.

Cellular Automata

Cellular Automata (CA) is a process where cells in a grid change properties, typically their color, based on the properties of their neighboring cells. The way in which they change can be specified by a set of rules. These rules are applied to all cells in parallel again and again, such that the state of the system of cells evolves with each iteration. While simple in concept, the global behavior that emerges from many cells obeying similar rules can be quite complex and, with appropriate rules, can resemble biological or mathematical processes. When implemented on computers, CA were one of the earliest forms of Artificial Intelligence (AI) or Artificial Life (A-Life) research. The 'classic' form is James Conway's *Game Of Life* (Gardner 1970) which sets rules about how cells arranged in a grid change state from one generation to the next. Cells can be alive (black) or dead (white) depending upon the combined state of all eight of its immediate neighbors. These patterns of black and white cells create interesting visual patterns, and potentially interesting graphical scores for musical patterns as well. It is the similarity of on/off states to the binary logic of 1s and 0s that most excited early researchers about the possibilities for computing with cellular automata.

CA rhythms (1 dimensional cellular automata)

In this example cellular automata data are mapped to rhythm. Rhythm is a more musically successful mapping of CA processes that pitch because it better suits the evolving repetition of the automata data. A one-dimensional matrix is all that is required to represent a rhythmic pattern and (i.e., an array or list of cells represents notes in the rhythm). A one-dimensional matrix is often depicted as series of cells with on(1) and off(0) states, as shown below.

```
10010101
```

A time series of these states is often shown as a list of matrices with each row being one generation. Four generations are shown below.

```
10010101
01010100
00111010
10100101
```

In the *RhtyhmicAutomata* program each cell in the array represents one semi-quaver and, in the score, notes are sounded on 'live' cells while rests are used where the cells are 'dead.' The rules that are applied to update the cells each iteration are the key to the musical style that emerges. These rules are, like traditional CA, based on the number of neighboring cells. Musically this relates to rhythmic density; the more neighbors a semi-quaver has the more densely populated is that area of the music. So, by varying the rules you can provide sparseness (density) tendencies. As well, rules influence the likelihood of cell change and thus the stability of the rhythmic patterns (how rapidly they evolve).

```
import jm.music.data.*;
import jm.JMC;
```

```
import jm.util.*;
```

The program imports the jMusic constants, the data types, and the `Util` package that contains the `Write` class.

```
public class RhythmicAutomata implements JMC{
    int barLength = 16;
    int[] bar = new int[barLength];
    int[] tempBar = new int[barLength];
    Part part1 = new Part("Hats", 0, 9);
    Part part2 = new Part("Rim Shot", 0, 9);
    Part part3 = new Part("Claps", 0, 9);
    Score score = new Score("AlgoRhythm", 84);
```

The class is declared and so are a number of class variables. Notice that an array of `int`'s called `bar` is declared. This holds the once dimensional cell matrix. The `tempBar` array is used when we apply the rules to evolve the array one generation.

```
public static void main(String[] args) {
    new RhythmicAutomata();
}
```

The `main()` method creates an instance of this class. Next we build the music one part at a time, bar by bar. The constructor makes a couple of method calls to fill the array (see details below), then sets up a loop that generates 23 bars of music, printing the state of the array to the terminal each time through.

```
public RhythmicAutomata() {
    initialise();
    makeMusic(part1, 42);
    for (int i=0; i<23; i++) {
        nextBar();
        makeMusic(part1, 42);
        printBar();
    }
    initialise();
    makeMusic(part2, 37);
    for (int i=0; i<23; i++) {
        nextBar();
        makeMusic(part2, 37);
        printBar();
```

```
    }
    initialise();
    makeMusic(part3, 39);
    for (int i=0; i<23; i++) {
        nextBar();
        makeMusic(part3, 39);
        printBar();
    }
    score.addPart(part1);
    score.addPart(part2);
    score.addPart(part3);
    Write.midi(score, "RhythmicAutomata.mid");
    Play.midi(score);
}
```

Set up an initial array of cells.

```
private void initialise() {
    System.out.println();
    System.out.println("==== Initialising automata array ====");
    for (int i=0; i<barLength; i++) {
        bar[i] = (int)(Math.random() * 2);
    }
    printBar();
}
```

The constructor calls many methods. The `initialise()` method is the first of them. It sets up an displays the data using `println` statements. The for-loop sets up the values of the cells choosing randomly between 1 and 0.

Display the matrix data at the command line.

```
private void printBar() {
    for (int i=0; i<barLength; i++) {
        System.out.print(bar[i] + " ");
    }
    System.out.println();
}
```

This method prints the contents of the array to the terminal as a string of 1s or 0s. Notice that the `System.out.print()` method does not add a carriage return, after each cell value is added a `System.out.println()` method adds the 'return' at the end of the line.

Applying the CA rules for one generation.

```
    private void nextBar() {
        int sum = 0;
        for (int i=0; i<barLength; i++) {
            for (int j=1; j<3; j++) {
                if (i-j > 0) sum += bar[i - j];
                if (i+j < barLength) sum += bar[i +j];
            }
            if (sum == 0) {
                if (bar[i] == 1) tempBar[i] = 0;
                else tempBar[i] = 1;
            }
            if (sum == 1) tempBar[i] = bar[i];
            if (sum == 2) tempBar[i] = bar[i];
            if (sum == 3) {
                if (bar[i] == 1) tempBar[i] = 0;
                else tempBar[i] = 1;
            }
            if (sum == 4) {
                tempBar[i] = 0;
                sum = 0;
            }
            bar = tempBar;
        }
    }
```

This is the guts of the program. In this method the rules are applied. First, the number of live (1) cells within the range up to three places either side of the current cell are counted. Depending upon its number of active neighbors a cell either lives or dies. If it has 1 or 2 neighbors it is unchanged, if it has 3 neighbors and is alive it changes its state, and if it has four neighbors it's getting too crowded and it dies. The `tempBar` array is used to store the values of the next iteration during this process, once completed its contents are transferred to the `bar` variable and become the current state.

Create one bar of music.

```
private void makeMusic(Part p, int pitch) {
    Phrase phr = new Phrase();
    for (int i=0; i<barLength; i++) {
        if (bar[i] == 0) phr.addNote(new Note (REST, SQ));
```

```
        else phr.addNote(new Note(pitch, SQ, (int)(Math.random() * 60 + 60)));
    }
    p.addPhrase(phr);
}
```

The `makeMusic()` method turns the 1s and 0s into notes and rests. Each phrase thus created is added to the part. This method is called once for each bar of music that is required.

Programming Practice

Run the *RhythmicAutomata* program as written then try to implements the following modifications.
- changing sounds
- changing tempo
- changing bar length
- adding another part
- capturing bars then playing in reverse order - going from cohesive -> random
- changing the rules
- making it take into account 3 neighbors each side rather than 2
- starting with composed patterns rather than random patterns

CA phrases (2D)

This is a simple example which uses the *Game of Life* rules. If a cell has too many or too few neighbors it dies (metaphorically from over crowding or lack of support) if it has a moderate number it lives or comes to life. Each generation (iteration) of the game results in a new pattern of dead and alive cells. The pattern of cells can be mapped to various musical elements.

The next example is the *AutomataMusic* program that creates a melody from the values in a two-dimensional cellular automata matrix. The visual appearance of the program is shown in figure 11.2. In the program the number of 'live' cells (black) are summed each generation and this number is used to specify the pitch. Each note has a sixteenth note rhythm value.

Figure 11.2. The visual output of the two dimensional CA example program.

Let's have a look at the source code.

```
import jm.JMC;
import jm.util.*;
import jm.music.data.*;
import jm.audio.*;
import jm.audio.synth.*;
import jm.music.tools.ca.*;
import jm.gui.ca.*;
```

We import the usual suspects for the jMusic data, and the audio classes for a simple synthesis output, and the util class for MIDI and AU file writing. To access the Cellular Automata classes in jMusic we need to import the jm.music.tools.ca.* and jm.gui.ca.* packages. Within these packages the jm.music.tools.CellularAutomata class is the engine room for this program, while the graphics are in the jm.music.tools.ca.DrawCA class.

```
public class AutomataMusic implements JMC{
    static boolean[][] cells = new boolean[10][10];
    int maxNotes = 100;
    Score score = new Score("The Cellular Drunk");
    Part piano = new Part("piano",0, 0);
    Phrase phr1 = new Phrase();
    Phrase phr2 = new Phrase();
    TriangleInst triInst = new TriangleInst(44100);
```

To specify the size of the cellular matrix (how many cells) a two dimensional array (an array of arrays - i.e., a matrix) called `cells` is declared. The size of the matrix is 10 cells by 10 cells, 100 in all. All the elements for a jMusic data structure are declared, score, parts and phrases.

The last two lines declare an audio instrument that is a raw triangle waveform.

```java
public static void main(String[] args){
    new AutomataMusic();
}
```

This simple `main()` method should be familiar by now to you. It creates a new instance of the class.

```java
public AutomataMusic() {
    int liveCellCounter;
    int noteNumber;

    CellularAutomata CA = new CellularAutomata(cells.length, cells[0].length,
        0.2, false);
    cells = CA.getAllStates();

    DrawCA DCA = new DrawCA(CA,"CA Music");
    DrawCA DCA2 = new DrawCA(CA,"Big Cellular Automata Music", 30, 10, 100);
```

The constructor has most of the hard-work within it. An instance of the Cellular Automata class called CA is declared. This class is one of the three used in this program. Having it separate keeps the details of the cellular automata code out of the way so we can focus on music, and also means that we can use it in a number of pieces without having to rewrite it or cut and paste code each time.

Two instances of the `DrawCA` class are declared. We use two simply to show that the class is flexible enough to draw a cellular matrix display at any specified size. Notice that the second declaration passes additional arguments to specify a non-default size.

```java
for (int i=0;i<maxNotes;i++) {
    CA.evolve();
    cells = CA.getAllStates();
    liveCellCounter = 0;
    for (int k=0; k<cells.length; k++) {
        for (int j=0; j<cells[0].length; j++) {
            if (CA.getState(k,j) == true) liveCellCounter++;
        }
```

```
        }
        noteNumber = liveCellCounter + (127 - cells.length*cells[0].length);
        Note n = new Note(noteNumber, SQ);
        phr1.addNote(n);

        try {
            Thread.sleep(100);
            System.out.println("Iteration " + i + " of + maxNotes);
        } catch (Exception e) {}
        DCA.repaint();
        DCA2.repaint();
    }
```

In this code block most of the important work is specified. A loop is set up to repeat for the maximum number of notes we want in our score.

The CA object has it's `evolve()` method called, which applies the rules to the matrix one time.

The for-loop goes through each cell and checks it's state (on or off, true or false) and keeps a tally in the `liveCellCounter` variable.

The tally of live notes is mapped to pitch, via the variable called `noteNumber`. So that we don't get very low notes the pitch is offset. In this case the pitch offset needs to be 27 because the maximum possible on-cells = 100 and the highest allowable MIDI pitch is 127. The mathematics might look a bit complicated, but that is to allow for a wide range of possible cell matrix sizes. Of course the larger the matrix the wider the probable pitch range.

A pause is inserted into the programs thread (100 milliseconds) so that the graphics don't go too fast. This deliberately slows down the running of the program - the things we do to look pretty!

Having used the cellular automata matrix we get it to redraw its appearance in the last couple of lines of the code segment. Each of the `DrawCA` objects has its `repaint()` method called.

```
    piano.addPhrase(phr1);
    score.addPart(piano);

    Write.midi(score, "AutomataMusic.mid");
    View.show(score, 330, 10);

    Write.au(score, "AutomataMusic.au", triInst);
    System.out.println(CA.toString());
```

After looping for a number of notes we end up with a phrase. This phrase is added to the piano part, then to the score. The score is written out as a MIDI file and as an audio file using the `triInst`. The score is also displayed using the jMusic piano-roll display, `View.show()`.

The Cellular Automata structure, when mapped to pitch in this way, creates a result that is not much different from randomness. This is to some degree a tendency of Cellular Automata but especially a limitation of our very simplistic mapping. More sophisticated work on music derived from Cellular Automata has been done by composers, in particular check out the work of Eduardo Miranda which is detailed in his book *Composing Music with Computers* (2001) and Dave Burraston (Burraston, Edmonds et al. 2004).

12: Making Waves

Sound in the physical sense can be understood as waves of air pressure moving from vibrating sources to our ears. The history of trying to understand sound waves goes back at least to Pythagoras and the ancient Greeks. It is also the case that larger scale musical structures, such as phrases, are also describes a curves. In this chapter, we will explore how wave functions, typically visualized as curves and contours, can be used as both a source for compositional ideas and as a way of rendering those compositions into audio files. But, before looking at mathematically generated curves and lines can translate into musical gestures we will look at how hand drawn curves can be turned into music.

Describing Musical Gestures as Curves

Sound waves, in the acoustic sense, are described in the computer as audio samples and digital wavetables. As we have discussed in previous chapters, this is the most fundamental way in which music, as digital audio, is described within the computer and we will examine this in again later in this chapter. However, there are other levels of abstraction at which we can describe music. In particular, at the note level where individual musical events are described and at the phrase, chord, chunk or building-block level where groups of notes are considered as a single entity. Waves, or more simply curves, can be used to describe paths for music at any of these levels of abstraction. For example, it is common to visualize samples as a describing a wave form, notes as a melodic curve, and phrase structures outlining a an arch form.

Curves, in mathematics, can have more formal description as functions, for example the sine function that describes a sine wave shape. In computer music we can combine the traditional thinking of musical structures as following contours with the mathematical descriptions of lines and cures as functions. In this chapter we will see examples of how musical gestures can be described in Java at different levels of abstraction and to varying degrees of description.

Sketch

The idea of mapping curves to musical parameters was used by the composer, instrument designer and architect Iannis Xenakis in designing his UPIC system in the late 1970s in France. The UPIC name is an acronym standing for Unité Polyagogique Information de CEMAMu. The system comprises a computer based synthesizer connected to graphic tablet. The user draws lines, which Xenakis referred to as arcs, on the tablet and these were interpreted by the system as any specified musical parameter. In this way the composer could sketch his/her musical ideas as shapes and then hear them back. The connection between Xenakis' activities as an architect and composer are obvious in this design of a sonic sketch pad. The pieces *Polytope de Cluny* (1972), *Mycenae Alpha* (1978) and *Taurhiphanie* (1987) are good examples of how Xenakis used the UPIC system.

The Sketch tool in jMusic is inspired by the UPIC system but is much more simple. It can display a score in a chromatic piano roll view, and allows the user to draw lines on a panel and these are played back mapped as melodic contours, with pitch on the vertical axis and time on the horizontal, as shown in figure 12.1.

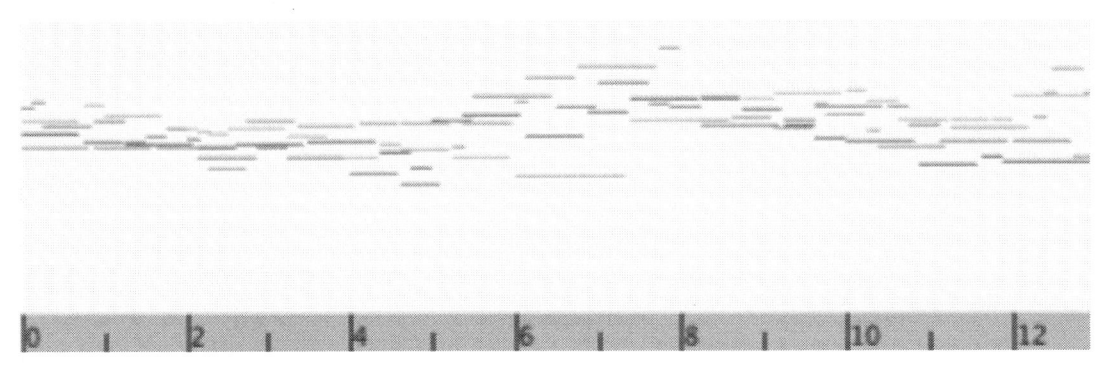

Figure 12.1: A Sketch display of a jMusic score.

In the spirit of sketching, the *FreeSketch* program opens a sketch window with a blank score. Dragging the mouse across the panel will create phrases. Selecting Play from the Sketch menu will play the score back using JavaSound's General MIDI sound bank.

```
import jm.JMC;
import jm.music.data.*;
import jm.util.View;

public class FreeSketch implements JMC {
    public static void main(String[] args) {
        Score s = new Score("Free Sketch", 120); View.sketch(s);
    }
}
```

The Sketch window is also available from the `HelperGUI` graphical interface has a `View.sketch()` button that displays the current composition and allows for free hand additions.

Generative Music

As we have seen in previous chapters, music can be composed in our imagination then transcribed into a code (Java, CPN or another), and it can be specified in broad outline and filled in by the algorithmic choices of the computer. In this section we see how music can arise as a sonic realisation of data; sonification. While all these practices are ways of generating music and sound, the term generative music usually implies that the music was created by a machine following an algorithm or heuristic principles. In a weak sense, all music made with Java could be said to be algorithmic and therefore generative, but in a strong sense of generative music the human control is secondary. A rich form of generative music is the sonification of mathematical functions and, since the current chapter is concerned with waveforms, sonification of wave functions are a good place to start.

Music from functions

A mathematical function describes a line or curve. These curves can be seen to describe a musical gesture, for example a melodic contour. A function can be mapped against any musical parameter, pitch in the case of melodic curve, or volume in the case of an amplitude envelope. The link between the function values and the musical parameters is entirely arbitrary; indeed a function may influence more than one parameter at a time. The function $x = 2 * y$ produces a straight line that moves twice as far in the horizontal direction (x) for every step it takes in the vertical direction (y). A graph of the function is shown in figure 12.2.

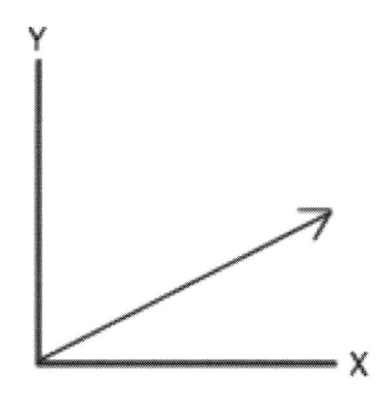

Figure 12.2: An analog trajectory.

From a statistical perspective a function is analogue, continuous and infinitely graded. However, when we map it against a chromatic note scale we get a quantized result, typical of a stepped digital output. An overlay of the stepping created by mapping the pitches is shown in figure 12.3.

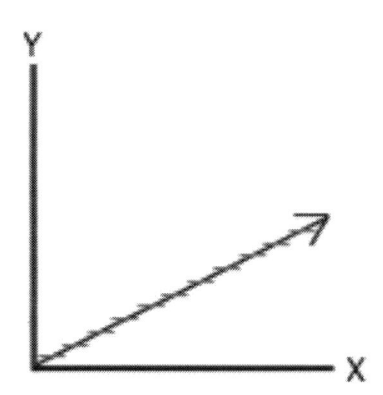

Figure 12.3: A trajectory with discrete steps.

Mapping the vertical position of the line to pitch and the horizontal length to rhythm value creates notes. Flatter, or more horizontal sections of the curve will create fewer and longer notes, while steeper more vertical sections will create more and shorter notes. We will now apply the function to notes mapping a sine wave shaped curve.

Sine wave melody

The simplest audio function is the sine wave. In this example, we will make a melody following the curve of a sine wave. It will not 'sound' like an audio sine wave – but we will get to that later in the chapter. Java has a built in method for the sine function, `Math.sin()` which we will use to do the more complicated math. The *SineMelody* program maps notes to once cycle of a sine wave curve. The pitch is calculated numerous times inside a for-loop where the variable `i` is incremented each time around.

```
int pitch = (int)(Math.sin(i/density) * 50 + 60);
```

The density variable adjusts how many notes are spread across each cycle of the sine wave. The extra math, `* 50 + 60`, is an offset to get the sine values into the range of MIDI pitches; this is an example of 'mapping' the sine data to pitch values.

The sine values relate to angles on a circle, and a full cycle of values goes once around the circle. This is why the for-loop repeats 2 `*` `PI` times. Results are multiplied by the density variable so we get a reasonable spread of values and to match the density divider in the sine function. The

SineMelody program extends `HelperGUI` the implementation of which has been shown previously, so only the `compose()` method is shown here.

```
public Score compose() {
    Score score = new Score("Sine melody", 130);
    Part p = new Part("Melody", MARIMBA, 0);
    Phrase phr = new Phrase();
    double density = 25.0;
    for (int i = 0; i < (2*3.14*density); i++) {
        int pitch = (int)(Math.sin(i/density) * 50 + 60);
        Note note = new Note(pitch, THIRTYSECOND_NOTE);
        phr.addNote(note);
    }
    p.addPhrase(phr);
    score.addPart(p);
    return score;
}
```

Extensions of this program could include changing the sine function for a different one. Some simple additive synthesis sonification is interesting to experiment with. Here, for example, is the code to sonify the result of adding this sine wave with another an octave above it (the fundamental with the first harmonic).

```
(int)((Math.sin(i/density) + Math.sin(i/density*2))/2*50+60);
```

The function shape in this example simply provides a melodic curve, and can be played back by any instrument.

Fractal music

Any mathematical function can be sonified in the way the sine function was above. Another popular set of functions to sonify are fractals. Fractal patterns are renowned for their self-similarity of structure. That is, patterns are one level are repeated at larger and smaller scales. The classic example in nature is the fern branch, where each sub-branch is a miniature version of the larger branch. Visualizations of fractal sets are also popular, depicted as colorful images of semi-organic appearance such as the Mandelbrot set. The inherent structure of fractal patterns has lead many to hope they may be useful in generating music. This turns out to be partially true, but like most mathematical music mappings, they work best when there are considerable constraints in place. The program `Fractal.java` implements a pitch mapping of fractals. It extends the `HelperGUI` which makes it convenient to generate new melodies one after another to observe the fractal patterns. In this example the pitches are constrained to the C major scale. Below is the code for making music by mapping fractals to pitch. The Fractal algorithm is based on one by R. F. Voss as cited in *Computer Music* by Charles Dodge and Jerse (1997:369).

```java
import jm.JMC;
import jm.music.data.*;
import jm.util.*;

public final class Fractal implements JMC {
    Score score = new Score("JMDemo - Fractal");
    Part part = new Part("Piano", PIANO);
    Phrase phr = new Phrase();

    float sum;
    float[] rg = new float[16];
    int k, kg, ng, threshold;
    int np = 1;
    int nbits = 1;
    int npts = 48; //number of notes
    float nr = (float)(npts);

    public static void main(String[] args){
        Fractal fract = new Fractal();
    }

    public Fractal() {
        part.addPhrase(phr);
        score.addPart(part);
        setupMath();
        calcNotes();
        output();
    }

    private void setupMath() {
        nr = nr/2;
        System.out.println("Calculating fractal melody. . .");
        while (nr > 1) {
            nbits++;
            np = 2 * np;
            nr = nr/2;
        }
        for (kg=0; kg<nbits; kg++) {
```

```java
                rg[kg] = (float)(Math.random());
            }
        }

        private void calcNotes() {
            for (k=0; k<npts; k++) {
                threshold = np;
                ng = nbits;
                while(k%threshold != 0) {
                    ng--;
                    threshold = threshold / 2;
                }
                sum = 0;
                for (kg=0; kg<nbits; kg++) {
                    if (kg<ng) rg[kg]=(float)(Math.random());
                    sum += rg[kg];
                }
                Note note = new Note((int)(sum/nbits*127), Q);
                phr.addNote(note);
            }
        }

        private void output() {
            View.show(score);
            Write.midi(score, "FractalMusic.mid")
        }
    }
```

More information about creating music from fractals can be found in "Computer Music" by Charles Dodge and Thomas A Jerse (1997), "Composing Music with computers" by Eduardo Miranda (2001), and "Fractals in Music" by Charles Madden (1999).

Audio Instruments

Audio instruments are at the core of jMusic's audio features, in the same way that Notes are at the centre of its musical structures. An instrument is an audio data generating class, that can be used to render scores as audio files based on digital audio data from either files or synthesis processes. The declaration of a new instrument is quite straight forward, as in this declaration of the `SineInst` instrument which is a simple sine wave oscillator.

```
Instrument sineWave = new SineInst();
```

There are a number of instruments that are included with the jMusic package, but not an exhaustive list. When designing jMusic we intended that people would build their own instruments so that their music takes on a unique character. Most instruments have constructors with options to specify sample rate and channels, and some instruments take arguments about timbral options such as filter cut-off frequency, modulation amounts, detuning, and so on. These vary from instrument to instrument, and when designing your own you can specify what suits your circumstances. A file destined for burning to an audio CD would be stereo and have a sample rate of 44100, as specified below.

```
Instrument sineWave = new SineInst(44100, 2);
```

Details of instrument design are covered in later chapters, for now we'll use instruments provided with jMusic. When a score is rendered to an audio file, each part specifies an instrument to use with a number in the same way General MIDI instrument numbers were specified.

```
Part arpPart = new Part("Arpeggio Part", 0);
```

Notice, that for parts intended for rendering to audio files, the channel argument is not required. It was used to specify a MIDI channel which is not relevant for audio. If a channel is included it will be ignored by the audio rendering process.

For scores that require more than one instrument we can create an array that holds all the instruments. For example,

```
Instrument[] ensemble = {sineWave, FMBrass, FatBass};
```

Parts access instruments according to the instrument location within the array. In this example, `sineWave` is instrument 0, `FMBrass` is instrument 1, and `FatBass` is instrument 2.

Write.au()

Rendering the score with the instruments will generate an audio file. This is done using the `au()` method of the `Write` class, and passing three arguments; the score, file name, and instrument (or instrument array). For example,

```
Write.au(score, "Arpeggio.au", sineWave);
```

Audio files generated by this method are in the au format. This format is well supported by Java but may not be supported by other applications you have. The file can easily be converted to another format by a program such as *Amadeus Pro*, *SoX*, *SoundHack*, or *Audacity*.

The rendered file will have one or more channels depending upon the instruments used. Most instruments default to mono (one channel) or stereo (two channels), but instruments, and the au format can support any number of channels. However, only mono and stereo files can be played back inside Java.

```
Play.au();
```

To play back an au file from disk us the `Play.au()` method, and pass it the file name to be played.

```
Play.au("Arpeggio.au");
```

For convenience, the HelperGUI can be used to play back an audio files from classes that extend it.

Audio rendering

Now, let's look at an example that uses these audio features of jMusic. In the *Arpeggio* program a score of a repeating phrase is created first. Then, a sine wave instrument is declared and used to render the score as an audio file to disk. Finally, the file is played back. This program has only three lines that make it different from the previous MIDI-based programs. These deal with the audio instrument declaration, file rendering, and file playback.

```
Instrument sineWave = new SineInst();
Write.au(score, "Arpeggio.au", sineWave);
Play.au("Arpeggio.au");
```

Here is a listing of the entire Arpeggio program.

```
import jm.JMC;
import jm.music.data.*;
import jm.music.tools.*;
import jm.util.*;
import jm.audio.*;

public class Arpeggio implements JMC {

    public static void main(String[] args) {
        new Arpeggio();
    }

    public Arpeggio() {
```

```
            int[] pitches = {D2, D2, D3, D3, A2, A3, F3, C3};
            Phrase arpPhrase = new Phrase();
            for (int i = 0; i < 16; i++) {
                int pitchIndex = (int)(Math.random() * pitches.length);
                Note n = new Note(pitches[pitchIndex], EIGHTH_NOTE);
                arpPhrase.addNote(n);
            }
            Mod.repeat(arpPhrase, 4);
            Part arpPart = new Part("Arpeggio Part", 0, arpPhrase);
            Score score = new Score("Arpeggio Score", 145, ArpPart);
            Instrument sineWave = new SineInst();
            Write.au(score, "Arpeggio.au", sineWave);
            Play.au("Arpeggio.au");
        }
    }
```

Seeing the audio data

While hearing the audio file is most important for music making, it is also interesting to see the data. The data can be visualised in the form of a graph plotting the values over time and as a list of raw numerical values. The values stored in the audio file are the momentary amplitude values from each sample time. The data can be plotted on an amplitude time graph, which will reveal the up and down 'wave' motion of the sound; a characteristic that leads it to be called a 'sound wave.' The values themselves are relative, rather than absolute. Their values depend upon the range and type of numbers used to store them. In the au (and most other) file formats, the data are integers and their range is determined by the bit resolution. Even more accuracy can be achieved by storing the data as floating-point values, which are how most professional-quality computer music applications, including jMusic, deal with the data. Normally, the range of floating point data is from 1.0 to –1.0, however, processing and addition of waveforms can involve higher numbers. The number of possible floating point values between 1 and –1 is also very large, providing exceptional resolution. When audio data is read or written to file from jMusic it is converted from floating point to integer values. We can see the waveform data plotted against time and the floating point sample values using an instrument specifically designed for this task, the `PrintSineInst` instrument.

Print instrument

The *PrintAudio* program prints the sample values out to the screen rather than to a file, so you can see what's going on. It consists of the three lines below inside the main method. Only a very short note is required because audio data rates can be thousands of samples per second, and in this display each line represents one value. In this program, a compact way of creating a simplistic jMusic score is shown where each music data object is taken as an argument to constructing the one that contains it. A file called name.au is written, but is empty and can be deleted.

```
Score s = new Score(new Part(new Phrase(new Note(C4, 0.01))));
Instrument inst = new PrintSineInst(4000);
Write.au(s, "name.au", inst);
```

The result of running this program will appear similar to figure 12.4. The 'o' characters plot the amplitude where higher values are to the right, and the precise sample values are shown in a column on the right of the display.

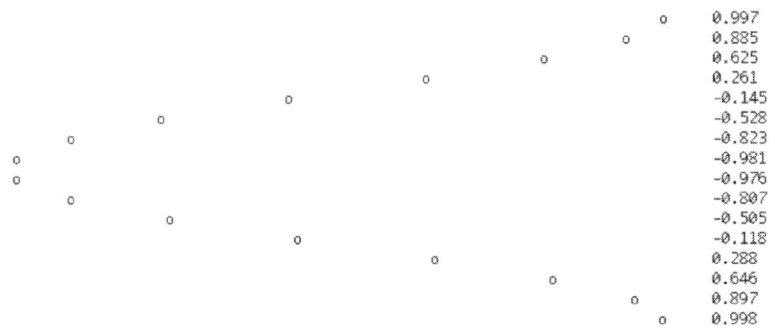

```
                                        o      0.997
                                    o          0.885
                                o              0.625
                            o                  0.261
                        o                     -0.145
                    o                         -0.528
                o                             -0.823
            o                                 -0.981
            o                                 -0.976
                o                             -0.807
                    o                         -0.505
                        o                     -0.118
                            o                  0.288
                                o              0.646
                                    o          0.897
                                        o      0.998
```

Figure 12.4. PrintAudio output.

There are a few of important things to notice about the data. The numbers are floating point values. All audio processing in jMusic happens as floating point numbers which ensures that the resolution (quality) is extremely high. The numbers are both positive and negative. The audio values centre around zero with louder values being those most distant from zero. The numbers are close to zero in value. Numbers produced by each note in jMusic are between -1.0 and 1.0 in value and so if three notes play at the same time their combined maximum value will be 3.0 or -3.0. Because the largest floating point values in Java can be in the millions you can see that there is plenty of head room in the use of floating point values (we can have very dense textures without the risk of distortion from clipping).

View.au()

A more conventional waveform display is available in jMusic and can be accessed with the View class. To see the output of the *Arpeggio* program using this viewer, add this line to the end of the program.

```
View.au("Arpeggio.au");
```

The .au() method takes the name of an audio file on the hard disk as an argument. At present only files in the .au format (the one used by jMusic and Java) can be read. The output will look similar to figure 12.5.

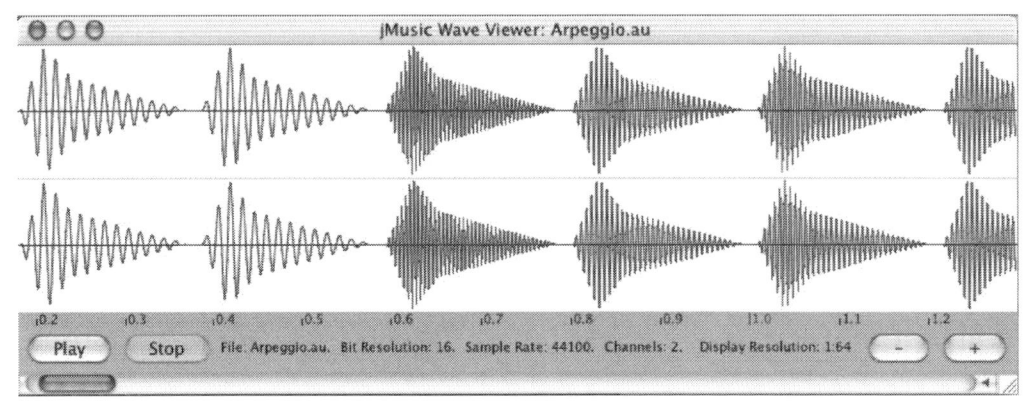

Figure 12.5. Wave viewer.

Viewing the waveform can reveal many attributes of the wave, some that can be heard others that cannot. For example, in figure 12.5 the duration (length) of each note is identical but notes of different pitches have a different texture due to the width of sine wave cycles. The wave viewer has many features that you can discover for yourself.

Here are a few of them; starting at the bottom.

- Scroll through the waveform with the horizontal scroll bar.

- Zoom in and out to see the wave a different resolutions using the '-' and '+' buttons or by dragging the time display ruler.

- Play the file with the 'Play' button. Use the 'Stop' button to halt playback.

- The time display ruler shows the position in time of the currently displayed wave section.

- Menu's duplicate many of the features just mentioned but also include;

- Opening a new file and quitting the viewer.

- Changing the colors of the display.

- Changing the height of the waveform display.

- Increasing the amplitude scaling (useful for inspection of quiet sections).

Making Music with Java

There is a View.au() button on the HelperGUI interface to allow display of composed files in the waveform viewer. The details required to make the HelperGUI work with audio are outlined below.

SineTest

This program generates sine waves with only a small frequency difference between them, the concurrent playback of these will produces audible 'beating' that emerges from the interaction between the sine waves. The speed of this beating is determined by the ratio between the sine wave frequencies. Listening for beating between sounds that are close in pitch is a common technique for tuning instruments, particularly stringed instruments such as guitar, violin, and piano.

```
import jm.JMC;
import jm.music.data.*;
import jm.midi.*;
import jm.util.Write;
import jm.util.Read;
import jm.util.View;
import jm.audio.Instrument;
import jm.music.tools.Mod;

public final class SineTest implements JMC{
    public static void main(String[] args){
        Score s = new Score();
        s.setTempo(60);
        Part p = new Part("Sine", 0);

        Phrase phr = new Phrase(0.0);
        for (int i=0; i<50;i++) {
            Note n = new Note(Math.random()*100+1000, 4.0);
            n.setPan(Math.random());
            Phrase phrase2  = new Phrase(n, Math.random()*30);
            p.addPhrase(phrase2);
        }
        p.addPhrase(phr);
        s.addPart(p);

        View.show(s);

        Instrument inst = new SineInst(22000);
```

```
            Write.au(s,"SineTest.au", inst);
    }
}
```

Rendering with samples

In this section, well see how pre-recorded audio can be read from disk and included as part of a composition. The audio file may be short, like a snare drum hit, or long, like a field recording from nature. A `Part` will correspond to the audio file when it is the sound source of an instrument. Therefore, `Notes` in that part are audio events that indicate when and for how long the sample is played within the score. An instrument that does this is the `SimpleSampleInst` instrument. Having the ability to use samples for rendering your compositions means you can access almost any sound (voices, instruments, sound effects, etc.) for your music - all you need do is record it as a digital audio file. The `SimpleSampleInst` allows jMusic scores to be rendered with digital audio recordings as sound sources. A simple analogy is to think of a MIDI sequencer sending 'notes' to a sampler for playback. Samples will playback for the duration of the note (or the length of the file, if that is shorter) by default, but the instrument can be set to play entire files regardless of the note duration. This later behavior is often used in drum machines. The `SimpleSampleInst` has three constructors.

```
    Instrument inst = new SimpleSampleInst("FileName.au");
```

The first constructor takes the filename as an argument. It sets other parameters to default settings, including the base frequency to 440 hertz (A4). The base frequency is the assumed pitch of the sample, and notes in the score at the base frequency (by default A4) will play back the sample at the recorded pitch. Notes with other pitches will cause the sample to play back higher or lower, relative to the base frequency.

```
    Instrument inst = new SimpleSampleInst("FileName.au", FRQ[C2]);
```

The second constructor takes the filename and a base frequency as arguments. It is common to use the JMC frequency constants for the frequency, but a double value indicating a specific frequency can be used. For example, `FRQ[C4]` is a constant specifying the frequency of middle C.

```
    Instrument inst = new SimpleSampleInst("FileName.au", FRQ[C2], true);
```

The third constructor adds an argument indicating whether or not the whole length of the sample regardless of the note's duration. The argument is a `Boolean` value (true or false). The default value is false, indicating that the sample will play for the duration of the note. You may have noticed that there have been no arguments for sample rate or number of channels, parameters that are often required for synthesis instruments. The `SimpleSampleInst` uses the sample rate and channel of the sample file, therefore the rendered file has the same specifications in this regard as the input sample.

Each SimpleSampleInst is associated with one audio file. A collage of sound files can be created using many instances of the `SimpleSampleInst`, and scores can combine sample-based and synthesis-based instruments. Also, remember that other instruments can be designed with additional features and controls that you may require. One current restriction is that each instrument used to render the a score must use the same sample rate and channel attributes.

The *SampleRender* program, shown below, uses the `SimpleSampleInst` to construct a short 'melody' from a spoken word sample.

```
import jm.JMC;
import jm.music.data.*;
import jm.util.*;
import jm.audio.*;

public class SampleRender implements JMC {
    public static void main(String[] args) {
        new SampleRender();
    }
    public SampleRender() {
        int[] pitchArray = {C4, G3, C4, E4, F4, G4, C5, G5, G4, G3, G2, C3};
        double[] rhythmArray = {1.0, 0.25, 0.25, 0.25,0.25,
                0.5, 0.5, 0.125, 0.125, 0.25, 0.5, 2.0};
        Phrase phr = new Phrase();
        phr.addNoteList(pitchArray, rhythmArray);
        Score score = new Score(new Part (phr));
        Instrument ssi = new SimpleSampleInst("Hi.au", FRQ[C4]);
        Write.au(score, "SampleRender.au", ssi);
        View.au("SampleRender.au");
    }
}
```

Rendering audio with any file

In the final analysis digital audio data is simply a list of numbers. Therefore, it is a logical step that any list of numbers can be turned into an audio file. All computer files consist of numbers and can therefore be sonified. The data in most files will simply sound like noise bursts because it is not intended to be organized in any musical way, nevertheless, this can still be an interesting exercise and a basis for creative musical application. jMusic includes an instrument specifically designed to read any file as sample data, the `TextInst` class. It can read a text file, such as a java source file, or any other file for that matter and, like all jMusic instruments, use the data to render a score. The code fragment below shows the details, minus the necessary Java class and method declarations. In this example the `TextInst` constructor does not take any arguments, instead when run it opens a file dialogue window to prompt for a file. Alternatively, a file name can be passed as a string to the instrument.

```
Score s = new Score(new Part(new Phrase(new Note(A4, 4.0))));
Instrument inst = new TextInst();
Write.au(s, "TextAudio.au", inst);
View.au("TextAudio.au");
```

Audio and the HelperGUI

We have mentioned that many of the audio features of jMusic are accessible via the `HelperGUI` and this section describes the details of this. When the `HelperGUI`'s Compose button is clicked the `compose()` method is run. Overriding the `compose()` method is required by programs wishing to use `HelperGUI` for MIDI and audio. It is assumed that the class that extends `HelperGUI` overrides the `compose()` method, and that method returns a score. This is the score that is used by `Write.au()`, `View.au()` and `Play.au()`. In addition, for audio, the `HelperGUI` class has an instrument array variable called `insts` which must be instantiated. When `insts` is not null, the `HelperGUI` enables the audio buttons. Here is an example of how the `insts` variable can be instantiated.

```
Instrument squareWave = SquareInst(44100, 2);
insts = new Instrument[] {squareInst};
```

Notice that the `insts` variable is not declared in this class because it is inherited from the `HelperGUI` class.

Adding audio to an arpeggio program

Let us now create an arpeggio class that overlaps several arpeggio patterns at one time and we will render it as both MIDI and audio files, the latter using the filtered sawtooth-wave audio instrument, *SawLPFInstF*. Each arpeggio line has its own pitch array, and each is kept in a separate part to enable different sounds to be used. An `arpeggiator()` method is used by each of the lines, and it takes a number of arguments allowing each line to produce a different outcome from the same method. Here is the full source code for the *ArpAudioMidi* program.

```
import jm.JMC;
```

```java
import jm.music.data.*;
import jm.util.*;
import jm.music.tools.Mod;
// This version creates several parts and adds them
// to a score. Several patterns can be used also.
// There is an accent added at quarter note intervals.
// The repeat length is modified to suite the pattern length.
public class ArpAudioMidi implements JMC {
    int[] pattern1 = {0,3,7,0};
    int[] pattern2 = {0,12,10,7,0,3,5,7};
    int[] pattern3 = {3,7,15,19};
    int[] progression = {0,2,0,5,0};
    int repeats = 8;
    double tempo = 130.0;
    Score arpScore = new Score("Argeggio Music", tempo);
    Part arpPart, arpPart2, arpPart3;

    public static void main(String[] args) {
        ArpAudioMidi myArp = new ArpAudioMidi();
        myArp.makeScore();
        myArp.saveAs();
    }
    public void makeScore() {
        // bass
        arpPart = new Part("Apreggio 1", SYNTH_BASS, 1);
        // part, root, arp pattern, random?
        arpeggiator(arpPart, C2, pattern1, true);
        arpScore.addPart(arpPart);
        // upper part
        arpPart2 = new Part("Apreggio 2", POLYSYNTH, 2);
        arpeggiator(arpPart2, C5, pattern2, false);
        arpScore.addPart(arpPart2);
        // middle part
        arpPart3 = new Part("Apreggio 3", SYNVOX, 3);
        arpeggiator(arpPart3, C3, pattern3, true);
        arpScore.addPart(arpPart3);
    }
    public void arpeggiator(Part arpPart, int rootNote, int[] pattern,
            boolean randomOrder) {
        for (int j=0; j<progression.length; j++) {
```

```java
                Phrase phr = new Phrase(j * repeats);
                for (int i=0; i<pattern.length; i++ ) {
                    if (randomOrder) {
                        phr.addNote(new Note(rootNote +
                            pattern[(int)(Math.random() * pattern.length)]
                            , SIXTEENTH_NOTE));
                    } else {
                        phr.addNote(new Note(rootNote + pattern[i],
                            SIXTEENTH_NOTE));
                    }
                }
                Mod.repeat(phr, repeats * 4/pattern.length);
                Mod.transpose(phr, progression[j]);
                Mod.accents(phr, 0.5);
                arpPart.addPhrase(phr);
            }
        }
        public void saveAs() {
            Write.midi(arpScore, "Arp4.mid");
            arpPart.setInstrument(0);
            arpPart2.setInstrument(0);
            arpPart3.setInstrument(0);
            Instrument inst = new SawLPFInstF(44100);
            Write.au(arpScore, "ArpAudio.au", inst);
        }
    }
```

Java Data Structures

Java provides a number of classes designed for storing data. Each of these has particular features that make it optimal for certain storage requirements. We will look at two of the most fundamental types, a fixed length list call an `Array` in Java, and a dynamic list call a `Vector` in Java.

Arrays

Arrays are data structures that contain a list of elements. Arrays are of a fixed size and hold data of a specific type. For example, `int[] myArray = new int[8];` declares a new array that can contain eight integer values. It is possible to create arrays of any Java data type. To assign an element to the first position in the array use the array name followed by the element to add to inside square brackets. For example, `myArray[0] = 34;`

To access an element in an array use the position in the array. To get the third element of `myArray` declared above, use `myArray[2];`. Notice that because we start counting at zero, 2 is the third element.

Vectors

Vectors are dynamic arrays of objects. Vectors can expand and contract as elements are added to them or deleted from them (unlike arrays that have a fixed size). To create a vector use the following code, `Vector myVector = new Vector();`.

To add an element to a vector use the `addElement()` method. For example, to add a note n to myVector use the code, `myVector.addElement(n);` vectors can only contain Java objects, and you can also add primitive types (such as int, float, double, or boolean) to a vector.

To retrieve an element from a vector use, `Note n2 = (Note)myVector.getElementAt(0);` This may look a bit complicated at first. It is necessary to specify the vector index to the `getElementAt()` method. It will be returned as type `object` from the array and therefore must be cast (converted) into the type required – in this case a `Note`.

Inheritance

Classes may extend another class, which means that the new class will inherit all the functionality of the previous class it extended. This is called inheriting the features of the class. The new class can then add more data or functionality as required. The notion of inheritance is an important aspect of object oriented programming. It is useful when class requirements are similar but not identical. A class with the overlapping functions can be created and each of the specific classes can extend the one with the base functionality. When a class is declared is may extend another class, like in this example;

```
public class Car extends MotorVehicle {
    ….class info. here …
}
```

An example of inheritance in the jMusic library is the `cpn` package that has classes to display a phase as common practice notation. Notes are displayed as CPN on a stave. All staves are similar, in that they have five lines and should display notes and rests, so jMusic has a `Stave` class that outlines these features. There is a `TrebleStave` and a `BassStave` class that each extend the `Stave` class. Each of these extended classes positions notes in a different location, for example middle C on the `TrebleStave` is one ledger line below the stave, while the same pitch in the

`BassStave` is positioned one ledger line above the stave. They also have different clefs displayed at the beginning of the stave. Otherwise they share functions including note images, dragging capabilities, rhythmic spacing and so on.

13: Sonic Spectra

Audio waveforms can be viewed from at least two perspectives, in the amplitude domain (as pressure changes over time) and in the frequency domain (as a summation of sine tones at different frequencies). In previous chapters we focused on audio in the time domain. In this chapter we will continue this by examining pitch and frequency in more detail, and explore aspects of sound spectra in the frequency domain including the harmonic series, timbre, and related compositional practices.

Music in the Physical World

Music is the perception of organized sound, and sound is created by moving objects. As a result it is not surprising that the studies of music and physics come together quite naturally. To create music or sound with a computer is to recreate the vibrating properties of physical or imaginary sonic devices and to stimulate loud speakers to produce these sounds. In the following sections we will look at some of the aspects of music and sound where physics plays an important role.

Pitch in hertz

Pitches sounds involve repeating waveforms, often called periodic waves, that have a fundamental pitch which is determined by how frequently the wave repeats. The time between the onset of each repletion is the period of the wave. Waveforms with a longer period have a lower fundamental frequency and pitch. Shorter periods equate to a higher fundamental frequency and pitch. The simplest periodic waveform is the sine wave, but all pitched sounds are periodic.

When `Notes` are constructed in jMusic their pitch can be specified as a MIDI note value or as a frequency in hertz. Notes can take an `int` or a `double` value as a pitch value. When taking an `int` value it is assumed that a MIDI note number (i.e., 60 = C4) are desired. When taking a `double` value for pitch, it is assumed the value is a frequency in hertz (i.e., 440.0 = A4). Because note frequency is represented as a double value (64 bit fractional) the pitch accuracy available in jMusic is ridiculously fine (e.g., 1026.08940567 Hz). This is great news for micro-tonal composers. When specifying the frequency value, division can be used as a convenient way of accurately calculating harmonic intervals from a fundamental. For example,

```
Note noteE5just = new Note(440.0 * 3 / 2, CROTCHET);
```

Microtonality

Each note on the piano, or any other instrument, has a particular frequency. The lower the note pitch, the slower the frequency. The frequency changes by a factor of two each octave. So when A4 has a frequency of 440 hertz, A5 is 880 hertz, A6 is 1720 hertz and A3 is 220 hertz, and so on. There are clearly many more frequencies than there are chromatic pitches, and in this section we will explore how to generate notes of any frequency.

The *PitchInHertz* example uses the `SineInst` instrument that produces a simple sine wave tone.

```
Instrument inst = new SineInst(22000);
```

The `SineInst` instrument is one of a number of instruments that ship with jMusic. The argument, 22000, specifies the sample rate. This will determine the quality and highest fundamental frequency of the sound. For sine waves, who don't have complex harmonics spectrum to consider, sample rate only influences the highest frequency that can be played. This highest playable frequency is determined the Nyquist frequency, which is approximately half the sample rate – in this case 11000 hertz. Higher sample rates will take longer to render and create larger files simply because the number of calculations and samples increase, but they will enable sounds of higher quality.

Pitches in this example are randomly chosen between 500 and 1500 hertz. The duration of each note (sine tone) is four beats. Because the default tempo is 60 bpm, four beats equals four seconds in duration.

```
Note note = new Note(Math.random() * 500 + 1000, 4.0);
```

There is likely to be some quite dissonant relationships (non simple ratios) between frequencies, when chosen at random. Interaction between these tones will cause an amplitude fluctuation effect called beating, which sound like a tremolo. Here is the complete code for *PitchInHertz*.

```
import jm.JMC;
import jm.music.data.*;
import jm.util.View;
import jm.util.Write;
import jm.audio.Instrument;

public final class PitchInHertz implements JMC {
    public static void main(String[] args) {
        Score score = new Score("Frequency Score");
        Part part = new Part("A Part", 0);
        for (int i=0; i<20; i++) {
```

```
            Note note = new Note(Math.random()*500+1000,4.0);
            note.setPan(Math.random());
            Phrase phrase = new Phrase(note, Math.random()*10);
            part.addPhrase(phrase);
        }
        score.addPart(part);
        Instrument inst = new SineInst(22000);
        Write.au(score, "SineTest.au", inst);
        View.print(score);
    }
}
```

Math Moment

Linear and non-linear: When considering the relationship between chromatic pitch and frequency it is clear that the two are not equal. In fact, the chromatic pitch scale is linear, every step is the same distance apart – one half-step (semitone), while the frequency scale is exponential, every octave step is double the previous one. We say that the frequency spectrum is non-linear. As well, the common practice notation stave is non linear also because a some steps between lines and spaces are a half-step (semitone) while others are a whole-step (tone). In many cases conversion between linear and non-linear systems can become quite complex. As you can imagine there are many non-linear systems, because any relationship that does not have a 1:1 ratio at each step is non-linear. Another example of nonlinearity is the loudness scale, measured in decibels. Decibels are measured on a logarithmic scale. However, MIDI velocity values and mixing desk sliders usually generate linear values, therefore conversion between these scales is almost always taking place in the software or hardware device. These linear and non-linear measuring relationships are not arbitrary, they are based on the way physical systems in our world operate and on how our brain perceives them, therefore they are systems we need to understand as we create music in Java.

Tuning systems

Tuning systems define a set of pitches at particular frequencies. In many cases (but not always) the tuning system defines a pitch pattern within one octave and relative to a starting pitch; a pattern which is repeated in higher and lower octaves. By convention, modern Western music uses the chromatic tuning system which divides and octave into twelve equal steps. Other tuning systems divide the octave into more or less steps, for example a pentatonic system would have five steps, and the relationship between steps may vary widely. Even the term octave, implying eight, is derivative of the western system of eight note scale, but we will use it here to describe a range between one frequency and another double it. As you can imagine the range of possible tuning systems is massive, and even the number of rational systems is very large indeed. We will only explore a few in this book. Each system has its own characteristic sound, and so the choice of tuning system has an important musical impact.

Many tuning systems derive frequencies from the integer ratios inherent in the harmonic series. For example, the ratios 1:2, 1:3, 2:3, 15:8, and so on. In fact, the chromatic system in common use is uncommon in this regard. Intervals that are tuned to integer ratios will sound without beating, as 'pure' intervals, however, these ratios only remain pure in one key. Therefore, designers of tuning systems make a trade-off between consistency of intervallic purity and freedom of harmonic modulation. As an example, we will compare the chromatic and just-tuned scales. The chromatic system maximizes the freedom of harmonic modulation while the just system maximizes intervallic purity. Below is a table with the ratios of each diatonic step in a Major scale with the intervallic ratios of each step to the root pitch.

	Root	2nd	3rd	4th	5th	6th	7th	Octave
Chromatic	1:1	1:1.06	1:1.26	1:1.33	1.49	1:1.68	1:88	2:1
Just	1:1	9:8	5:4	4:3	3:2	5:3	15:8	2:1

The chromatic scale, as previously mentioned, divides the octave into twelve equal steps, and this means that some intervals are slightly sharp (above) the just interval, while others are slightly flat (below). The just system focuses on making important intervals beat-free, including the perfect fourth, fifth and both major and minor thirds. An advantage is that primary triads sound quite pure, but the disadvantage is that the size of half steps (semi-tones) is uneven and some can be quite dissonant.

The example program *TuningSystems* renders a score in four different tuning systems for easy comparison. As well as chromatic and just, the pythagorean and mean tuning systems are used. Each tuning system is represented in the program as an array of frequency multipliers for each step in the scale. These values are relative to the chosen root frequency.

```
double[] pythagorean = {1.0, 1.053, 1.125, 1.185, 1.265, 1.333,
     1.404, 1.5, 1.58, 1.687, 1.778, 1.898};
```

The pitches are represented as MIDI note numbers, 60, 61 and so on, and these are converted into the appropriate frequency depending upon their scale degree. Where `i` is the index to the current note in the phrase.

```
double pitch = FRQ[pitches[i]-degree] * pythagorean [degree] * octave;
```

The scale degree and octave need to be calculated for each note prior to this frequency calculation.

```
int degree = pitches[i]%12;
```

```
    double octave = (int)(pitches[i] / 12 - 5) * 2.0;
    if (octave == 0) octave = 1;
    if (octave < 0) octave = -1 * (octave/1.0);
```

Here is the full code for the tuning systems example:

```java
import jm.music.data.*;
import jm.JMC;
import jm.util.*;
import jm.audio.Instrument;

public final class TuningSystems implements JMC{
    public static void main(String[] args){
        new TuningSystems();
    }
    // Batok Mikrokosmos
    public TuningSystems() {
        // soprano
        int[] pitchSop = {G4,A4,B4,BF4,A5,AS5,B4,A4,BF4,AF4,G4,A4,B4,BF4,
                C5,CS5,D5,CS5,B4,C5,BF4,C5,B4,A4,BF4,G4,D5,CS5,B4,C5,BF4,
                C5,B4,A4,BF4,G4,REST,E4,A4,BF4,REST,E4,A4,B4,REST,
                E4,A4,C5,REST};
        double[] rhythmSop = {Q,Q,Q,Q,Q,Q,Q,Q,Q,Q,Q,Q,Q,Q,Q,2.5,
            Q,Q,Q,Q,Q,Q,Q,Q,Q,Q,Q,Q,Q,Q,Q,Q,Q,Q,Q,
            C,Q,Q,Q,C,Q,Q,Q,C,Q,Q,Q,2.5};
        // alto
        int[] pitchAlto = {G4,D4,CS4,D4,G4,D4,A3, REST, E4,DS4,CS4,
                REST,D4,CS4,B3,FS4,CS4,REST,FS4,CS4,REST,FS4,CS4,REST,F3};
        double[] rhythmAlto = {DC,C,DC,C,DC,C,2.5,DC,C,DC,C,DC,C,DC,C,
            Q,Q,DC,Q,Q,DC,Q,Q,DC,2.5};
        //set up the instruments
        Instrument insts = new SquareLPFInst(44100);
        //test
        Phrase phr = new Phrase();
        for (int i=0; i<56; i++) {
            phr.addNote(new Note(i+24, SQ));
        }
        Score s = new Score(new Part(phr));
        // tuning system frequency ratios
        double[] chromatic = {1.0,1.059,1.122,1.189,1.26,1.335,1.414,1.498,
                1.587, 1.682, 1.782, 1.888};
```

```java
        double[] pythagorean = {1.0,1.053,1.125,1.185,1.265,1.333,1.404,1.5,
            1.58, 1.687, 1.778, 1.898};
        double[] just = {1.0,1.067,1.125,1.2,1.25,1.333,1.406,1.5,1.6,1.667,
            1.8, 1.875};
        double[] mean = {1.0,1.07,1.118,1.196,1.25,1.337,1.398,1.496,1.6,
            1.672, 1.789, 1.869};
        //create a score and render it as an audio file
        Score chromaticScore = new Score("Chorale", 130);
        chromaticScore.addPart(createPart(pitchSop, rhythmSop, 0, chromatic));
        chromaticScore.addPart(createPart(pitchAlto, rhythmAlto, 1,
            chromatic));
        Write.au(chromaticScore, "ChromaticTuning.au", insts);
        //create and render a score
        Score pythagoreanScore = new Score("Chorale", 130);
        pythagoreanScore.addPart(createPart(pitchSop, rhythmSop, 0,
            pythagorean));
        pythagoreanScore.addPart(createPart(pitchAlto, rhythmAlto, 1,
            pythagorean));
        Write.au(s, "PythagoreanTuning.au", insts);
        //create and render another score
        Score justScore = new Score("Chorale", 130);
        justScore.addPart(createPart(pitchSop, rhythmSop, 0, just));
        justScore.addPart(createPart(pitchAlto, rhythmAlto, 1, just));
        Write.au(justScore, "JustTuning.au", insts);
        //create and render yet another score
        Score meanScore = new Score("Chorale", 130);
        meanScore.addPart(createPart(pitchSop, rhythmSop, 0, mean));
        meanScore.addPart(createPart(pitchAlto, rhythmAlto, 1, mean));
        Write.au(meanScore, "MeanTuning.au", insts);
    }
    /*
    * This method converts the pitch and rhythm data into notes
    * and packs them into a part with a specified tuning system.
    */
    private Part createPart(int[] pitches, double[] rhythms, int instrument,
            double[] modeRatios) {
        Part part = new Part("", 0); //instrument);
        Phrase phrase = new Phrase();
        // add notes
        for (int i=0; i<pitches.length; i++) {
```

```
            if (pitches[i] == REST ) {
                int pitch = REST;
                phrase.addNote(new Note(pitch, rhythms[i]));
            } else {
                int degree = pitches[i]%12; // assumes we're in C maj or A min
                double octave = (int)(pitches[i] / 12 - 5) * 2.0;
                if (octave == 0) octave = 1;
                if (octave < 0) octave = -1 * (octave/1.0);
                double pitch = FRQ[pitches[i] - degree] * modeRatios[degree] *
                    octave;
                phrase.addNote(new Note(pitch, rhythms[i]));
            }
        }
        part.addPhrase(phrase);
        return part;
    }
}
```

The Harmonic Series

Complex sounds, such as those in the acoustic world, have a wave shape that is more complex than a single sine wave. The more complex the waveform, the more uneven and jagged the waveform looks, and the more bright or harsh it will sound. This complexity is the result of combining many sine waves of different frequencies together. Each different frequency is known as an overtone. While the frequencies of musical sounds has been studied for thousands of years, since the ancient Greeks, the fact that sound timbre can be described as combined overtones of different frequencies was proved mathematically by Joseph Fourier in the 17th Century. He showed that for periodic waveforms the sine wave components are restricted to integer multiples of the fundamental frequency. Such that if the fundamental frequency is 100 hertz, the component sine waves are at frequencies of 100, 200, 300, 400 hertz, and so on. An overtone at these simple multiples of the fundamental is known as a harmonic, and the set of all these harmonics make up the harmonic series. The processes of deconstructing a sound into its harmonic components is called a Fourier analysis in recognition of this discovery.

Additive synthesis

As we have seen, the sine wave is the basis of textual spectra. Additive synthesis uses multiple sine waves to create complex timbres, and provides detailed control over spectral development because each partial (sine wave component) can have its own temporal evolution by controlling individual amplitude and frequency envelopes. Additive synthesis provides maximum specificity over the timbre of the sound, however, it also requires the most detailed setting of parameters and values, can be computationally expensive, and dynamic changes such as oscillator balance at different dynamics can be awkward to implement. Each partial requires its own sine wave oscillator and the number of partials determines the level of waveform detail. Typically between about six and twenty partials are used, with each set to a frequency in the harmonic series. The outputs from each partial are added together to generate a complete sound.

Score-based spectrum

We can achieve an interesting musical result using simple instruments, such as a sine wave, with appropriate scores. The *AddingSineWave* program is an example which plays on this psychoacoustic effect by laying multiple sine waves as notes (chords) within a score. The sine wave notes create a complex timbre based on the harmonic series. Ever-changing relationships between the onset, duration and amplitude of overlapping notes result in an evolving overall timbre. In order to get more natural sounding results two factors are scaled against the harmonic number, their amplitude and duration. This mimics the case in acoustic sounds where higher harmonics have increasing less energy and so their amplitude is softer and they fade out more quickly. This is achieved by dividing amplitude and rhythm values by the harmonic number, indicated in the code below as the i index variable. The score created in *AddingSineWaves* is made up of four note clusters. Each comprises a part with nine single note phrases.

```
Part cluster = new Part();
double rootFrequency = Math.random() * 700 + 100;
for (int i = 1; i < 10; i++) {
    Phrase harmonic = new Phrase((counter) * 2.0 + Math.random() * 0.02);
    Note n = new Note(i * rootFrequency, 2.0 * Math.random() + 1.0 / i,
        (int)((Math.random() * 90 + 30) / i));
    harmonic.addNote(n);
    cluster.addPhrase(harmonic);
}
```

The notes are rendered to an audio file using a sine wave instrument, `SineInst`. This program is a simple example of how sine waves combine to form complex timbres and how jMusic composition can blur the distinction between score and sound, in this case creating timbre from texture.

More jMusic Instruments

In this section we will look at how the concepts of adding audio waveforms of different frequencies can be applied to creating synthesis instruments in jMusic.

Instrument-based spectrum

A more traditional approach to additive synthesis is to render a single note with an instrument that generates a complex waveform via additive synthesis. This is the approach used in the *AdditiveTimpani* program. In this program the definition of overtone frequencies and amplitudes is directed toward the instrument. The score itself is quite simple, with one note for each sound event – in this case Timpani hit. The `AddSynthInst` instrument is used and accepts the following arguments:

```
int - sample rate
double[] - frequency multipliers
double[] - amplitude multipliers
double[][] - break point envelope values for each overtone
```

The values for some of these arguments are shown below.

```
private double[] freqVals = {1.0,1.42,1.53,1.77,1.94,2.01,2.4};
private double[] volVals = {1.0,0.8,0.7,0.6,0.5,0.3,0.1};
```

Notice, that there are seven arguments for both `freqVals` and `volVals`, one for each of seven overtones. The `freqVals` data are used as a multiplier of the fundamental, which is derived from the note pitch. The `volVals` data are used to scale the volume of each overtone, notice that the higher overtones have less volume. A second aspect of the volume for each overtone is its envelope. The envelope data for the fundamental are shown below. Envelopes are covered in more detail in a later chapter, for now it is sufficient to understand that the data are pairs of Cartesian points describing the shape of the loudness contour of the overtone.

```
private double[] pointArray1 = {0.0,0.0,0.002,1.0,0.3,0.4,0.7,0.05,1.0,0.0};
```

An array for each envelope can be provided and collected as a two dimensional array (an array of arrays) before being passed to the `AddSynthInst` constructor. In *AdditiveTimpani* only three envelope arrays are created and are reused many times to save some effort.

```
Instrument inst = new AddSynthInst(44100, freqVals, volVals, points);
```

A timpani sound is somewhat pitched but still has a distinctive noisiness characteristic of percussive sounds. The frequency ratios used in this example reflect this imperfection by being values close to, but not exactly, integer multiples. Working out what frequencies and envelopes to use for a particular sound could take a great deal of experimentation but, fortunately, tables of spectral data for many acoustic instruments have been published. One of the earliest and most well known collections is Jean-Claude Risset's *Introductory Catalogue of Computer-Synthesized Sounds* (1969).[1]

Below is the full code for the *AdditiveSynthesis* program, and the code for the `AddSynthInst` jMusic instrument.

AdditiveTimpani

```
import jm.JMC;
import jm.music.data.*;
import jm.audio.*;
import jm.util.*;

public final class AdditiveTimpani implements JMC{
    // Set up overtone attributes
    private double[] freqVals = {1.0, 1.42, 1.53, 1.77, 1.94, 2.01, 2.4};
    private double[] volVals = {1.0, 0.8, 0.7, 0.6, 0.5, 0.3, 0.1};
    private double[] pointArray1={0.0,0.0,0.002,1.0,0.3,0.4,0.7,0.05,1.0,0.0};
    private double[] pointArray2={0.0,0.0,0.05,1.0,0.2,0.3,0.6,0.05,1.0,0.0};
    private double[] pointArray3={0.0,0.0,0.01,1.0,0.2,0.2,0.5,0.05,1.0,0.0};
    private double[][] points =
        new double[freqVals.length][pointArray1.length];
    // Set up music attribute sets
    private int[] pitches = {D3, C3, F2, A2};
    private double[] rhythms = {2.0, 1.0, 0.5, 0.5};

    public static void main(String[] args){
        new AdditiveTimpani();
    }
    public AdditiveTimpani() {
        Score score = new Score("Timpani Score", 120);
        Part part = new Part("Timp. Part", 0);
        Phrase phr = new Phrase(0.0);
        for (int i=0; i<16; i++ ) {
            Note note = new Note(pitches[(int)(Math.random() *
                pitches.length)], rhythms[(int)(Math.random() *
                rhythms.length)]);
```

---

[1] Risset's collection was reprinted in 1994 with an audio CD as, *Computer Music Currents 13*, Wergo (WER 2033-2).

```
            note.setDuration(note.getRhythmValue() * 2.5);
            phr.addNote(note);
        }
        part.addPhrase(phr);
        score.addPart(part);
        // Construct the double array of break point envelope
        points[0] = pointArray1;
        points[1] = pointArray2;
        for (int i=2; i<freqVals.length; i++) {
            points[i] = pointArray3;
        }
        // Create instrument, render and view score.
        Instrument inst = new AddSynthInst(44100, freqVals, volVals, points);
        Write.au(score, "AdditiveTimpani.au", inst);
        View.au("AdditiveTimpani.au");
    }
}
```

AddSynthInst

```
import jm.audio.io.*;
import jm.audio.synth.*;
import jm.music.data.Note;
import jm.audio.AudioObject;
import jm.audio.Instrument;

public final class AddSynthInst extends Instrument{
        private double[] overtoneRatios;
        private double[] overtoneVolumes;
        private double[][] allEnvPoints;
        private double[] envPoints={0.0,0.0,0.05,1.0,0.15,0.4 0.9,0.3,1.0,0.0};
        private int sampleRate;

        public AddSynthInst(int sampleRate){
            this.sampleRate = sampleRate;
            double[][] tempPoints = new double[5][];
            for (int i=0; i<5; i++) {
                    tempPoints[i] = envPoints;
            }
            allEnvPoints = tempPoints;
            double[] temp1 = {1.0f, 3.0f, 5.0f, 7.0f, 9.0f};
```

```
                this.overtoneRatios = temp1;
                double[] temp2 = {1.0f, 0.5f, 0.35f, 0.25f, 0.15f};
                this.overtoneVolumes = temp2;
        }
        public AddSynthInst(int sampleRate, double[] overtoneRatios,
                    double[] overtoneVolumes, double[][] envPointArray) {
                this.overtoneRatios = overtoneRatios;
                this.overtoneVolumes = overtoneVolumes;
                allEnvPoints = envPointArray; //tempPoints;
                this.sampleRate = sampleRate;
        }
        public void createChain(){
                Envelope[] env = new Envelope[overtoneRatios.length];
                Volume[] vol = new Volume[overtoneRatios.length];
                Oscillator[] osc = new Oscillator[overtoneRatios.length];
                for (int i=0;i<overtoneRatios.length;i++){
                        osc[i] = new Oscillator(this, Oscillator.SINE_WAVE,
                                    this.sampleRate,2);
                        osc[i].setFrqRatio((float)overtoneRatios[i]);
                        env[i] = new Envelope(osc[i], allEnvPoints[i]);
                        vol[i] = new Volume(env[i], (float)overtoneVolumes[i]);
                }
                Add add = new Add(vol);
                    StereoPan span = new StereoPan(add);
                SampleOut sout = new SampleOut(span);
        }
}
```

Timbral morphing

Risset composed works using additive synthesis based on his spectral analysis of acoustic instruments, including a series titled *Mutations* released on INA-IMG in 1987. *Mutations* exploits one of the distinct advantages of additive synthesis, precise control of each partial, to morph—or mutate—from one spectrum to another. He achieves this by cross fading the envelopes of particular harmonics to gradually change the timbre over time.

The *Morph* program emulates this technique. It plays a single note with the `AddMorphInst` instrument. This instrument has partials with two sets of envelopes. One envelope begins quickly and dies down gradually, and a second set start gradually and ramp up toward the end of the note. The first envelope is applied to each odd partial which produces a hollow clarinet-like sound, while the second envelope is applied to partials with asymmetric ratios that produce a gong-like timbre. The note, therefore, sounds as if it gradually transforms form a clarinet to a gong.

The *Morph* example uses the `AddMorphInst` instrument (detailed below) to create a simple audio output.

```java
import jm.JMC;
import jm.music.data.*;
import jm.audio.*;
import jm.util.*;

public final class Morph implements JMC{
    public static void main(String[] args){
        new Morph();
    }

    public Morph() {
    Score score = new Score(new Part(new Phrase(new Note(C3, 10.0))));
    Instrument inst = new AddMorphInst(22050);
    Write.au(score, "Morph.au", inst);
    View.au("Morph.au");
    }
}
```

The `AddMorphInst` class describes an An additive synthesis instrument implementation which cross fades between two different spectra.

```java
import jm.audio.io.*;
import jm.audio.synth.*;
import jm.music.data.Note;
import jm.audio.Instrument;

public final class AddMorphInst extends Instrument {
    // class variables
    /** the relative frequencies which make up this note */
    private double[] freqVals = {1.0, 3.0, 5.0, 7.0, 9.0, 1.0, 0.5699, 0.57,
        0.92, 1.1999, 1.2, 1.7, 2.74, 3.0, 3.76, 4.07, 7.3, 9.4, 10.0};
    /** the volumes to use for each frequency */
    private double[] volVals = {1.0, 0.7, 0.5, 0.3, 0.2, 1.0, 0.8, 0.75, 0.7,
        0.65, 0.6, 0.55, 0.5, 0.45, 0.4, 0.35, 0.3, 0.15, 0.1};
    /** The points to use in the construction of Envelopes */
    private double[] pointArray1 = {0.0, 0.0, 0.1, 1.0, 0.3, 0.4, 1.0, 0.0};
    private double[] pointArray2 = {0.0, 0.0, 0.5, 0.2, 0.8, 1.0, 1.0, 0.0};
```

```java
        private double[][] points = new double
            [freqVals.length][pointArray1.length];
    /** Pan */
    private float pan;
    /** The sample Rate to use */
    private int sampleRate;
    /** The Oscillators to use for each frequency specified */
    private Oscillator[] osc;
    /** The envelope to apply to each Oscillator's output */
    private Envelope[] env;
    /** The volume to apply to each envelopes output */
    private Volume[] vol;
    // Constructor
    public AddMorphInst(int sampleRate){
        this.sampleRate = sampleRate;
        // set up envelope points
        for (int i=0; i<7; i++) {
            points[i] = pointArray1;
        }
        for (int i=7; i<freqVals.length; i++) {
            points[i] = pointArray2;
        }
    }
    public void createChain() {
        //define the audio chain(s)
        osc = new Oscillator[freqVals.length];
        env = new Envelope[freqVals.length];
        vol = new Volume[freqVals.length];
        for (int i=0;i<freqVals.length;i++){
            osc[i] = new Oscillator(this, Oscillator.SINE_WAVE,
                this.sampleRate, 2);
            osc[i].setFrqRatio((float)freqVals[i]);
            env[i] = new Envelope(osc[i], points[i]);
            vol[i] = new Volume(env[i], (float)volVals[i]);
        }
        Add add = new Add(vol);
        StereoPan span = new StereoPan(add);
        SampleOut sout = new SampleOut(span);
    }
}
```

14: Interactivity

This book has focused on musical composition with Java, and the approach as generally been to write and run programs that render output as either MIDI or audio files. Some interactivity was introduced in when using the `HelperGUI` class to present a visual interface that allowed you to change variables then rerun your program, that is, interactivity assisted with rapid re-rending of music without the need to recompile and restart your programs. In this chapter we will examine how your programs can run in real-time, by this we mean how they can generate music on the fly, playing back note by note as the music is generated. This will allow us to interact with the music to effect it during creation. This style of interactivity is common these days with faster computers can could more accurately be described as being instrument building or performing, than composing, but these boundaries are increasingly meaningless.

Real-time music generation

In order to playback the music as it is created (in real-time) jMusic uses a different structure from what we've used for composition. Notes are still the primary musical object, but phrases, parts and scores are replaced by the `RTLine` and `RTMixer` class. A class that extends `RTLine` is responsible for 'producing' notes as requested. A class that extends `RTMixer` coordinates a number of `RTLines` to keep them in sync. Instruments are required to play the notes and these are declared by your application and passed to the `RTLine`. Figure 14.1 provides an overview of this structure.

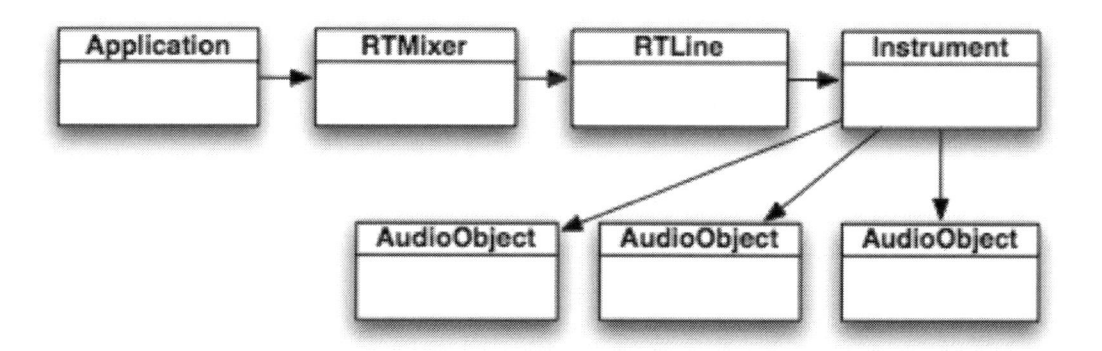

Figure 14.1. The structure of a simple real-time class hierarchy in jMusic.

The heart of real-time audio playback in jMusic is the RTLine class. Your real-time program must have a class that extends RTLine and overrides the getNote() method. Inside the get-Note() method should be code that composes the music note by note; returning one note at a time. This method will be called again and again as required. Here is the code for *BassLineA*, a class that extends RTLine and part of in our first real-time example program.

```
import jm.music.rt.RTLine;
import jm.audio.Instrument;
import jm.music.data.Note;

public class BassLineA extends RTLine {
    private Note n = new Note(36, 1.0);
    private int pitch = 36;
    private int[] intervals = {0, 0, 0, 4, 7, 10, 12};
    private double panPosition = 0.5;

    public BassLineA (Instrument[] instArray) {
        super(instArray);
    }

    public synchronized Note getNote() {
        n.setPitch(pitch +
        intervals[(int)(Math.random() * intervals.length)]);
        n.setDynamic((int)(Math.random()* 5 + 120));
        n.setPan(panPosition);
        n.setRhythmValue((int)(Math.random()*2+1) * 0.25);
        n.setDuration(n.getRhythmValue() * 0.9);
        return n;
    }
}
```

Music Moment

The algorithm in *BassLineA* makes a random selection from pitches above the root note as specified in the intervals array. The rhythm value is chosen randomly between an sixteenth and an eighth note. While this works OK, we can get a more interesting result using a random walk to select pitches to give a greater sense of melodic shape, and if we use a Gaussian distribution we will get the occasional large leap to add interest. The rhythms can be made more musical by weighting the probabilities so that longer notes fall on the down beats, thus giving a greater sense of pulse.

This `BassLineA` class is called by another class named `RTComposition`. Notice that the `BassLineA` constructor requires an array of instruments to be passed to it. Correspondingly, the `RTComposition` class creates an array of one instrument to pass to `BassLineA`.

```java
import jm.JMC;
import jm.music.data.*;
import jm.audio.*;
import jm.music.rt.RTLine;

public class RTCompositionA implements JMC {
    private RTMixer mixer;
    private BassLineA bassLine;

    public static void main(String[] args) {
        new RTCompositionA();
    }

    public RTCompositionA() {
        int sampleRate = 44100;
        int channels = 2;
        RTSawLPFInstA synthBass = new RTSawLPFInstA(sampleRate,
            1000, channels);
        Instrument[] insts = new Instrument[] {synthBass};

        bassLine = new BassLineA(insts);
        bassLine.setTempo(104);

        RTLine[] lineArray = new RTLine[] {bassLine};
        mixer = new RTMixer(lineArray);
        mixer.begin();
    }
}
```

The `RTComposition` class first creates an instrument with the desired sample rate and the number of channels (2 indicating stereo). The instrument, named `synthBass`, is added to an instrument array, named `insts`, and is used as an argument when constructing an instance of the `BassLineA` class, named `bassLine`.

Having created the bass line and provided it with a synth bass instrument, the next step in jMusic real-time audio is to mix all the lines together using the `RTMixer` class. In this example there is only one line, but it must still be passed in an array to the mixer. Once the `RTMixer` instance, named `mixer`, is created we start the music playing by calling the mixer's `begin()` method.

This example relies on a third class that defines the instrument used to play the notes. The code for the instrument is below. As we've seen with previous jMusic instruments the `createChain()` method has the critical elements. You will notice that it is a subtractive synthesis instrument comprised of a sawtooth oscillator, filter, and amplitude envelope.

```java
import jm.audio.Instrument;
import jm.audio.io.*;
import jm.audio.synth.*;
import jm.music.data.Note;
import jm.audio.AudioObject;

public final class RTSawLPFInstA extends Instrument {
    private int sampleRate;
    private int filterCutoff;
    private int channels;
    private Filter filt;

    public RTSawLPFInstA(int sampleRate, int filterCutoff, int channels)
    {
        this.sampleRate = sampleRate;
        this.filterCutoff = filterCutoff;
        this.channels = channels;
    }

    public void createChain() {
        Oscillator wt = new Oscillator(this, Oscillator.SAWTOOTH_WAVE,
            this.sampleRate, this.channels);
        filt = new Filter(wt, this.filterCutoff, Filter.LOW_PASS);
        Envelope env = new Envelope(filt, new double[]
            {0.0, 0.0, 0.05, 1.0, 0.9, 1.0, 1.0, 0.0});
        Volume vol = new Volume(env);
        StereoPan pan = new StereoPan(vol);
    }
}
```

The `Filter` object, named `filt`, in the `RTSawLPFInst` class is declared as an instance variable, while all other `AudioObjects` in the chain are local variables. This is in preparation for the next stage of our real-time journey where we will control the filter cutoff position from a graphical interface.

Real Time GUI Control

The first step for our graphical interface will be to add Start and Stop buttons to begin and end (or pause) the bass line playback. The interface makes use of Java GUI libraries and the Action-Listener interface is used to react to users clicking on the buttons. Below is a revised version of the RTComposition class with the added GUI code. The classes BassLineA and RTSawL-FOInstA are unchanged.

```java
import jm.JMC;
import jm.music.data.*;
import jm.audio.*;
import jm.music.rt.RTLine;

import java.awt.*;
import java.awt.event.*;
import javax.swing.event.*;
import javax.swing.*;

public class RTCompositionB implements JMC, ActionListener {
    private RTMixer mixer;
    private BassLineA bassLine;
    private JButton goBtn, stopBtn;
    private boolean firstTime = true;

    public static void main(String[] args) {
        new RTCompositionB();
    }

    public RTCompositionB() {
        int sampleRate = 44100;
        int channels = 2;
        RTSawLPFInstA synthBass = new RTSawLPFInstA(sampleRate, 1000,
            channels);
        Instrument[] insts = new Instrument[] {synthBass};
        bassLine = new BassLineA(insts);
        bassLine.setTempo(104);
        displayGUI();
```

```java
    }

    private void displayGUI() {
        JFrame window = new JFrame("Real-Time Bass Line");
        window.setDefaultCloseOperation(JFrame.EXIT_ON_CLOSE);
        window.setSize(50, 250);
        JPanel panel = new JPanel(new BorderLayout());
        window.getContentPane().add(panel);

        goBtn = new JButton("Start");
        goBtn.addActionListener(this);
        panel.add(goBtn, "West");
        stopBtn = new JButton("Stop");
        stopBtn.addActionListener(this);
        panel.add(stopBtn, "East");

        window.pack();
        window.setVisible(true);
    }

    public void actionPerformed(ActionEvent e) {
        if (e.getSource() == goBtn) {
            if (firstTime) {
                RTLine[] lineArray = new RTLine[] {bassLine};
                mixer = new RTMixer(lineArray);
                mixer.begin();
                firstTime = false;
            } else mixer.unPause();
            goBtn.setEnabled(false);
            stopBtn.setEnabled(true);
        }

        if (e.getSource() == stopBtn) {
            mixer.pause();
            goBtn.setEnabled(true);
            stopBtn.setEnabled(false);
        }
    }
}
```

The additional methods in this class are `displayGUI()` and `actionPerformed()`. The awt and swing packages are imported for the interface components. The `displayGUI()` method is called at the end of the constructor and the button clicks will initiate the `actionPerformed()` method because the buttons are registered with the `ActionListener`. There is a Boolean flag named `firstTime` that is used in the `actionPerformed()` method when the `goBtn` is clicked. When `firstTime` is true, the mixer is declared and started, then `firstTime` is set to false. On subsequent clicks on the `stopBtn` and `goBtn` the mixer is paused or unpaused.

The next extension to the *RTComposition* program is to add a fader that controls of the filter cutoff. This requires the addition of a `JSlider` and a `JLabel` component. The `ChangeListener` interface is used to detect adjustment of the slider, and information from this is passed to the `RTMixer` (see figure 14.1) and the label value is updated.

```java
import jm.JMC;
import jm.music.data.*;
import jm.audio.*;
import jm.music.rt.RTLine;

import java.awt.*;
import java.awt.event.*;
import javax.swing.event.*;
import javax.swing.*;

public class RTCompositionC implements JMC, ActionListener,
          ChangeListener {
    private RTMixer mixer;
    private BassLineC bassLine;
    private JButton goBtn, stopBtn;
    private boolean firstTime = true;
    private JSlider cutoff;
    private JLabel value;

    public static void main(String[] args) {
        new RTCompositionC();
    }

    public RTCompositionC() {
        int sampleRate = 44100;
```

```java
        int channels = 2;
        RTSawLPFInstC synthBass = new RTSawLPFInstC(sampleRate, 1000,
            channels);
        Instrument[] insts = new Instrument[] {synthBass};

        bassLine = new BassLineC(insts);
        bassLine.setTempo(104);

        displayGUI();
    }

    private void displayGUI() {
        JFrame window = new JFrame("Real-Time Bass Line");
        window.setDefaultCloseOperation(JFrame.EXIT_ON_CLOSE);
        window.setSize(50, 250);
        JPanel panel = new JPanel(new BorderLayout());
        window.getContentPane().add(panel);

        goBtn = new JButton("Start");
        goBtn.addActionListener(this);
        panel.add(goBtn, "West");
        stopBtn = new JButton("Stop");
        stopBtn.addActionListener(this);
        panel.add(stopBtn, "East");

        cutoff = new JSlider(1, 1, 100, 10);
        cutoff.setEnabled(false);
        cutoff.addChangeListener(this);
        panel.add(cutoff, "Center");

        value = new JLabel("1000");
        panel.add(value, "South");

        window.pack();
        window.setVisible(true);
    }

    public void actionPerformed(ActionEvent e) {
        if (e.getSource() == goBtn) {
            if (firstTime) {
```

```java
                    RTLine[] lineArray = new RTLine[] {bassLine};
                    mixer = new RTMixer(lineArray);
                    mixer.begin();
                    firstTime = false;
                    cutoff.setEnabled(true);
                } else mixer.unPause();
                goBtn.setEnabled(false);
                stopBtn.setEnabled(true);
            }
            if (e.getSource() == stopBtn) {
                mixer.pause();
                goBtn.setEnabled(true);
                stopBtn.setEnabled(false);
            }
        }

        public void stateChanged(ChangeEvent e){
            if (e.getSource() == cutoff) {
                value.setText("" +(cutoff.getValue() * 100));
                mixer.actionLines(
                new Integer(cutoff.getValue()*100), 1);
            }
        }
    }
```

The *RTCompositionC* program requires new versions of the line and instrument classes; `BassLineC` and `RTSawLPFInstC`. These classes each have an additional method to handle parsing the filter cutoff value. When the slider value is adjusted, a reference to the slider value is sent as an `Integer` along with an arbitrary reference number that indicates the value is a filter cut off value. This process, that jMusic uses to sending values to the filter, may seem somewhat complex but it is flexible enough to allow any number of controllers to be sent to any number of audio objects in instruments. The important line from the `stateChanged()` method is this.

```
mixer.actionLines(new Double(cutoff.getValue() * 100.0), 1);
```

The `actionLines()` method is the first step in a series of message passing steps to get the controller information from the application class to the correct `AudioObject`, in this case an instance of the `Filter` class. The path is depicted in figure 14.2. The application passes the value(s) to the `RTMixer` which broadcasts it to all `RTLines` registered with the mixer. The

RTLine broadcasts the value(s) to all it's instruments, which in turn pass the value(s) on to the appropriate audio units they contain.

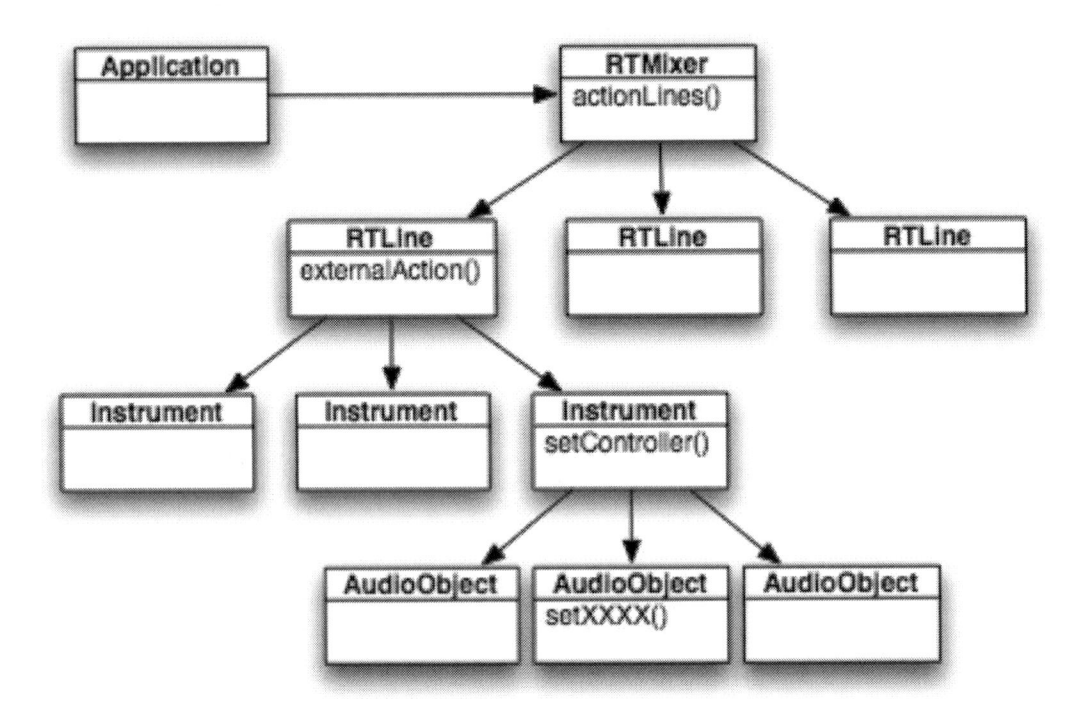

Figure 14.2. The path a control message follows from application to audio object.

The mixer, as a result of extending the RTMixer class, will broadcast this information to any of the RTLine instances that are registered with the mixer by calling a special method named externalAction(). In this case there is only one RTLine registered with the mixer, an instance of BassLineC. Like all classes that extend RTLine, the BassLineC class can override the RTLine method called externalAction() which takes an array of doubles.

```
public synchronized void externalAction(Object obj, int actionNumber) {
    if (actionNumber == 1) {
        double filterCutoff = ((Double)obj).doubleValue();
        for (int i=0;i<inst.length;i++) {
            double[] values = {filterCutoff};
            inst[i].setController(values);
        }
    }
}
```

This method is the only difference between the classes `BassLineA` and `BassLineC`. It is called from the mixer class which passes an object with the controller value (in this case a Double) and an `actionNumber`. In the `RTCompositionC` class we assigned the filter cutoff as action number 1. The value has to find its way to the `Filter` object which is in the instrument. So the next step is to pass the cutoff value to each instrument in the line. There is only one value in this case, but it is possible for there to be more, so we pass the value as an element in a double array. The value is passed to the `setController()` method of the instrument.

```
public void setController(double[] controlValues){
        filt.setCutOff(controlValues[0]);
}
```

The `setController()` method is the only addition to the `RTSawLPFInstC` class. Any instrument that wants to receive controller messages in this way needs to implement this method. It's job is to pass the controller value to the `Filter` instance, named `filt`. It does this by calling the `setCutOff()` method and passing the first (zeroth) element in the array.

In summary, the process of adjusting the filter cutoff from the slider involves four steps;

1) get the slider value and pass it (or a scaled version of it) to the mixer along with a controller index;

2) the mixer will broadcast the data to all lines;

3) the lines will pass on the information to any associated instruments and;

4) the instruments pass the value to the relevant audio object (in this case the filter object).

Figure 14.3: The control interface with a pan and filter cutoff sliders.

Programming Practice

As an exercise try adding a pan slider to your GUI interface, as shown if figure 14.3. The procedure for passing the controller information is quite similar to what was used for the filter cutoff. Remember to make the `StereoPan` object in the instrument an instance variable, and also remember to change the `panPosition` variable in the `BassLine` class otherwise the next note will reset the changed pan position. As assistance, here are the important methods from the `RTLine` and `Instrument` classes.

```
public synchronized void externalAction(Object obj, int actionNumber) {
    if (actionNumber == 1) {
        double filterCutoff = ((Double)obj).doubleValue();
        for (int i=0;i<inst.length;i++) {
            double[] values = {filterCutoff, -1};
            inst[i].setController(values);
        }
    }
    if (actionNumber == 2) {
        panPosition = ((Double)obj).doubleValue();
        for (int i=0;i<inst.length;i++){
            double[] values = {-1, panPosition};
            inst[i].setController(values);
        }
    }
}
public void setController(double[] controlValues) {
    if (controlValues[0] >= 0) filt.setCutOff(controlValues[0]);
    if (controlValues[1] >= 0) pan.setPan(controlValues[1]);
}
```

External Control

We have seen how controlling a real-time music program can be achieved using the standard computer interfaces (mouse and keyboard) via GUI components. It is often desirable to use other physical interfaces for music programs, including piano-like keyboards, physical fades and dials or more experimental interfaces such as data gloves and electronic sensors. These interfaces often use the MIDI standard to communicate and in this section we'll show how to respond to and send MIDI messages. It is also possible to record audio using the computer and it is also possible to have our programs respond to that audio input in real time. In the later part of this section we'll see how to achieve this with jMusic.

MIDI input and output

The Musical Instrument Digital Interface (MIDI) protocol work by sending messages. There are a number of message types including note on and off, control change, program change, and system exclusive messages. The messages come in a package but Java has libraries that construct and deconstruct these to and from their constituent parts. jMusic adds an easy to use layer on top of the standard Java libraries that does the most commonly required tasks. The `jm.midi.MidiCommunication` class provides this functionality. It is an abstract class, this means that it cannot be used directly but must be extended. See the `MidiComTest` example below for an example. There is one abstract method that must be overridden also, the `handleMidiInput()` method which manages incoming MIDI data. The other important method is `sendMidiOutput()` which enables you to control external MIDI devices by sending messages to them. Both these methods act in real-time, that is they operate immediately they are called and there is no scheduling of events built into the `MidiCommunication` class (but of course you could add that if you wanted). The `handleMidiInput()` and `sendMidiOutput()` methods take four arguments, which are aspects of the MIDI message. To fully appreciate these arguments it is necessary to understand how a short MIDI message is constructed.

A standard short MIDI message is made up of three bytes; a status byte and two data bytes. The structure of a MIDI message is shown in figure 14.4. The status byte contains two parts, the type of message (note on, controller etc.) and the channel for the message (remembering that the MIDI specification allows for 16 channels – 0 to 15), The two data bytes contain different information depending on the message type but always have values between 0 and 127. For example, in the Note On and Note Off messages the first data byte has the pitch of the note and the second it's velocity (dynamic), while for a Controller message the first data byte contains the controller number (e.g. 7 for volume) and the second data byte contains the controller value.

Status Byte

| Type | Channel | | Data 1 | | Data 2 |

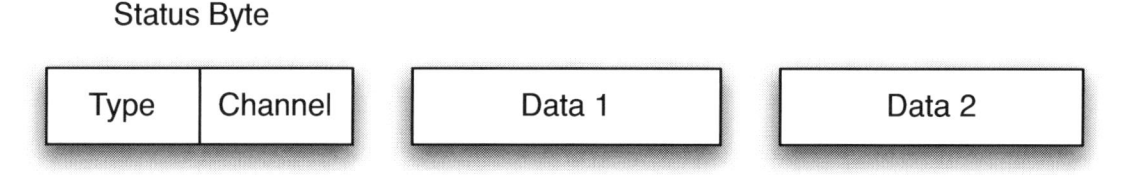

Figure 14.4. The structure of a short MIDI message.

The methods in the `MidiCommunication` class take four arguments and behind the scenes the type and channel are combined to form a status byte. The value of the status byte is simple the sum of the type and channel values.

It is possible for a computer system to have several MIDI ports, or destinations, some of them to internal software synthesizers and others to external synthesizers or other devices. MIDI messages need to be sent to the appropriate port. To assist with this setup, the `MidiCommunication` class when constructed presents a window with a list of all available MIDI ports from which the user can select the ones they want to use. This window is presented twice, first for the selection of the MIDI input port then for selection of the MIDI output port. The communicating to the MIDI hardware is a system-dependent operation and Java support for this can vary between computer operating systems.

The *MidiComTest* program is an example of how to use the `MidiCommunication` class in an application.

```
import jm.midi.MidiCommunication;

public class MidiComTest extends MidiCommunication {

    public static void main(String[] args) {
        new MidiComTest();
    }

    public MidiComTest() {
        sendMidiOutput(176, 0, 7, 80); // volume
        sendMidiOutput(144, 0, 60, 100); // note on
        try {
            Thread.sleep(500);
        }catch(Exception e) {}
        sendMidiOutput(128, 0, 60, 0); // note off
    }

    public void handleMidiInput(int type,int channel,int data1,int data2) {
        System.out.println("MIDI IN - [type: " + type + "]
            [Channel: " + channel + "] [Data byte 1: " + data1 + "]
            [Data byte 2: " + data2 + "]");
    }
}
```

Appendix A: Constants in the JMC

These words and abbreviations can be used in place of numbers in classes that implements the JMC interface. In many cases one value is represented by a series of alternate words, for example, the rhythm value 1.0 can be QUARTER_NOTE, Q, CROTCHET, or C. Notice that most of the constants are in upper case, which makes them easier to recognize amongst the Java code. Java is a case sensitive language and so they must be written using the case that appears here. Their numerical values are not shown here, but you can consult the jMusic documentation for the exact value of each constant.

RhythmValues

C, CD, CDD, CROTCHET, CROTCHET_TRIPLET, CT, DC, DDC, DDEN, DDHN, DDM, DDQ, DDQN, DEMI_SEMI_QUAVER, DEMI_SEMI_QUAVER_TRIPLET, DEN, DHN, DM, DOTTED_CROTCHET, DOTTED_EIGHTH_NOTE, DOTTED_HALF_NOTE, DOTTED_MINIM, DOTTED_QUARTER_NOTE, DOTTED_QUAVER, DOTTED_SEMI_QUAVER, DOTTED_SIXTEENTH_NOTE, DOUBLE_DOTTED_CROTCHET, DOUBLE_DOTTED_EIGHTH_NOTE, DOUBLE_DOTTED_HALF_NOTE, DOUBLE_DOTTED_MINIM, DOUBLE_DOTTED_QUARTER_NOTE, DOUBLE_DOTTED_QUAVER, DQ, DQN, DSN, DSQ, DSQT, EIGHTH_NOTE, EIGHTH_NOTE_TRIPLET, EN, ENT, HALF_NOTE, HALF_NOTE_TRIPLET, HN, HNT, M, MD, MDD, MINIM, MINIM_TRIPLET, MT, Q, QD, QDD, QN, QNT, QT, QUARTER_NOTE, QUARTER_NOTE_TRIPLET, QUAVER, QUAVER_TRIPLET, SB, SEMI_QUAVER, SEMI_QUAVER_TRIPLET, SEMIBREVE, SIXTEENTH_NOTE, SIXTEENTH_NOTE_TRIPLET, SN, SNT, SQ, SQD, SQT, THIRTYSECOND_NOTE, THIRTYSECOND_NOTE_TRIPLET, TN, TNT, TSN, TSNT, WHOLE_NOTE, WN

Pitches

A0, A1, A2, A3, A4, A5, A6, A7, A8, F0, F1, F2, F3, F4, F5, F6, F7, F8, AFN1, AN1, AS0, AS1, AS2, AS3, AS4, AS5, AS6, AS7, AS8, ASN1, B0, B1, B2, B3, B4, B5, B6, B7, B8, F0, F1, F2, F3, F4, F5, F6, F7, F8, BFN1, BN1, BS0, BS1, BS2, BS3, BS4, BS5, BS6, BS7, BS8, BSN1, C0, C1, C2, C3, C4, C5, C6, C7, C8, C9, F0, F1, F2, F3, F4, F5, F6, F7, F8, F9, CN1, CS0, CS1, CS2, CS3, CS4, CS5, CS6, CS7, CS8, CS9, CSN1, D0, D1, D2, D3, D4, D5, D6, D7, D8, D9, F0, F1, F2, F3, F4, F5, F6, F7, F8, F9, DFN1, DN1, DS0, DS1, DS2, DS3, DS4, DS5, DS6, DS7, DS8, DS9, DSN1, E0, E1, E2, E3, E4, E5, E6, E7, E8, E9, F0, F1, F2, F3, F4, F5, F6, F7, F8, F9, EFN1, EN1, ES0, ES1, ES2, ES3, ES4, ES5, ES6, ES7, ES8, ES9, ESN1, F0, F1, F2, F3, F4, F5, F6, F7, F8, F9, F0, F1, F2, F3, F4, F5, F6, F7, F8, F9, FFN1, FN1, FS0, FS1, FS2, FS3, FS4, FS5, FS6, FS7, FS8, FS9, FSN1, G0, G1, G2, G3, G4, G5, G6, G7, G8, G9, GF0, GF1, GF2, GF3, GF4, GF5, GF6, GF7, GF8, GF9, GFN1, GN1, GS0, GS1, GS2, GS3, GS4, GS5, GS6, GS7, GS8, GSN1, REST

Dynamics
F, FF, FFF, FORTE, FORTISSIMO, MEZZO_FORTE, MEZZO_PIANO, MF, MP, P, PIANISSIMO, PP, PPP, SILENT

Panning
PAN_CENTER, PAN_CENTRE, PAN_LEFT, PAN_RIGHT

General MIDI program changes
AAH, ABASS, AC_GUITAR, ACCORDION, ACOUSTIC_BASS, ACOUSTIC_GRAND, ACOUSTIC_GUITAR, AGOGO, AHHS, ALTO, ALTO_SAX, ALTO_SAXOPHONE, APPLAUSE, ATMOSPHERE, BAG_PIPES, BAGPIPE, BAGPIPES, BANDNEON, BANJO, BARI, BARI_SAX, BARITONE, BARITONE_SAX, BARITONE_SAXOPHONE, BASS, BASSOON, BELL, BELLS, BIRD, BOTTLE, BOTTLE_BLOW, BOWED_GLASS, BRASS, BREATH, BREATHNOISE, BRIGHT_ACOUSTIC, BRIGHTNESS, CALLOPE, CELESTA, CELESTE, CELLO, CGUITAR, CHARANG, CHIFFER, CHIFFER_LEAD, CHOIR, CHURCH_ORGAN, CLAR, CLARINET, CLAV, CLAVINET, CLEAN_GUITAR, CONCERTINA, CONTRA_BASS, CONTRABASS, CRYSTAL, CYMBAL, DGUITAR, DIST_GUITAR, DISTORTED_GUITAR, DOUBLE_BASS, DROPS, DRUM, DX_EPIANO, EBASS, ECHO, ECHO_DROP, ECHO_DROPS, ECHOS, EL_BASS, EL_GUITAR, ELECTRIC_BASS, ELECTRIC_GRAND, ELECTRIC_GUITAR, ELECTRIC_ORGAN, ELECTRIC_PIANO, ELPIANO, ENGLISH_HORN, EPIANO, EPIANO2, FANTASIA, FBASS, FIDDLE, FINGERED_BASS, FLUTE, FRENCH_HORN, FRET, FRET_NOISE, FRETLESS, FRETLESS_BASS, FRETNOISE, FRETS, GLOCK, GLOCKENSPIEL, GMSAW_WAVE, GMSQUARE_WAVE, GOBLIN, GT_HARMONICS, GUITAR, GUITAR_HARMONICS, HALO, HALO_PAD, HAMMOND_ORGAN, HARMONICA, HARMONICS, HARP, HARPSICHORD, HELICOPTER, HONKYTONK, HONKYTONK_PIANO, HORN, ICE_RAIN, ICERAIN, JAZZ_GUITAR, JAZZ_ORGAN, JGUITAR, KALIMBA, KOTO, MARIMBA, METAL_PAD, MGUITAR, MUSIC_BOX, MUTED_GUITAR, MUTED_TRUMPET, NGUITAR, NYLON_GUITAR, OBOE, OCARINA, OGUITAR, OOH, OOHS, ORCHESTRA_HIT, ORGAN, ORGAN2, ORGAN3, OVERDRIVE_GUITAR, PAD, PAN_FLUTE, PANFLUTE, PBASS, PHONE, PIANO, PIANO_ACCORDION, PIC, PICC, PICCOLO, PICKED_BASS, PIPE_ORGAN, PIPES, PITZ, PIZZ, PIZZICATO_STRINGS, POLY_SYNTH, POLYSYNTH, PSTRINGS, RAIN, RECORDER, REED_ORGAN, REVERSE_CYMBAL, RHODES, SAW, SAWTOOTH, SAX, SAXOPHONE, SBASS, SEA, SEASHORE, SFX, SGUITAR, SHAKUHACHI, SHAMISEN, SHANNAI, SITAR, SLAP, SLAP_BASS, SLOW_STRINGS, SOLO_VOX, SOP, SOPRANO, SOPRANO_SAX, SOPRANO_SAXOPHONE, SOUNDEFFECTS, SOUNDFX, SOUNDTRACK, SPACE_VOICE, SQUARE, STAR_THEME, STEEL_DRUM, STEEL_DRUMS, STEEL_GUITAR, STEELDRUM, STEELDRUMS, STR, STREAM, STRINGS, SWEEP, SWEEP_PAD, SYN_CALLIOPE, SYN_STRINGS, SYNTH_BASS, SYNTH_BRASS, SYNTH_CALLIOPE, SYNTH_DRUM, SYNTH_DRUMS, SYNTH_STRINGS, SYNVOX, TAIKO, TELEPHONE, TENOR, TENOR_SAX, TENOR_SAXOPHONE, THUMB_PIANO, THUNDER, TIMP, TIMPANI, TINKLE_BELL, TOM, TOM_TOM, TOM_TOMS, TOMS, TREMOLO, TREMOLO_STRINGS, TROMBONE, TRUMPET, TUBA, TUBULAR_BELL, TUBULAR_BELLS, VIBES, VIBRAPHONE, VIOLA, VIOLIN, VIOLIN_CELLO, VOICE, VOX, WARM_PAD, WHISTLE, WIND, WOODBLOCK, WOODBLOCKS, XYLOPHONE

General MIDI drum and percussion sounds
ACOUSTIC_BASS_DRUM, ACOUSTIC_SNARE, BASS_DRUM_1, CABASA, CHINESE_CYMBAL, CLAVES, CLOSED_HI_HAT, COWBELL, CRASH_CYMBAL_1, CRASH_CYMBAL_2, ELECTRIC_SNARE, HAND_CLAP, HI_BONGO, HI_MID_TOM, HI_WOOD_BLOCK, HIGH_AGOGO,

HIGH_FLOOR_TOM, HIGH_TIMBALE, HIGH_TOM, LONG_GUIRO, LONG_WHISTLE, LOW_AGOGO, LOW_BONGO, LOW_CONGA, LOW_FLOOR_TOM, LOW_MID_TOM, LOW_TIMBALE, LOW_TOM, LOW_WOOD_BLOCK, MARACAS, MUTE_CUICA, MUTE_HI_CONGA, MUTE_TRIANGLE, OPEN_CUICA, OPEN_HI_CONGA, OPEN_HI_HAT, OPEN_TRIANGLE, PEDAL_HI_HAT, RIDE_BELL, RIDE_CYMBAL_1, RIDE_CYMBAL_2, SHORT_GUIRO, SHORT_WHISTLE, SIDE_STICK, SPLASH_CYMBAL, TAMBOURINE, VIBRASLAP

Scales and modes
AEOLIAN_SCALE, BLUES_SCALE, CHROMATIC_SCALE, DIATONIC_MINOR_SCALE, DORIAN_SCALE, HARMONIC_MINOR_SCALE, INDIAN_SCALE, LYDIAN_SCALE, MAJOR_SCALE, MELODIC_MINOR_SCALE, MINOR_SCALE, MIXOLYDIAN_SCALE, NATURAL_MINOR_SCALE, PENTATONIC_SCALE, TURKISH_SCALE

Tuning systems
EQUAL, JUST, MEAN, PYTHAGOREAN

Audio waveforms
COSINE_WAVE, PULSE_WAVE, SABERSAW_WAVE, SAWDOWN_WAVE, SAWTOOTH_WAVE, SINE_WAVE, SQUARE_WAVE, TRIANGLE_WAVE

Audio noise types
BROWN_NOISE, FRACTAL_NOISE, SMOOTH_NOISE, STEP_NOISE, WHITE_NOISE

Phrase position alignments
AFTER, BEFORE, CENTER_ALIGN, CENTER_ON_END, CENTER_ON_START, CENTRE_ALIGN, CENTRE_ON_END, CENTRE_ON_START, END_ON_CENTER, END_ON_CENTRE, END_TOGETHER, START_ON_CENTER, START_ON_CENTRE, START_TOGETHER

Appendix B: Methods in the Mod class

These are the methods of the Mod class in jMusic. Only the methods taking a phrase as an argument. Most Mod class methods are overloaded to accept Parts, Scores and CPhrases as arguments in place of phrases. Some similar method signatures have been omitted from this list, for a full list consult the jMusic documentation.

accents(Phrase phrase, double meter, double[] accentedBeats, int accentAmount)

Increase the dynamic of notes at regularly occurring pulse locations which generates the sound of regular meter.

addToDuration(Phrase phrase, double amount)

Vary the duration of each note in the phrase by the specified amount.

addToLength(Phrase phrase, double amount)

Vary both the rhythm value and duration of each note in the phrase by the specified amount.

addToRhythmValue(Phrase phrase, double amount)

Vary the rhythm value of each note in the phrase by the specified amount.

append(Phrase phrase1, Phrase phrase2)

Adds phrase2 to the end of phrase1.

bounce(Phrase phrase)

Adjusts all Note pan values to alternate between extreme left and right from note to note.

changeLength(Phrase phrase, double newLength)

Alters the phrase so that it's notes are stretched or compressed until the phrase is the length specified.

compress(`Phrase phrase, double ratio`)

A compressor/expander routine.

crescendo(`Phrase phrase, double startTime, double endTime, int startDynamic, int endDynamic`)

Provides a linear dynamic value increase across the range specified.

cycle(`Phrase phrase, double numBeats`)

Extends the phrase by repeating it until it is as long as the specified length.

cycle(`Phrase phrase, int numNotes`)

Extends the phrase by repeating it until it contains the number of notes as specified by `numNotes`.

decrescendo(`Phrase phrase, double startTime, double endTime, int startDynamic, int endDynamic`)

Provides a linear dynamic value decrease across the range specified.

diminuendo(`Phrase phrase, double startTime, double endTime, int startDynamic, int endDynamic`)

Provides a linear dynamic value decrease across the range specified.

elongate(`Phrase phrase, double scaleFactor`)

Stretch the time of each note in the phrase by `scaleFactor`

expandIntervals(`Phrase phrase, double amount`)

Vary the interval between notes scaling by the specified amount to each interval.

fadeIn(Phrase phrase, double fadeLength)

Linearly increases from zero the dynamic in the phrase.

fadeOut(Phrase phrase, double fadeLength)

Linearly decreases from zero the dynamic in the phrase.

fillRests(Phrase phrase)

Lengthens notes followed by a rest in the phrase by creating one longer note and deleting the rest.

increaseDuration(Phrase phrase, double multiplier)

Vary the duration of each note in the phrase by the multiplier.

increaseDynamic(Phrase phr, int amount)

Increases the dynamic by a certain amount - obviously a negative number will decrease it.

inversion(Phrase phrase)

Mirror the pitch of notes in the phrase around the first note's pitch.

merge(Phrase phrase1, Phrase phrase2)

Combines the phrases from a second CPhrase into the first.

mutate(Phrase phrase, int pitchCount, int rhythmCount, int[] pitches, int lowestPitch, int highestPitch, double[] rhythms)

Mutates the phrase by changing pitches and rhythm values.

normalise(Phrase phrase)

Increases dynamic values so that the loudest is at maximum level.

palindrome(`Phrase phrase, boolean repeatLastNote`)

Extend the phrase by adding all notes backwards.

quantize(`Phrase phrase, double qValue`)

Quantizes start times of notes within the phrase to the closest qValue.

randomize(`Phrase phrase, int pitchVariation, double rhythmVariation, int dynamicVariation`)

Adjusts Note values to any value plus or minus a specified amount.

repeat(`Phrase phrase, int n`)

Makes the phrase n times as long by repeating.

retrograde(`Phrase phrase`)

Reverse the order of notes in the phrase.

rotate(`Phrase phrase, int numSteps`)

Move the notes around a number of steps as specified by numSteps which each step involving the first note becoming the second, second the third, and so forth with the last becoming first.

shake(`Phrase phrase, int amount`)

Randomly adjusts all Notes' dynamic value to create uneven loudness.

shuffle(`Phrase phrase`)

Randomize the order of notes in the phrase without repeating any note.

shuffle(`Score score`)

Randomly order notes within each phrase.

slurDown(Phrase phrase)

All descending sequences of notes are slurred by having their duration extended to 100% of the rhythm value.

slurUp(Phrase phrase)

All ascending sequences of notes are slurred by having their duration extended to 100% of the rhythm value.

spread(Phrase phrase)

Randomly sets the pan position of all notes across.

tiePitches(Phrase phrase)

Joins consecutive notes in the phrase that have the same pitch, creating one longer note.

tieRests(Phrase phrase)

Joins consecutive rests in the phrase creating one longer note.

transpose(Phrase phrase, int transposition)

Transpose the phrase up or down in semitones.

transpose(Phrase phrase, int transposition, int[] mode, int key)

Transpose the phrase up or down in scale degrees.

varyLength(Phrase phrase, double minLength, double maxLength)

Adjusts all note duration values to vary randomly between specified values.

Appendix C: Installing jMusic

Install Java

First, visit the `java.sun.com` site to install Java Standard Edition. Macintosh users note that Java is pre-installed on OS X.

Below are the instructions for downloading and installing jMusic.

Install jMusic on Linux / Unix

1. Download and install Java from Sun. (Skip this step if you have a Java already.)

2. Download the `jmusic_1.5.tar.gz` file from SourceForge and uncompress.

3. Place the `jmusic.jar` file and `inst` directories in your Java class path. This is usually done by editing your shell .*rc file (in OS X or in Linux a ~/.bashrc file) and add the location of the jMusic directories to the class path environment variable.

4. (Optional) To use the MidiShare package (msjm) for MIDI input and output you will need to download and install MidiShare from Grame, including the Java developer kit with the grame.jar file. You should run msconnect to connect the various midi input/output sources that you might have.

Eg. (for the tcshell) setenv CLASSPATH ${home}/jmusic/lib/jmusic.jar/:${home}/jmusic/inst/:.

Eg. (for the bash shell) export CLASSPATH=.:$HOME/jMusic/jmusic.jar:$HOME/jMusic/inst/

Note: The jmqt package requires Apple's QuickTime and will not run on Lunix or Unix. It has been deprecated since the introduction of JavaSound. You can safely ignore it.

Install jMusic on Mac OS X

1. From `http://sourceforge.net/projects/jmusic/download` the `jmusic_1.5.tar.gz` file from and uncompress. Place the jMusic folder in your user directory. e.g., `/User/andrew/jMusic`

2. Place the `jmusic.jar` file and the `inst` directory in your Java class path by modifying your `.profile` file (see below).

3. Open a terminal window (or quit and reopen if already open) to initiate the .profile file. (The terminal app is in the /Applications/Utilities/ directory.) Use the commands `javac filename.java` or `java filename` to run Java file using jMusic.

4. (Optional) To use the `MidiShare` package (`msjm`) for MIDI input and output you will need to visit `http://midishare.sourceforge.net/` and download and install `MidiShare`. You should run `msconnect` to connect the various midi input/output sources that you might have. All the files need to go in the working directory. The `grame.jar` needs to be added as an environment variable in the classpath. For example, `setenv CLASSPATH :${home}/jMusic/graeme.jar`

Note: The `jmqt` package uses Apple's QuickTime for music playback. It has been deprecated since the introduction of JavaSound. You can safely ignore it.

Creating a .profile file.

Assume you have put the jMusic folder in your User directory, use a text editor to create a file called .profile with the following (single) line in it. In OS X not all text editors can read or write files starting with a dot, as these are generally hidden. We suggest that you open a terminal and use the *pico* editor to create and or edit your `.profile` file. Navigate to your home directory by typing `cd ~`. In the terminal type `pico .profile` then add the line below (assuming you put jMusic in your home directory).

export CLASSPATH=.:$HOME/jMusic/jmusic.jar:$HOME/jMusic/inst/

Save the file in your user directory. e.g: `/User/andrew/.profile`

Create (or edit an existing) a `.profile` file in the same directory by typing `pico .profile`. Add the following line to the file:

. .bashrc

Save the file in your user directory. e.g: `/User/andrew/.profile`

Install jMusic on Microsoft Windows

1. Install Java if its not already installed. Download the latest Java SDK installer from Sun. Run the executable and follow the on-screen prompts to install.

2. From `http://sourceforge.net/projects/jmusic/download` the `jmusic_1.5.tar.gz` file from and unzip it to `c:\jmusic`.

3. Some environment variables must be set before jMusic can be run successfully. Under Win2000, NT or XP.

   * Open the System Properties Dialog. (By right-clicking My Computer and going to Properties OR by naviagting through Start | Settings | Control Panel | System)

   * Choose the Advanced tab

   * Click Environment Variables...

   * Ensure that a variable called CLASSPATH exists and it contains c:\jmusic\jmusic.jar;c:\jmusic\inst

4. You may wish to try creating, compiling and running a simple jMusic program to test if the tools has been set up correctly. Here is a tutorial to try which will work on all flavours of Windows.

5. (Optional) To use the MidiShare package (msjm) for MIDI input and output you will need to visit http://midishare.sourceforge.net/ and download and install MidiShare. You should run msconnect to connect the various MIDI input/output sources that you might have. The midishare user file is called midishare186.zip The midishare developer file is called midishare2000.zip They are in the same ftp folder, and the layout is a bit confusing (careful). You need to put the dlls that you want to use, as well as the midishare32dll (which has all the important native classes) into the system folder, so that they can be awakened at midishare startup time. Make sure the .ini files are put into the windows folder.

For even more information on getting going with Java try the getting started instructions from Sun's Java homepage.

References

Burraston, D., E. Edmonds, et al. (2004). Cellular Automata in MIDI based Computer Music. International Computer Music Conference. Miami, ICMA: 71-81.

Cook, N. (1990). Music, Imagination and Culture. Oxford, Oxford University Press.

Cook, P. R. (2002). Real Sound Synthesis for Interactive Applications, A. K. Peters.

Cope, D. (2001). Virtual Music: Computer synthesis of musical style. Cambridge, MA, MIT Press.

Dodge, C. and T. A. Jerse (1997). Computer Music. New York, Schirmer Books.

Gardner, H. (1985). The Mind's New Science: A History of the Cognitive Revolution. New York, Basic Books.

Gardner, M. (1970). "Mathematical Games: the fantastic combinations of John Conway's new solitaire game of 'life'." Scientific American 223(4): 120-123.

Lindley, C. A. (2000). Digital Audio with Java. Englewood Cliffs, N.J, Prentice Hall.

Madden, C. (1999). Fractals in Music: Introductory mathematics for musical analysis. Salt Lake City, High Art Press.

Miranda, E. R. (2001). Composing Music with Computers. Oxford, Focal Press.

Moore, F. R. (1991). "The Dyfunctions of MIDI." Computer Music Journal 12(1): 19-28.

Niemeyer, P. and J. Knudsen (2000). Learning Java. Seastopol, California, O'Reilly & Associates.

Reynolds, C. W. (1987). "Flocks, Herds, and Schools: A distributed behavioral model." Computer Graphics 21(4): 25-34.

Risset, J.-C. (1969). Introductory Catalogue of Computer-Synthesized Sounds. Murray Hill, NJ, Bell Laboratories.

Roads, C. (1996). The Computer Music Tutorial. Cambridge, MA, MIT Press.

Schwanauer, S. and D. Levitt (1993). Machine Models of Music. Cambridge, MA, MIT Press.

Scruton, R. (1983). "Understanding Music." Ratio 25: 97-120.

Selfridge-Field, E. (2001). Composition, Combinatronics, and Simulation: A historical and philosophical enquiry. Virtual Music: Computer synthesis of musical style. D. Cope. Cambridge, MA, The MIT Press: 187-220.

Xenakis, I. (1971). Formalized Music: Thought and Mathematics in Composition. Bloomington, Indiana University Press.

Printed in Great Britain
by Amazon